Praise for *The Opposite of Happiness*

'Beautifully written, intensely thoughtful and emotionally gripping . . . Anyone interested in the unhappy moiety of human experience will find this book fascinating and informative'

– Roy F. Baumeister, former president of the International Positive Psychology Association and coauthor of *The Power of Bad*

'A must-read for anyone who wants to understand the full breadth of the human experience. *The Opposite of Happiness* refuses to promise that it can fix you, which may be why, by the last page, it so nearly does'

– Max Bennett, author of *A Brief History of Intelligence*

'Loewenstein, a founder of behavioral economics and one of the field's most creative scholars, has written a clever, insightful and often personal tour of the worst parts of life . . . *The Opposite of Happiness* is a brilliant, humane and unexpectedly delightful book about the many varieties of human misery'

– Paul Bloom, professor of psychology at the University of Toronto and author of *Psych*

'This brilliantly crafted book explains – in the deepest and most satisfying way possible – why we're consigned to experience sadness, anxiety, fear, loneliness and other flavors of misery. When you finish, you'll know yourself better, you'll understand the people you care about better and you'll feel like you're on a first-name basis with . . . the leading scholar on how emotions shape our every decision'

– Angela Duckworth, *New York Times* bestselling author of *Grit*

'This is not a self-help book, except that it will probably make you wiser, more socially connected and, yes, happier. I suppose that's what happens when you spend a few hours in the company of one of the world's great thinkers'

– Eli J. Finkel, bestselling author of *The All-or-Nothing Marriage* and host of the *Love Factually* podcast

'Insightful, personal and compelling, *The Opposite of Happiness* expertly explores the dark side of our emotional lives'

– Daniel Gilbert, Edgar Pierce Professor of Psychology at Harvard University and *New York Times* bestselling author of *Stumbling on Happiness*

'Blending beautiful writing, surprising humor, gripping stories and cutting-edge science, *The Opposite of Happiness* reveals why negative emotions are not a flaw in the system, but the system itself. This is a rare book that will both unsettle and enlighten you – and change forever how you understand your own inner life'

– Sonja Lyubomirsky, Distinguished Professor of Psychology at the University of California, Riverside and author of *The How of Happiness*

'This profound and deeply personal book will change how you understand yourself and your emotions. Loewenstein – one of the most influential behavioral scientists in history – brings decades of research to bear on this exploration of human suffering, examining emotions ranging from envy and shame to anxiety and regret'

– Katy Milkman, James G. Dinan Professor at the Wharton School of the University of Pennsylvania and author of *How to Change*

'This book weaves fascinating findings from social psychology about the emotions that cause bad feelings with deeply personal reports from a remarkable "Misery Survey" into a great read that will be interesting to all and helpful to many by revealing the origins and the meaning of diverse kinds of misery'

– Randolph Nesse, MD, author of *Good Reasons for Bad Feelings*

'An enormously enjoyable tour of the miseries. Loewenstein has recast *The Inferno* with sound science, wit and wise advice'

– Martin E. P. Seligman, PhD, Fox Leadership Professor of Psychology at the University of Pennsylvania and author of *Learned Optimism*

'A magnificent achievement. It's all about misery and suffering, but it elevates the spirit. It's teeming with wisdom, insight, empathy and sparkle. One of the best books I have ever read'

– Cass R. Sunstein, Robert Walmsley University Professor at Harvard University and author of *Manipulation*

'*The Opposite of Happiness* does for *feeling* what Kahneman's *Thinking, Fast and Slow* does for thinking'

– John Tierney, former *New York Times* columnist and coauthor of *The Power of Bad* and *Willpower*

The Opposite of Happiness

ALSO BY GEORGE LOEWENSTEIN

It's on You: How Corporations and Behavioral Scientists Have Convinced Us That We're to Blame for Society's Deepest Problems (coauthored with Nick Chater)

Exotic Preferences: Behavioral Economics and Human Motivation

The Opposite of Happiness

HOW BAD FEELINGS MAKE AND BREAK US

George Loewenstein

WILLIAM COLLINS

William Collins
An imprint of HarperCollins*Publishers*
1 London Bridge Street
London SE1 9GF

WilliamCollinsBooks.com

HarperCollins*Publishers*
Macken House,
39/40 Mayor Street Upper
Dublin 1
D01 C9W8
Ireland

First published in Great Britain in 2026 by William Collins
First published in the United States in 2026 by Harper,
an imprint of HarperCollins*Publishers*

1

A catalogue record for this book is available from the British Library

ISBN 978-0-00-875640-6 (hardback)
ISBN 978-0-00-875641-3 (trade paperback)

Designed by Kyle O'Brien

Set in Adobe Garamond Pro by Six Red Marbles UK, Thetford, Norfolk

Printed and bound in the UK [using 100% renewable electricity at CPI Group (UK) Ltd]

FSC
www.fsc.org
MIX
Paper | Supporting responsible forestry
FSC® C013604

To Matthew

Call no man happy until he is dead.

—Solon

Contents

Introduction

In March 2019, the economist Alan Krueger—who had served as assistant treasury secretary in the Obama administration and was widely seen as a contender for the Nobel Prize—was found dead at his home in Princeton, New Jersey. The cause, according to a statement from his family, was suicide. Krueger's death at fifty-eight cut short one of the most successful, creative, and idealistically oriented careers in my field. And it came just nine months after the chef and television personality Anthony Bourdain hanged himself at a luxury resort in France. In both cases, the people left behind wondered how someone with such a rich life, with so many projects in the works, so beloved by their families, so admired by their peers, could do it.

It was no mystery to me. The news of those deaths reached me during one of the most miserable periods of my life. I thought about suicide constantly. I never seriously considered acting on those thoughts—I've seen too many lives shattered by the suicide of someone close to impose that on my family—but I've never been more depressed than I was then.

At one point, I told a friend it felt as if a switch had flipped in my brain, and like in a bad dream, I couldn't figure out how to flip it back. I'd been through milder depressions before, and I knew on some level that these feelings would almost certainly pass. After all, much of my research deals with this very phenomenon—how hard it is, when caught in one emotional state, to imagine ever feeling differently—a phenomenon I once labeled an "empathy gap."

But that knowledge didn't help me at all. Intellectually, I knew my pain would probably end. Emotionally, it felt endless. This book grew out of that dark period—partly as a way to make something of my misery, partly as a way to connect with others going through miseries of their own.

Turning personal struggles into research questions has been one of the through lines of my professional life. As an economist who studies how psychology shapes decision making—often in ways that defy rational models—I tend to start with something I've experienced: a feeling I've had, a misery I've endured, a story (from a colleague or a book) that stuck with me. In fact, I think of my research as a kind of storytelling. And like many novelists, I often don't know where the story is going when I begin.

Although this book draws on a wide range of research from psychology, economics, and the cognitive sciences, it's more personal than anything I've ever written—rooted in my own experiences and those of my friends, students, and colleagues. After I committed to writing it, I developed the odd habit of asking people to name their greatest form of misery—the feeling or psychic state that causes them the most suffering.

You might imagine this made me unpopular—and maybe it did, though it's possible my popularity was already so low it couldn't drop any further (what social scientists call a *floor effect*). But the answers were fascinating. One friend, without hesitation, said: *humiliation*. He then told me two harrowing stories—one of which appears in the chapter on shame that was inspired by him. Another said: *regret*, and described a specific experience that still haunts him years later. Maybe the bluntness of my question invited blunt responses, but I can't recall a single person who couldn't come up with an answer that made me wince in sympathy.

In short, there was no shortage of misery.

Yet when I scanned the popular science shelves for works on this subject, I found almost nothing. There were dozens of books about *happiness*—many of them built on research I know well and, in a few cases, helped produce—but very few books about the opposite of happiness, the darker side of the emotional spectrum. The myriad happiness books promise a lot, offering a buffet of strategies (many contradictory) for living a better life. But I've always found them vaguely irritating. I doubt any of them would help me, or anyone else, find lasting happiness. I'm not even sure that happiness is a goal worth pursuing.

As I will explain in the coming pages, many of the things people do to avoid suffering or find satisfaction—chasing ambitious goals, clinging to hope, suppressing painful thoughts, striving for control, protecting their pride—don't just fail to deliver happiness; they often make our misery worse. This book is about why that happens. It's about the miseries that evolution designed us to feel, and how our efforts to escape them so often sharpen the sting.

Woe Is (Not Just) Me

The focus of this book is not on physical or external sources of misery like disease or poverty, but on psychic suffering—miseries manufactured in the mind. Many of these are, admittedly, "first-world problems"; none involves violence, sickness, homelessness, or the many forms of objective hardship that vast numbers of people are born into or endure during the course of life. But privilege offers no exemption from misery, as the two suicides I just referred to so clearly illustrate.

Although I began the project to make sense of my own suffering, I offer in these pages no tips and precious little advice. This is *not* a self-help book. Let me be clear: I don't know how to spare anyone—including myself—from misery. One of the book's central arguments is that misery is inescapable. It's not some malfunction or a bug in the system. It *is* the system. Evolution didn't design us to be happy; it designed us to survive and reproduce—and, as it turns out, that design comes with a lot of built-in suffering.

But even if we cannot escape misery, we can certainly better understand it. And as the saying goes, "to understand is to forgive." That phrase is usually meant to apply to others, but it can be applied to oneself as well. Maybe understanding why we are unavoidably miserable can at least help us to blame *ourselves* less—removing guilt (about being unhappy) from the already toxic stew of negative emotions that so many of us experience. (I discuss these second-order "meta-emotions"—emotions about emotions—in Chapter 4).

Of course, understanding is hard to achieve in isolation. Most of us don't think clearly about our own misery until we've tried putting it into words—and that usually happens, if it happens at all, in conversation. Sharing, confessing, venting, commiserating—all this is a way of testing our private anguish against the backdrop of other people's experience. Often, that's when we discover that what feels like a shamefully unique misery is in fact disturbingly common.

Yet not everyone has the opportunity, or inclination, to share. Research suggests that women share more than men. That's partly because women, on average, have more close relationships and thus more people to confide in. For many men, their closest relationship is with their "significant other," and that is often the *last* person with whom they can share the things that weigh on them the most. (Being best friends with your spouse may sound ideal, but it carries a hidden risk: like investing all your money in the company you work for, it leaves you undiversified. If the relationship ends and you're in need of comfort, the only person you have to turn to may be the one person you can no longer bear to talk to.)

The observation that women share more than men obscures a more interesting pattern that my colleagues and I discovered in our research. In a paper titled "He Said, She Said," Erin Carbone, Irene Scopelliti, Joachim Vosgerau, and I report the finding that men and women are actually quite similar when it comes to how likely they are to share positive things (which are often about themselves). Where they differ is in their tendency to share negative thoughts, feelings, and experiences: men tend to keep bad things bottled up, whereas women unburden themselves to others.

On this dimension, I seem to fall on the female end of the distribution. Perhaps it's the result of growing up in a female-dominated household, or maybe it's just my temperament, but I've always tended to overshare, almost exclusively when it comes to negative experiences. This habit has had one unexpected benefit: it's taught me just how widespread misery really is. Whether it's back pain, digestive issues, insomnia, parenting struggles, or plain old depression, it's remarkable how often the person I'm speaking to either suffers from the same thing or knows someone who does.

Of course, it's possible that people feel a need to reciprocate confessions and fabricate woes (or exaggerate real ones) to match my own, but I doubt that explains everything. After all, how many people are going to feign suffering from digestive issues just to make me feel better? The more I shared and prodded others to reciprocate, the more I became convinced that vast numbers of people are leading what Thoreau famously called "lives of quiet desperation."

One of my most vivid experiences along these lines involved a problem I struggled with as an adolescent—one I was deeply ashamed of and discussed with no one: a difficulty urinating in public bathrooms. I suspected it meant something significant about me—perhaps that I was a latent homosexual (in fact, a gay friend in high school who was always convinced that I, too, was gay noticed my "issue" and offered that very interpretation).

I suffered in silence, often creating elaborate work-arounds to avoid exposure. Imagine my surprise, then, when in graduate school at a dinner with friends—and mixed company, no less—one casually mentioned suffering from what he jokingly called "stage fright" in public restrooms. No one seemed put off or surprised by his admission; they treated it as nothing more than an amusing personal quirk.

Later, I learned there's a psychological term for this: *paruresis*, or shy bladder syndrome, which reportedly ranks second only to public speaking as a common social phobia. Once I was attuned to its prevalence, I began to see it everywhere. For instance, in the building where I work, one of the bathrooms has urinals that lack partitions. Despite its central location in a building notorious for its paucity of bathrooms, these urinals are virtually unused. This makes me wonder: *How many of us are hiding parts of ourselves that we're profoundly ashamed of—things that are either exceedingly common or that no one would even blink at if they came out casually?*

The illusionist Derren Brown spent sixteen years hiding the fact that he was gay, convinced it was a terrible secret. *No one must ever know*, he thought. Later he realized how "silly" it had been to suffer in silence—"Because," he said, "when you do eventually come out, you realize no one gives a fuck."

From Economy to Misery

This is not meant to be an authoritative guide to every form of psychic suffering, but rather one scientist's bird's-eye view of the subject, shaped by broad reading, personal experience, and, in many cases, my own research. The aim is not to do justice to the vast academic literature on every emotion I discuss, but to step back and ask why misery—across its many forms—plays such a defining role in the human experience.

I come to this question from an unusual angle. In the late 1980s, I helped create the field of behavioral economics, which applies insights from psychology to understand how and why people actually make seemingly irrational decisions—not just about money, but also about time, effort, relationships, risk, and their own well-being. While the interdisciplinary nature of behavioral economics has shaped my thinking in many areas, it has also placed me in an intellectual no-man's-land: too psychological for economists to consider me one of their own, too economic for acceptance into the ranks of psychologists.

In this book, I draw more from psychological than economic literature, with one notable exception. The person I quote more than anyone else is, in fact, the forefather of all economists, the Scottish Enlightenment philosopher Adam Smith—coiner of the "invisible hand," hero of libertarians and free marketeers. What, you may ask, is someone like Smith doing in a book about feelings, good or bad?

Seventeen years before he published *The Wealth of Nations*, Smith wrote a penetrating inquiry into human nature titled *The Theory of Moral Sentiments* that closely anticipates—and partially inspired—the perspective I share in this book. His writing is elegant and persuasive, and worth reproducing for that reason alone. But, part of the reason I quote so frequently from Smith is to challenge his popular image as a poster boy for unfettered capitalism. Smith is best known for the "invisible hand" metaphor—the idea that individuals, by pursuing their own well-being in free markets, inadvertently promote the public good. Yet in this earlier book Smith made clear that people are poor judges of what's in their self-interest and that much of their economic activity is based not on its rational pursuit but on a widespread delusion. That delusion is that happiness lies just beyond some imagined finish line—a better house, financial security, more time, greater respect—and that reaching it will at last bring peace of mind.

At numerous points in his book, Smith expresses skepticism about such pursuits, and in an especially vivid passage, he recounts how those of us who work so hard to get the things we think we want will come to realize—long after it is too late for a course correction—how little satisfaction they bring us in the end. Wealth and greatness, he concludes, "are mere trinkets of frivolous utility, no more adapted for procuring ease of body or tranquility of mind, than the tweezer-cases of the lover of toys." (Apparently, tweezer-cases were quite the rage in eighteenth-century Glasgow.)

It is tempting to think that this delusion, once properly identified, could be somehow corrected. Smith begs to differ. He saw it as an inevitable and, more to the point, *necessary* feature of human life, the very force propelling civilization forward:

> It is this deception which rouses and keeps in continual motion the industry of mankind. It is this which first prompted them to cultivate the ground, to build houses, to found cities and commonwealths, and to invent and improve all the sciences and arts, which ennoble and embellish human life; which have entirely changed the whole face of the globe.

In the end, Smith seems to be describing two invisible hands at work: one that pushes us forward, promising happiness just out of reach, and another that yanks us back toward dissatisfaction when those promises inevitably fail.

Downward Trajectories

This book is divided into two parts. Part 1 examines why misery is so central to the human experience. In it I enumerate the evolutionary, psychological, and social quirks that make negative feelings more powerful, persistent, and pervasive than positive ones. I discuss why this imbalance exists, and how it evolved to keep our ancestors alive, even as it poisons our inner life.

I begin with a chapter on **emotions**, which reprogram the mind and body. Next, I introduce **empathy gaps**—psychological blind spots that prevent people from understanding other peoples' emotions, or accurately imagining their own future or past feelings. These gaps explain why we often feel isolated in our misery—because we *are*!—and why so many of us repeatedly make decisions that undermine our well-being.

From there, I examine the thorny subject of **self-esteem**, which people wrongly think of as an independent source of inner strength, but which actually has less to do with the self than with others. I also explore the **inner conflicts** we face when different parts of ourselves want different things—or when we condemn ourselves for wanting the "wrong" thing. These internal struggles amplify feelings of guilt, shame, and inadequacy, and they help explain a disturbing truth: We are often the architects of our own misery. Not only literature, but daily life, in my experience, is filled with people who are—frequently and painfully—their own worst enemy.

I then explore even more spectacular forms of **self-sabotage**—how people actively undermine themselves at critical moments by choking under pressure or chickening out. Next, I turn to **intrusive thoughts and memories**—those unwelcome ambushers of the mind that defy control, indeed most persistently when we attempt to suppress them. In the final two chapters of Part 1, I reveal the dark side of two seemingly positive psychological forces. The first is **hedonic adaptation**, which is often celebrated for its restorative powers: it helps us recover, emotionally, from disappointments, losses, and even profound injuries. But this same mechanism also ensures that our happiness never lasts—and, more troublingly, that the pains we experience in life hit harder and linger longer than commensurate pleasures. The second supposedly positive force is **hope**, which for all its virtues can perversely prolong suffering, trapping people in situations that might otherwise be escaped and making some bad outcomes far worse than they need to be.

Whereas Part 1 explains why misery exists and how it works in general terms, Part 2 dissects its individual specimens—each chapter devoted to a distinct variety of psychic pain. In each, I speculate about the evolutionary function the emotion may have served, then explain how it arises, how it affects our behavior, and—perhaps most importantly—what it feels like.

For this last question, I draw heavily on an unpaid survey I conducted with more than five hundred individuals who have volunteered, over the years, to participate in my research. In this "Misery Survey" I asked people to identify their most intense and persistent form of misery, to tell me a story about it, to rate how bad it was (on a zero-to-ten badness scale), and to share any personal insights they had—essentially a more formalized version of the questions I'd been asking my friends for years.

A distinctive feature of the Misery Survey is that each participant was randomly assigned to reflect on a specific negative emotion—envy, say, or shame—and asked whether they suffered from that kind of misery in particular. If they said they did not, then they were presented with another negative emotion, again at random, and this process repeated until they either found one that resonated or exhausted the list of twelve (which almost never happened). This design made it possible to distinguish between miseries that many people feel affect them deeply and personally (like anger or anxiety) and those that trouble a more select few (like jealousy or guilt).

What surprised me most, however, was not the prevalence of any one misery but the depth of them all. Some of the stories people shared were almost unbearably painful to read—a pale reflection, I can only imagine, of what it must be to actually live through them. Many of these heartrending accounts appear throughout the book, interwoven with the science, to remind us that while we can talk about misery in the abstract, it is never abstract to those experiencing it.

I begin Part 2 with a chapter on the hell of **waiting**, which shows that waiting for something bad is often more painful than enduring the event itself, and that, perversely, waiting for something good is often distressing, too. The misery of waiting gives way to **boredom** in the following chapter. I explain why it only *seems* like a paradox that we feel increasingly bored in an age of unlimited options for mental stimulation. The next misery is **anger**—not the kind of mild righteous indignation that can, in fact, sometimes be pleasurable, but the kind of corrosive anger experienced when one is the helpless victim of another person.

A pair of chapters on **envy** and **jealousy** comes next, in which I untangle their subtle but crucial differences: Envy arises from wanting what others have, while jealousy stems from the fear of losing something we already possess. Both distort how we see others—and ourselves. One of the primary forces driving jealousy is a fear of **rejection**, which is the subject of the next chapter—an experience that is not only among the most painful, but also among the most common.

As the descent into the depths of awfulness continues, I turn to **guilt**, the misery of moral failure, which drives us to seek forgiveness for things we've done—or merely imagined doing. Then comes **shame**, its deeper and crueler cousin, which eats at our identity: not merely the sense that we've acted badly (as with guilt), but the conviction that we *are* bad—or at least that other people think so.

Anxiety follows, in which the mind exhausts itself trying to anticipate every possible danger—trapping us in a cycle of rumination and imagined catastrophe. Then **regret**, which forces individuals to relive their mistakes—including, commonly, the roads not taken. The penultimate misery—and ultimate social pain—is **loneliness**. It hijacks the body's stress systems, and feeds on itself: the lonelier we feel, the harder it becomes to reach out. Often framed as a problem of social isolation—of how many connections we have or how often we interact with others—I argue that loneliness is actually more about seeing ourselves as unlovable or unlikable.

Finally, at the bottom of the pit is **depression**: the last misery in this book, and the one that launched this whole infernal journey for me. Any of the earlier miseries I describe—rejection, guilt, anger, anxiety—can, if left to fester, tip into this numbing, self-perpetuating form of suffering. And unlike those other miseries, whose evolutionary purposes are at least seemingly graspable, depression's function remains deeply obscure. That inscrutability only deepens its menace, making it feel less like a survival mechanism and more like a psychic curse.

Together, these twenty chapters illuminate the cunning ways the psyche conspires to make us miserable. Each person's experience of misery may be idiosyncratic—shaped both by biography and biology—but no one is exempt. If at times this book feels like the nonfiction equivalent of a Hieronymus Bosch painting—an underworld of suffering that sprawls in every direction—this is by design; I am merely giving the subject of misery the harsh treatment it deserves. If there's any light to be found in the darkness, it's this: while we may suffer alone, we are never alone in suffering.

PART 1

Why We Suffer

1

Because Misery Is the Price of Survival

Life for the emotional is comprised of dizzying revolutions of the clock, for *what they want* changes so rapidly that *who they are* is constantly in question. If the emotional man one day loves Samantha and the next Sally, then who is he? If I went to bed one night loving Chloe and awoke the next morning hating her, then who was "I"?

—Alain de Botton, *On Love*

A Bomb in My Inbox

I'm not prone to substance abuse, but like many academics I have at least one intractable addiction: email. One February morning, I made the mistake of indulging this addiction while I waited for my friend Jules to pick me up for a day of skiing. Having studied curiosity—and the dangers of satisfying it—I made a second mistake when I opened a message from a colleague at another university with whom I'd had, up until then, less than uniformly positive interactions and, hence, from whom I had no reason to expect good news.

My trepidation was more than borne out. As I read the message, I realized that it wasn't addressed *to* me, but was *about* me. The message had been intended for a third party, and the sentiments expressed about me did not make for a favorable beginning to a day of skiing—nor any day for that matter.

As I sat there reading and rereading the message that I wasn't supposed to have received, I felt a wave of heat and pressure in my head, my muscles tensed, and I started sweating—the unmistakable physical signs of anger and hurt. Immediately I began to compose in my mind a return message that was intended to inflict the same pain in the sender that his email had created in me. My goal was to send off this message quickly, before departing, so I could discharge the feelings before spending the day on the slopes. I felt completely confident that sending such a message was the right thing to do and that it was something that I would never regret because I would always feel exactly as I did at that moment.

So much for the benefits of studying emotions!

Fortunately, the doorbell rang before I was able to transfer the message from my head to the computer, and my impatience to get the message out was supplanted by the desire not to keep Jules waiting. So I got into Jules's car, vented to him for the hour that it took us to get to the ski slopes, and continued to fume whenever we took a break from skiing and the memory of the offending message rushed back into consciousness. Late in the day, however, I began to "cool off." It gradually came back to me that I'd sent plenty of similar messages to friends complaining about third parties—even, occasionally, about people I would consider friends. But, up to that point, I had enjoyed, to the best of my knowledge, the superior fortune of sending them to their intended recipients rather than their targets.

By the end of the day, I could even begin to catch a glimmer of my persecutor's perspective. Perhaps I *could have* cited his work more generously. And hadn't I experienced similar feelings myself toward others, on occasion, though perhaps done a better job of suppressing my anger, or at least its expression?

Armed with such insights and another hour of counseling from Jules during the drive back, when I got home that evening I sent back a conciliatory, dispassionate response. That response avoided the nasty escalation that would almost certainly have followed from the message I had intended to send that same morning, and it probably left the unfortunate sender with the feeling (at least until he reads this) that he had truly misunderstood me—that, contrary to sentiments expressed in his message, I must be an exceptionally warm, generous, fair-minded individual (a perfectly accurate description, of course!).

This episode brought home, once again, the power emotions have over us. But it also raised a deeper question: What do our emotions reveal—and what do they obscure? Was the "real" me the vengeful person composing an angry reply at 9 a.m., or the calm and reasonable one who wrote back at 6 p.m.?

That uncertainty reflected a broader issue that I'd been grappling with as an emotion researcher. Despite more than a decade of studying feelings, I still couldn't answer the most basic question: *What is an emotion?* Not just in terms of brain circuits or physiological responses, but in terms of their purpose. Why do we have them? And why do so many of them make us miserable?

An Answer, Millions of Years in the Making

These questions were very much on my mind in the summer of 2002, when I codirected a five-week workshop on emotions and decision making at the Center for Advanced Study in the Behavioral Sciences, tucked into the hills behind Stanford. My codirector was Roy Baumeister, arguably the most influential living psychologist, whose work on self-control, aggression, meaning, and sexuality had shaped much of the field—and my own thinking.

The participants—all junior faculty—brought an impressive range of perspectives. One of them was an evolutionary psychologist who struck me as both extremely sharp and slightly exhausting. Evolutionary psychologists tend to work on inherently interesting topics—like sex and violence—but they also have a habit of spinning pat little Paleolithic fables about how every human behavior evolved. In these stories, each preference or feeling is traced back to a specific adaptive problem faced by our forebears. For instance, because women historically bore the greater costs of pregnancy and child-rearing, they evolved stronger preferences for mates with resources and status, whereas men, more concerned with fertility, sought out youth and physical attractiveness. Amos Tversky, a giant in my field, memorably called such accounts "just-so stories"—tidy ex post facto explanations that sound plausible yet are impossible to verify without a time machine.

That skepticism shaped my own view of evolutionary psychology. In my experience, the best theories are not the ones that explain everything too easily, but the ones that make sense of facts that otherwise resist explanation. So I was surprised when, toward the end of the workshop, this same participant handed me a paper that reshaped my whole thinking about emotions.

It was written by her advisers, Leda Cosmides and John Tooby, who (until Tooby's death in 2023) codirected the Center for Evolutionary Psychology at UC Santa Barbara. Their account of emotion helped me make sense of a decade's worth of scattered findings—some from my own research, others from the broader literature—that I'd never quite been able to connect.

I already knew, for instance, that emotions weren't just feeling states like being happy, sad, or angry. Researchers such as NYU's Joseph LeDoux had persuaded me that the emotions we consciously experience are just the tip of the iceberg—the visible surface of a deeper, more intricate system, most of which operates outside our awareness. I knew emotions were linked to motivation—it's no accident that the word *emotion* contains *motion*. I also knew emotions had what psychologists call *valence*: some feel good, others bad. But the distinction wasn't always clean. Anger, for example, could feel either good or bad depending on the context. Nostalgia could feel good and bad at once.

From my own work, I knew that emotions didn't just shape how we feel—they changed how we think, decide, and behave. I'd run experiments showing that sadness or disgust could flip familiar decision-making patterns, altering how people valued their possessions or spent their money. I'd also found that people became more willing to take risks—or break moral rules—when sexually aroused or craving a fix, and that outside those states, they were terrible at predicting how those feelings would affect them (more on that in the next chapter).

What I didn't have was the bigger picture—an account of what emotions are *for*. Cosmides and Tooby offered a compelling answer. Their theory was more expansive than anything I'd encountered. They argued that, as our ancestors evolved—much of it before modern humans even existed—certain recurring situations proved critical to survival and reproduction: fighting, falling in love, fleeing predators, losing social status. To deal with these challenges, humans developed all-encompassing responses—what Cosmides and Tooby called "superordinate programs"—that not only motivated us to act, but helped us, at least in our ancestral environments, to act effectively.

They described the brain as a collection of specialized circuits, each honed via natural selection to help solve a specific kind of problem: regulating digestion, tapping into energy stores, narrowing the focus of attention, modulating facial expressions. Emotions, they proposed, orchestrate these subsystems, rapidly and automatically switching some on, dampening others, and coordinating them to meet an adaptive challenge.

Consider fear. When we enter a fearful state, certain circuits (those involved in sleep, for instance) are switched off, while others (those enhancing our ability to evade predators or defend ourselves) are ramped up. Our muscles tense, our breathing rate increases, our body is flooded with stress hormones like adrenaline and cortisol. The digestive system powers down, even halting saliva production (hence the dry mouth that, perversely, often accompanies public speaking). Our senses sharpen, attuning us to subtle cues like the creak of a floorboard or the hint of a footstep. Our memory becomes more precise, focusing on potential hiding places or escape routes.

The effect of such an emotion is not reducible to a single feeling, brain region, or physiological change. Emotions sweep through us, altering how we perceive the world, restructuring our memories, reshaping our judgments, and driving our actions. My takeaway from their article was that emotions don't just influence us—they *reprogram* us. When we're in different emotional states, it's almost as if we become different people—like the vengeful person I was the morning I received the errant email and the reflective one who wrote back later that evening.

As tormenting as these shifts can sometimes be, they are not signs that our emotional system is malfunctioning, but evidence that it is doing precisely what it was designed to do: help our early human ancestors survive long enough to pass on their genes. As the evolutionary psychiatrist

Randolph Nesse puts it: "Natural selection does not give a fig about our happiness. In the calculus of evolution, only reproductive success matters." Most of the psychological distress we feel today isn't caused by actual physical or social danger, Nesse points out, but by a system calibrated in our ancestral environment to err on the side of caution. From our evolved brain's perspective, the cost of a false alarm—of feeling bad when nothing is wrong—is small. The cost of missing a real threat could be fatal. The result is an emotional system built for vigilance, not peace of mind.

Evolution, it seems, must be cruel to be kind.

Acting Lessons

As much as I liked thinking of emotions as programs, I wanted to put some proof behind the theory, to be sure that I hadn't just fallen for another particularly compelling just-so story. An opportunity presented itself in 2008, when I attended a talk by some Carnegie Mellon University (CMU) colleagues that felt less like an academic symposium and more like a magic show.

A team of researchers led by the computer scientist Tom Mitchell and the neuroscientist Marcel Just had seemingly discovered a way to read people's minds. Or, more accurately, they had harnessed what was then a hot new technique called *machine learning* to see whether computers could be trained to distinguish patterns of brain activity associated with different thoughts.

In the training phase, they scanned participants' brains while showing them images of ordinary objects—a hammer, say, or an egg—and used these new statistical tools to learn the distinctive neural patterns associated with thinking about each one. Then came the test. The same participants were shown the objects again, in random order, and the system tried to identify—based solely on brain activity—which object they were viewing. It succeeded, with impressive accuracy.

As soon as I saw the results, which were later published in the journal *Science*, I wondered whether a similar technique could be used to "mind-read" not just what a person was seeing, but what they were feeling. Such a tool would be enormously valuable to emotion researchers—who typically depend on notoriously unreliable self-reports to determine whether someone is happy, sad, jealous, or bored.

There was, however, a big problem. Predictive machine learning algorithms require large quantities of training data because the electrical signals picked up by the brain scanner—a functional magnetic resonance imaging (fMRI) machine—are extremely noisy. To train the algorithm to decipher emotions in the same way it distinguished between thoughts about hammers and eggs, we needed to be able to induce different emotional states over and over again. This was easy to do with words or pictures, which don't lose their meaning even if someone is exposed to them multiple times. But emotions, whether conscious or not, must be *encoded* in the brain before they can be *decoded* by a machine. That is, we needed to get people to actually *feel* these emotions on demand, and repeatedly.

For a few emotions, like disgust, you can elicit the emotion in question quickly and reliably by showing someone disgusting pictures or film clips. (I've often had success with the toilet scene from *Trainspotting*.) But what about jealousy? Or happiness? How could we get people to genuinely experience those emotions, and do so frequently and consistently enough for the machine learning analysis to pick it up?

A member of the research team, my then-colleague Karim Kassam, had a brilliant idea. In addition to its reputation for science and engineering, my university (CMU) also has a renowned drama school. Who better than a Method actor to induce different emotional states, rapidly and repeatedly? We recruited ten seasoned acting students, conducted training sessions, and then asked them to self-induce nine different emotional states—anger, disgust, envy, fear, happiness, lust, pride, sadness, and shame—while we scanned their brains.

Each emotion was presented using one of two alternating word cues, so we could be confident that we were capturing emotional states rather than responses to the words themselves. To confirm that the actors were genuinely experiencing the emotions—and not merely simulating them—we also compared the brain activity from self-induced disgust with the scans we obtained by showing participants disgusting images. Much to the actors' credit, the patterns were indistinguishable.

I was struck by the results. First, the algorithm could identify, with a high degree of accuracy, whether someone was feeling happy, or lustful, or angry, simply by recognizing patterns in their brain activity. Although the people we scanned were psychologically and temperamentally distinct, their brains appeared to encode these nine emotions in remarkably similar ways. That consistency allowed us to train the model on data from nine actors, and then successfully predict the emotional states of the tenth—the so-called holdout actor.

What's more, the neural signatures of each emotion weren't confined to a single location in the brain. Instead, each emotional state corresponded to a distinctive pattern distributed across at least five different regions. These ranged from regions unique to humans and other primates that emerged relatively recently in evolutionary history to ancient structures that we share with reptiles.

It was once thought that specific emotions were housed in specific brain regions—fear in the amygdala, disgust in the insula. And while it's true that certain areas are more active during certain emotions, our study suggested a more complex picture. Emotions don't activate one region. They recruit multiple circuits simultaneously, in predictable combinations. It seemed to me like a glimpse of Cosmides and Tooby's theory in action: a reprogramming process, visible on the scanner, as each emotion reconfigured the brain.

While our findings supported the idea that emotions can reprogram us—and offered a promising tool for researchers—they sent a little chill down my spine (though *chill* was not among the states we examined). My wife's father, a psychotherapist and a truly delightful person, used to tell his children, "Never be ashamed of your thoughts; you can only be judged for your actions." But the ability to read people's emotional states, potentially against their wishes, seemed to open up a new and troubling frontier—one in which people might one day be judged, or even punished, for things going on entirely within their minds.

The Negativity Bias

The findings from the brain-scanning study didn't just confirm that emotions reprogram us. They also hinted at something deeper and more unsettling: that our emotional system tilts toward the negative. Of the nine emotions we asked actors to self-induce, it was the negative ones—anger, disgust, sadness—that produced the most distinct patterns of activation and were, hence, easiest to tell apart. The positive emotions, by contrast, were fuzzier and more easily confused. In fact, we only included two positive emotions—pride and happiness—in part because there just aren't that many to choose from.

Tolstoy's famous opening to *Anna Karenina* about happy families being all alike but unhappy ones each being unhappy in their own way applies just as well to feelings. There are simply more ways to feel bad than to feel good—and more words to describe those bad feelings. English is bloated with terms for anger, anxiety, sorrow, shame, jealousy, regret. When it comes to the positive side of the spectrum, the vocabulary thins out fast. Indeed, we lack satisfactory terms for a range of positive feelings, such as the pleasure of waiting for something good to happen or the absence of hunger or pain. Research on autobiographical memory shows that people's self-reports of emotional reactions to adverse experiences tend to reveal exquisite differentiation between different negative emotions, but the same is not true of recollections of positive experiences.

In some essential respects, our emotions resemble basic physiological feeling states like hunger and thirst that the body uses to protect itself. Each of these states comes equipped with a *stick* that will punish us if a need isn't addressed. We feel pangs of hunger when we lack nutrition; the intensifying agony of thirst when we lack hydration; the (curiously unnamed, at least in English) discomfort associated with the need to urinate or defecate; physical pain when we get hurt; and the misery of being too hot or too cold when our body temperature deviates from its set point. These sensations feel bad, and for obvious evolutionary reasons, each feels bad in its own way: hunger doesn't feel like pain, and pain in your leg doesn't feel like pain in your stomach. Each signal points to a different remedy, and we usually know exactly what needs to be done to stop the "beating."

Most of these systems also offer a carrot—a burst of pleasure when the need is being met. Scientists call this *alliesthesia*: food tastes better when we're hungry, cool water feels better when we're hot. But the asymmetry is striking. Quite simply, the stick is mightier than the carrot. Discomfort persists—hunger gnaws, thirst intensifies, pain sharpens—until the problem is solved. Pleasure, by contrast, tends to be brief. Once we've eaten or cooled off, we don't continue to feel good about it. The system shuts off, and the carrot, once delivered, is quickly forgotten.

The carrot also requires forward thinking—we have to recognize that food will taste good if we eat it, and then act on that recognition. The stick, by nature of its immediacy, does not require forward thinking. Our response to pain and suffering is usually automatic (like removing your hand from a hot frying pan). Perhaps this explains why, when people are asked to match adjectives to their respective categories, they are much quicker—by more than a third of a second—to pair pain-related words with the concept of pain than they are to match pleasure-related words with pleasure.

At first glance, emotions like anger, sadness, pride, or disgust might seem different from biological drives like hunger or thirst. But the difference is mostly one of complexity, not kind. Like those bodily systems, emotions feel good or bad, and they push us toward action. But, while hunger and thirst come with both a carrot and a stick, most emotions only come with a stick. They are not there to reward us. They're there to motivate us—often through discomfort—to change our behavior in ways that, over evolutionary time, helped our ancestors survive.

Most emotion researchers agree that there's a small set of "basic" or "core" emotions shared across cultures, though they differ on which emotions make the list. The most common version includes six: sadness, anger, disgust, fear, surprise, and happiness. Of these, four are unambiguously negative. One—happiness—is clearly positive. And one—surprise—can go either way, depending on what's popping out of the box. Some researchers have proposed adding shame—tellingly, another negative.

Not only are there more negative emotions than positive ones, but the negative ones tend to overpower the positive. Psychologists Paul Rozin and Edward Royzman captured this dynamic with a vivid metaphor: drop a cockroach into a vat of wine, and the whole thing is ruined; pour fine wine onto a cockroach, and it does nothing to improve the roach. This "roach effect" applies broadly. If you're in acute pain, no amount of beauty, humor, or pleasure will cancel it out. It's hard to imagine someone enjoying a sunset or a symphony while passing a kidney stone. While no amount of good can neutralize the truly bad, even a trace of bad can ruin something good. How much pleasure remains in a fine meal after a loved one makes a thoughtless comment (or, just as likely, bristles after *you* said the wrong thing)?

This "negativity bias," as it is commonly called, arises early in childhood, has been documented in all cultures in which it has been explored, and has also been observed in nonhuman primates and even birds. As with so much else, Adam Smith intuited the negativity bias long before the term was coined. "Pain," he wrote, "is, in almost all cases, a more pungent sensation than the opposite and correspondent pleasure. The one almost always depresses us more below the ordinary, or what may be called the natural state of our happiness, than the other ever raises us above it."

"What Good Are Positive Emotions?"

Even though, or perhaps especially because, this is a book about unhappiness, it is worth noting that, despite the huge focus of the media and popular literature on happiness, psychologists have been largely flummoxed when it comes to explaining what function positive emotions serve, and there is far less consensus on this issue than there is on the function of negative emotions. In a paper about positive emotions, the emotion researcher Charles Carver asks, "What are positive feelings? Do they have a purpose? How do they arise?"

It is unlikely that any emotion expert, including Carver, would pose an analogous question about whether negative emotions have a purpose. Likewise, one of the most highly cited articles on positive emotions, by Barbara Fredrickson, states that "psychology's knowledge base regarding positive emotions is so thin that satisfying answers to the question 'What good are positive emotions?' have yet to be articulated." Fredrickson goes on to describe how different negative emotions but not different positive ones are associated with identifiably different facial expressions, whereas all positive emotions simply result in a generic smile.

Likewise, different negative emotions have at least crudely different measurable bodily effects (such as changes in heart rate and skin temperature), whereas different positive emotions have so far not been found to produce distinguishable bodily responses. Research also shows that negative emotions (just like pain and other unpleasant physiological feeling states) are much more likely than positive ones to lead the person experiencing them to try to make sense of them—to figure out what is causing the negative emotion and what types of steps could be taken to alleviate it.

All this points to a simple and sobering conclusion: our emotions were built to keep us alive and reproducing, not to keep us happy. That's the central thesis of this book—that misery is not a glitch in the system but a feature of it, and perhaps the defining one. From an evolutionary standpoint, positive emotions may serve mostly as contrasts—reprieves from the real work of avoiding pain, correcting mistakes, and navigating threats. Think of it as a version of the "good cop, bad cop" routine: The bad cop—our negative emotions—does all the work, pushing, interrogating, keeping us on edge. The good cop—our positive feelings—earns goodwill simply by offering a break from the brutality.

In this sense, as Schopenhauer once observed, positive emotions aren't really positive at all. "What is commonly called happiness," he wrote, "is really and essentially always *negative*"—a momentary absence of suffering, a brief pause between the relief of one painful desire and the onset of the next.

The Stone Age Mind

The Stanford biologist Robert Sapolsky spent the early years of his career living in mud-and-dung huts in Kenya, tracking baboons across the savannah. His research focused on their social hierarchies and stress responses. But eventually, his curiosity led him to a more peculiar species: humans. In his seminal 1994 book *Why Zebras Don't Get Ulcers*, Sapolsky explores why stress is so much more damaging for us than for other animals.

For most other species in the animal kingdom, stress is a short, adaptive burst—a response to immediate physical danger. "We're not normal animals," Sapolsky says. "For 99 percent of the beasts on the planet, stress is three minutes of screaming terror after which it's over. And what do we do? We turn on the same stress response for thirty-year mortgages."

While the health impacts of chronic stress—including elevated risk of heart disease and diabetes—are now well-documented, Sapolsky's insight applies far beyond stress alone. Negative emotions of all kinds, once useful for solving specific survival problems, now linger in our minds and bodies long past their original utility. The machinery of emotion was shaped by natural selection over eons, but it hasn't had time to catch up with the rapid changes of the last ten thousand years—a blink in evolutionary time. As Cosmides and Tooby put it: "Our modern skulls house a stone-age mind."

For most of human history, we lived in small, interdependent bands of hunter-gatherers. In that world, loneliness, for instance, was a sharp, adaptive cue—a signal that we had drifted too far from the group. But today, nearly 60 percent of the global population live in urban areas, surrounded by other people but increasingly unmoored from community. Technology mediates more and more of our social connections, but it doesn't always satisfy our need to belong.

As Sapolsky noted in *Why Zebras Don't Get Ulcers*, pathogens like bacteria and viruses evolve faster than we do, which makes fighting infections a perpetual arms race. But there's a parallel struggle unfolding in our emotional lives. We may not have viruses that target happiness, but we do have commercial interests that thrive on our distress. Pharmaceutical companies sell more drugs when we can't sleep or feel depressed. Social media platforms hijack our motivational circuits to keep us scrolling—never mind if we're miserable.

The same pattern we see with loneliness holds for the other negative emotions we'll examine in this book, like boredom, impatience, and anxiety. All of them evolved as short-term signals—to shift our attention, spur us to act, or prepare us for a threat. And they still sometimes achieve those ends. But in the modern world, those signals are triggered more often, in contexts in which they're less helpful, and resolved less easily. Because of this mismatch between design and environment, the very mechanisms that once helped us survive now often just make us suffer.

To be clear, this mismatch isn't the root cause of our misery. As I argued earlier in this chapter, the human mind was never designed for happiness in the first place. Our emotional systems evolved to prioritize threats over comfort, loss over gain, and bad over good. Across the broad sweep of human history, that negatively tuned nature has held us in good stead. Our emotions have been an engine of survival and progress—even if the experience of them was rarely comfortable for the individuals involved.

But today, those same emotions are increasingly out of sync. They haven't changed. But the world has. Compared to earlier epochs of human development, many aspects of life have actually improved: we live longer, lose fewer children, and enjoy unprecedented material comfort and safety. And yet, subjectively, we are not thriving. Reports of anxiety, loneliness, and depression have increased significantly in recent decades, with especially sharp rises among young people. We are arguably more miserable now than we were built to be. The rest of this book is an attempt to understand why.

2

Because We Can't Bridge the Empathy Gap

We feel in one world, we think, we give names to things in another; between the two we can establish a certain correspondence, but not bridge the gap.

—Marcel Proust, *The Guermantes Way*

A Problem That Cannot Be Shared

In November 1992, Mike Stroud, a British physician with a passion for adventure, embarked on a journey that would test the limits of human endurance. Along with his partner, the famed explorer Sir Ranulph Fiennes, he set out to cross the frozen continent of Antarctica on foot without any help from animals, machines, or other humans—something no one had ever done before. For ninety-seven days, the two men dragged their nearly five-hundred-pound sledges across an endless expanse of ice, battling hunger and exhaustion as the elements laid waste to their bodies. Both men suffered horribly as wind and subzero temperatures gnawed at their extremities, but Fiennes had a much worse case of frostbite, which slowly began to eat away at his fingers and toes. Midway through the journey, he was hobbling in agony. Stroud felt helpless as he watched his typically stoic partner sink further into misery with every excruciating step.

"I could do nothing," Stroud confessed in his memoir, "but reassure him that I understood, though I didn't really. Pain is a problem that cannot be shared."

As Stroud perceives here, the empathy we claim to feel for others when they are suffering is often just an illusion. We cannot truly share a feeling like pain, hunger, or anger unless we are experiencing that same feeling ourselves. This is part of the reason why we often feel personally isolated when we are in the grip of a strong emotion like depression or grief, as if no one quite understands what we are going through. Odds are, they don't.

If anything, the kind of physical pain that Stroud observed in his partner is perhaps the *easiest* type of feeling to relate to. Fiennes's wound was external; Stroud could *see* the effect of the frostbite as it eroded his partner's forefoot. Even more viscerally, he could *smell* his rotting flesh. Often we feel a wave of disgust or nausea when we observe a gruesome wound or a bone that is obviously broken. In such cases, we are engaging in a kind of emotional translation, using our feelings of disgust as a proxy to perceive the intensity of someone else's pain.

This reflex is so strong that we can experience extreme empathic distress on behalf of a wounded person who himself actually feels no pain. This was illustrated vividly by the case of Edward Gibson, the "human pincushion." A vaudeville performer who was born congenitally unable to experience pain, Gibson would walk onto the stage and ask a man from the audience to stick fifty to sixty pins into him up to his head, then he would pull them out one by one as spectators gasped or sometimes grew faint. As the writer David B. Morris noted, "It is clear that Gibson's audience, no doubt reflecting a general human response, found themselves incapable of imagining a truly pain-free existence. They instinctively supplied the pain he did not feel."

Yet there are many types of physical pain—not to mention seemingly endless varieties of psychological pain, which we will explore in the coming chapters—that have minimal outward manifestations and don't trigger any discernible visceral reactions in us when we encounter them in others. When someone is suffering from these internal miseries, we may feel compelled to say things like "I feel your pain," especially if we've endured something similar in our own lives, but usually we are lying to ourselves as well as to them. Whatever sympathy we experience in such cases is purely of the cerebral kind, which is to say not much sympathy at all.

Adam Smith understood this. In *The Theory of Moral Sentiments*, he wrote that our sympathies naturally gravitated more toward visible pains than those that lurked beneath the surface. "We conceive in a much more lively and distinct manner the pain which proceeds from an external cause, than we do that which arises from an internal disorder." While the sight of a physical wound or fracture might elicit an immediate and visceral reaction, Smith observed that internal suffering—whether physical or psychological—leaves us grasping at an abstract sense of what the afflicted person might be enduring.

"When we condole with our friends in their afflictions, how little do we feel in comparison to what they feel?" he wrote. "We may even inwardly reproach ourselves with our own want of sensibility."

Like many of Smith's observations, this rings profoundly true for me. I try to be compassionate when a friend shares some personal misery. But my deepest, most visceral feelings of empathy come not when I learn of an individual's plight, but retrospectively, when I have a closely related experience and suddenly think to myself, *Oh,* that *is what they were feeling.*

On one occasion, when my back suddenly "went out" when I was carrying rocks to construct an outdoor sauna, my almost instantaneous response was a surge of empathy for a friend who had been long complaining of back pain. Of course, I had expressed sympathy, and maybe even attempted to convey understanding, but it was only when I was immediately feeling what he was experiencing—or at least a small taste of it—that the words truly (but belatedly) aligned with emotions in my mind.

It occurs to me that, while I am unable to truly fathom the feelings of my friends and relatives until I've experienced their plight myself, I have no such trouble empathizing with the suffering (or joy) of a fictional character in a great novel. This seems like a paradox.

Freud once remarked that "creative writers are valuable allies" because they grasp truths about the mind that philosophy and science often struggle to articulate. That's part of the reason I turn to literature again and again in this book. But that alone doesn't explain why I find myself more moved by the silent desperation of the title character in Tolstoy's grim novella *The Death of Ivan Ilyich* than by a neighbor's chronic illness. I suspect it has something to do with the skill of novelists—the best among them don't just describe emotions; they make us feel them. In Ivan's case, we feel the isolating horror of dying from a nameless internal illness while everyone around him seems almost inconvenienced by the event. "The awful, terrible act of his dying was, he could see, reduced by those about him to the level of a casual, unpleasant, and almost indecorous incident (as if someone entered a drawing room diffusing an unpleasant odour). What most tormented Ivan Ilyich was that no one pitied him as he wished to be pitied." In his memoir, the poet Christian Wiman describes a similar kind of emotional exile as he endured an excruciatingly painful treatment for a rare form of bone marrow cancer:

"Though I have in my life experienced gout, bladder stones, a botched bone marrow biopsy and various other screamable insults, until recently, I had no idea what pain was. It *islands* you. You sit there in your little skeletal constriction of self, of disappearing self, watching everyone you love, however steadfastly they may remain by your side, drift farther and farther away."

For those of us at the bedside watching a loved one endure acute physical or psychic pain, the hardest part is not simply witnessing the suffering but facing the truth that we cannot cross into their experience or carry even the smallest share of their burden.

Empathy Gaps

While it is almost impossible to empathize with someone when you are not literally sharing their pain, you might be surprised to discover it is equally impossible to empathize with yourself—to imagine how *you* would feel, or act, when in a different emotional state from the one you're in now. The term that I came up with to describe this phenomenon is an *empathy gap.*

The idea first came to me back in the 1990s, when my standard jogging route took me up Pittsburgh's notoriously long and steep Greenfield Hill. On the ascent, I would always grow tired and miserable. My pace declined, my motivation flagged. By the time I reached the top I was on my last leg, cursing myself for soldiering up the hill yet again, swearing this was the last time, and even doubting I could make it back to the starting point. Descending the other side, however, as soon as I caught my breath I instantly forgot my former pain and wondered what all the fuss had been about. Once I noticed the pattern, I began to see it everywhere.

I observed, for example, that when I got an invitation to travel to give a talk in a different time zone, it mattered what time zone I was in when I got the invitation. If well rested, in my home time zone, I would think, *No big deal,* about making a long trip and would likely accept. However, if I was jet-lagged in a different time zone when the invitation came in, and in touch with the misery of travel, I would be far more likely to decline.

Empathy gaps can come in many varieties. There are *hot-to-cold* gaps in which one is in an affectively charged state—e.g., hungry, cold, angry, sleepy, or sexually excited—and trying to imagine how one would feel and behave if *not* in that state. And there are *cold-to-hot* gaps in which one is in an affectively "cold," or emotionally neutral, state and trying to imagine how one would act or behave in a hot state. Empathy gaps can occur prospectively, retrospectively, or interpersonally. Over-shopping on an empty stomach is a classic manifestation of a prospective hot-to-cold empathy gap, and believing, right after a big lunch, that one is going to have a light dinner is a prospective cold-to-hot empathy gap.

Mike Stroud, once he made it home from his death-defying Antarctic adventure, experienced a more extreme version of this same kind of emotional blindness—a retrospective cold-to-hot empathy gap: "Even though I can clearly remember saying to myself every day of the journey 'I must never do this again,' I don't feel now as I did then. The *memory deficit* is playing its tricks already."

The issue is not a deficit of *memory* but rather of *feeling*; because he is in a different affective state, he is in many respects a different person from the one who suffered through all the pains and privations of the ninety-seven-day polar trek. And so you might ask—as I did of myself in the last chapter, under more prosaic circumstances—who is the *real* Stroud? The man, starving and exhausted, who committed countless times to never attempt such a reckless adventure again? Or the man, warm in his room, who callously ignores his former self's protestations as he begins to devise fresh adventures that will plunge him once more into the brink?

In some cases, empathy gaps give us the courage to take risks and embark on difficult challenges that we might later deem incredibly meaningful. But in other cases, they lead us to make decisions that are, in hindsight, catastrophic—and not just for us. We underestimate how much we'll suffer, or overestimate how much others can bear. We plan to say no, but end up saying yes (or remaining silent). We picture ourselves keeping calm, then explode. We think we'll have "just one drink," or that we will leave our car at the bar and call an Uber after we've had one too many.

These aren't only errors in judgment. They are engines of misery. In the previous chapter, I described how strong emotions reprogram us so completely that, in their grip, we become almost unrecognizable—even to ourselves. Empathy gaps are the impenetrable gulf between one emotional state and another. Unable to see past what we feel, we make costly mistakes—or assume, falsely and sometimes fatally, that our misery will never end.

The Heat of the Moment

Sex provides one of the more vivid illustrations of the way empathy gaps can impair our judgment. When in the thrall of passion, people often do things that they couldn't have imagined themselves doing beforehand and that they can't make sense of "the morning after." Along with my colleagues Dan Nagin and Ray Paternoster, I once presented eighty male undergraduates from the University of Maryland with a date-rape scenario involving a woman named Susan. Students were told to imagine that they had met Susan at a bar one night and went back to her apartment:

> After listening to music for a few minutes, Susan turns down the lights and begins to kiss you and rub your penis through your pants. In response, you begin to kiss and fondle Susan's breasts. You then reach under her skirt and begin to touch her. She allows you to do this, and after several minutes you attempt to remove Susan's clothes. Susan tells you that she thinks she is not interested in having sex but does not try to physically stop you.

The subjects were then asked to rate, on a 0-to-100-percent scale, the likelihood they would either: (1) "stop kissing and fondling her immediately when she expressed a lack of interest in sex"; (2) "verbally coax her to let you remove her clothes"; and (3) "have sex with her even if she protested."

Subjects were randomly assigned to one of three groups. In the "sexual arousal" condition, they viewed photographs of nude women before reading the scenario and predicting their behavior. In the "no arousal" condition, they viewed photographs of similarly attractive but fully clothed women before reading the scenario and predicting their behavior. And, in the "prior arousal" condition, they viewed the provocative photographs on one day, then returned to answer the questions on the following day.

Our main prediction, which was supported, was that sexually excited subjects would be more able to imagine themselves behaving in a forceful manner than those who were unaroused. The mean self-predicted likelihood of "pushing the issue" (which mainly meant verbally coaxing Susan) when she said "no" was 80 percent in the immediate-arousal condition but only 50 percent in the no-arousal condition—a large and statistically significant difference.

What about the third, prior arousal, condition? Hopefully you, the reader, noticed and wondered about that one. It has a backstory.

In 1994, I took a leave of absence from my job at Carnegie Mellon University and followed my wife, Donna Harsch, a historian of Germany, to Berlin. At a party we had been invited to (a disappointingly rare occurrence), I struck up a conversation with a legal scholar, who introduced herself as a close associate of Catharine MacKinnon, the feminist legal theorist known for her fierce opposition to pornography. MacKinnon's research focused on women's rights and sexual abuse and exploitation. She was quite a controversial figure, famous both for her views—she cast pornography as a civil rights violation and form of human trafficking—and her personal life. In the early 1990s she dated (and at one point was engaged to) Jeffrey Masson, a Sanskrit scholar who, due to his turbulent experience as head of the Freud Archive, was the subject of a book by *The New Yorker* writer Janet Malcolm, to whom he famously bragged that he had had sex with over one thousand women.

When I told MacKinnon's colleague about our experimental design, which then included only two conditions—viewing nude photos or clothed photos—her reaction startled me: "You are creating rapists by showing them pornography!"

Though the charge seemed absurd to me, given the prevalence of nudity in all kinds of media, it gave me pause, and, after recounting it to my collaborators, we decided to include an additional experimental treatment—the *prior*-arousal condition, in which participants viewed the nude images one day, but only answered the scenario questions the next. If we were "creating rapists"—whipping men up into a lasting state of sexual aggression—then these participants should have responded to the "date rape" scenario more aggressively than those who had never seen the arousing images. Our aim was to show that this was not the case.

Results from this treatment reassured us—indeed, they more than reassured us, because, surprisingly, respondents in this condition expressed a *lower* likelihood that they would misbehave than those in the no-arousal control condition. We conjectured that they *had* been aroused when they viewed the nude pictures, couldn't get in touch with that arousal a day later when they answered the questions (due to a retrospective cold-to-hot empathy gap), and concluded that they were not the type of person who would be likely to misbehave in the "heat of the moment."

The gap between the judgments people make in a neutral state versus the heat of the moment suggests that many people would do things when they were sexually aroused that they would later regret. Sure enough, in 2007, a team of Dutch researchers tested whether empathy gaps might explain the "morning after syndrome"—the self-recrimination that occurs when one is in a cold state, recalling excesses committed in a hot state (typically when intoxicated and/or sexually excited).

Their study had three phases, in each of which subjects performed a different task. In the first phase, subjects were asked to describe a sexual act that they performed in the past and now regretted. In the second phase, they were randomly assigned to either a sexual-arousal or no-arousal condition. Participants in the arousal condition watched a ten-minute erotic film, and those in the no-arousal condition watched a ten-minute film depicting an (unarousing) runway fashion show. In the final phase, subjects were presented with the description of the sexually regrettable behavior that they had described roughly ten minutes earlier and were asked to evaluate it. Consistent with a hot-to-cold empathy gap, men who were sexually aroused were less likely to judge themselves harshly as compared with those who were not sexually aroused.

A Taste for Torture

In some situations—sex being a classic example—being in a "hot" state, in the grip of a strong emotion, can lead us to make reckless or immoral choices that we would easily recognize as wrong in a calmer state of mind. But in other cases, the problem is the opposite: being in a "cold" or emotionally neutral state can blind us to the suffering of others, which we would easily recognize if we could experience even just a small dose of their pain.

Although the United States is a signatory to the Geneva Conventions, which prohibit torture, in the aftermath of the 9/11 attacks, the George W. Bush administration began to authorize the use of torture in interrogations of alleged terrorists held at Guantanamo Bay and "enemy combatants" captured on the battlefields in Iraq and Afghanistan. When these practices were eventually challenged by legislators and the courts, the administration refined its definition of torture to include the most blatant techniques, such as electric shock, but did not categorize other techniques such as sleep deprivation, waterboarding, and forced immobility as torture.

In a *Fresh Air* interview, *New York Times* national security reporter Scott Shane referenced a largely forgotten 1956 article in the *Archives of Neurology and Psychiatry*. The piece, written by two physicians hired by the US Department of Defense, was an early psychological assessment of what the Bush administration dubbed "enhanced interrogation techniques"—the same methods used by the Soviet KGB. The techniques included isolation, exposure to cold, food and sleep deprivation, and the forced maintenance of painful physical positions. "The living organism cannot entirely withstand such assaults," wrote the authors of the report:

> Another technique widely used is that of requiring the prisoner to stand throughout the interrogation session or to maintain some

> other physical position which becomes painful. This, like other features of the KGB procedure, is a form of physical torture in spite of the fact that the prisoners, and KGB officers alike, do not ordinarily perceive it as such. Any fixed position which is maintained over a long period of time ultimately produces excruciating pain.

These same techniques were widely used at Guantanamo and in Iraq and Afghanistan, and the position of the Bush administration was that none of it constituted torture. As Shane noted, Donald Rumsfeld, the former defense secretary who oversaw interrogation policy during much of this period, begrudgingly withdrew some techniques after public criticism. In one memo, Shane said, Rumsfeld scoffed at objections to prolonged standing, remarking that he personally "stood for eight hours a day" at work, so he "didn't really see why this was such a big deal for the prisoners."

Part of the problem, I think, is that the people designing these interrogation policies had no idea what it actually felt like to be on the receiving end. Along with two colleagues, Loran Nordgren and Mary-Hunter Morris, I conducted a series of studies exploring how hot-to-cold empathy gaps affect perceptions of torture. We asked participants whether specific interrogation tactics should be classified as torture or merely as "enhanced" techniques.

Our studies focused on three methods: exposure to cold temperatures, sleep deprivation, and social isolation. Some participants were exposed to small doses of the relevant discomfort. Based on the hot-to-cold empathy gap, we predicted—and found—that those who experienced even a small "taste" of the pain were more likely to judge the technique as torture and to oppose its use. In the sleep-deprivation study, for example, we asked participants enrolled in an executive MBA course—who tend to be chronically sleep-deprived—either before or after a three-hour evening class whether sleep deprivation should be classified as torture. Those asked at the end of class, when they were presumably sleepier, were significantly more likely to say yes.

As in the earlier sexual arousal study involving the hypothetical date with Susan, we also included a "day delay" condition to test how long these empathy effects last. In the torture study focusing on cold exposure, participants read a short description of an interrogation tactic: "Exposing detainees to cold weather is a common interrogation tactic. This tactic involves keeping a detainee in a near-freezing room with little clothing on for up to five hours at a time."

Participants were randomly assigned to one of three groups. In the cold condition, they submerged one arm in a bucket of ice water while making their judgments. In the control condition, they placed their arm in room temperature water. In the prior-cold condition—the analog to the prior-day-arousal condition—participants made their judgments ten minutes after removing their arm from the ice water, by which point they no longer felt cold.

As predicted, participants in the cold condition judged the cold-room tactic to be significantly more painful than those in the control group. The same gap emerged between the cold and prior-cold conditions, suggesting that people need to be actively experiencing discomfort to fully appreciate its severity. Just having experienced it recently isn't enough. That finding challenges the assumption that people with prior exposure to these techniques—such as military interrogators who are subjected to them during training—are in a better position to assess their ethicality.

It also undercuts arguments like Rumsfeld's, which rely on vague personal analogies. Standing for eight hours in an office isn't the same thing as being forced to stand, sleep-deprived and under duress, in a windowless cell.

One of the most notorious forms of torture (calling it by the term it merits) used by the US Armed Forces was "waterboarding," which involves strapping a person down, covering their face with cloth, and pouring water over it to simulate drowning. Waterboarding should have been particularly difficult to justify since the US had previously argued in court that enemy soldiers who employed the technique committed war crimes. The difficulty of appreciating the horror of miseries one isn't currently being subjected to was grimly, albeit somewhat amusingly, illustrated by the Chicago radio host "Mancow" Muller, who had dismissed the procedure's seriousness and volunteered to undergo it, expecting to "laugh it off." In footage he recorded of the event, however, he quits within seconds and concedes that waterboarding is "far worse than I expected . . . and I hate to admit this: it's absolutely torture." The writer Christopher Hitchens also subjected himself to this technique for an article in *Vanity Fair* and wrote that the experience left a lasting psychological imprint: "If waterboarding isn't torture, then nothing is."

The empathy gap doesn't just distort how we judge others. It also warps how we judge our past selves. People who break under torture—especially from methods like isolation or cold that seem, in retrospect, relatively minor—often carry deep shame. The Russian historian Irina Scherbakova, who conducted hundreds of interviews with victims of Stalin's terror, found that those who had betrayed friends or confessed to false crimes under interrogation—often from methods as deceptively tame as prolonged standing or sleep deprivation—were among the most haunted decades later. Looking back, they struggled to understand how they could have once capitulated to what seemed like "mild" coercion.

That inability to reconcile one's own breaking point with the apparent mildness of the method is not unique to Stalin's victims. In the aftermath of the Korean War, the US Air Force commissioned a social scientist named Albert Biderman to study why so many captured American POWs had cooperated with their Communist captors. Analyzing the experiences of 220 repatriated servicemen, Biderman found that the most effective forms of coercion weren't necessarily the most brutal. Instead, they were often subtle, slow-building, and hard to recognize, such as alternating kindness with humiliation or enforcing petty, arbitrary rules.

The less obvious the force, the more likely it was that prisoners would fail to register what was happening as torture. And because they couldn't see the external pressure clearly, they believed they had broken of their own volition. That belief—that they had failed a basic test of strength or character—left them riddled with guilt. In Biderman's words, the "disabling effects of guilt" eroded their ability to resist further, undermined their sense of agency, and left them tormented by the conviction that they had collapsed from within.

The trauma of torture may last a lifetime. But the ability to truly empathize with someone else's—or even one's own—experience of it seems to disappear almost as soon as the torture ends.

Design or Defect?

Why do we have empathy gaps? Why should we systematically mis-predict how powerfully emotions will change our behavior, our judgment, and our desires? One possibility is that the empathy gap serves some evolutionary function. Some have proposed that poor memory of the pain of childbirth, for instance, was necessary for the perpetuation of the species. As the writer Francine Prose once commented, "Our very survival as a species depends on the fact that our memory of pain and fear is—blessedly, mercifully—short. After giving birth to my first child, I thought, as so many do, that no reasonable woman would ever endure childbirth twice. And it wasn't until I was in labor with my second son that I remembered how I could possibly have thought something like that."

My guess, however, is that poor memory for pain did not evolve for such a reason. For one thing, it seems unlikely that early humans were even aware of the connection between sex and procreation. For another, the sex drive seems to be particularly effective in displacing exactly such long-term considerations, just as it leads people to have unsafe sex or go to bed with the wrong person—even when they know better.

In my opinion, the explanation for hot-to-cold empathy gaps is more prosaic. As Cosmides and Tooby have argued, the function of emotions is to reprogram us. When we're in a strong emotional state—angry, afraid, aroused, in pain—we don't just feel differently; we think differently. Our perceptions shift. Our priorities rearrange themselves. Things that once felt important, essential, or desirable can suddenly seem irrelevant, absurd, or even repulsive.

Once an emotion fades, we may remember what we said or did, and even have an idea of how we felt. But we lose access to the mental world that went with that emotion—the hunger, panic, desire, and certainty that made it feel so real and urgent at the time.

Why do we have these blind spots? I suspect the reason is simple: nature just isn't perfect. Maybe, in another million years, we'll have evolved to bridge the gap.

No Exit

On the morning of April 11, 1987, Primo Levi, the celebrated Italian author of *Survival at Auschwitz,* stepped out the door of his apartment in Turin and, according to police reports, flung himself over the fourth-floor banister. Elie Wiesel, another Holocaust survivor, attributed Levi's death to the trauma he suffered during the war: "Primo Levi died at Auschwitz 40 years later."

Yet by most accounts, Levi's final days were consumed not by memories of the past, but by miseries of the present. He was severely depressed, as his biographer Ian Thomson later wrote. He was suffering from intense prostate pain. He couldn't sleep. He had been on a roller coaster of drugs—antidepressants and antipsychotics—meant to pull him out of his slump. Nothing worked. He could barely summon the energy to phone a friend or run himself a bath. He had no interest in talking about anything except how depressed he was. Intellectually, he understood that the darkness might lift, as it had during previous episodes. But, he told a doctor friend, it didn't feel that way: "I know that this phase will pass, just as the others have done, but I'm aware of this only at the rational level; my overriding impression is that it will last forever and that I will never find an exit out."

Thankfully, the vast majority of people who experience major depressive episodes do not die by suicide. Yet there is reason to believe that many who do are falling victim to an empathy gap—one so profound it makes it impossible to imagine ever feeling better. "Levi had reached that phase of the disease," Thomson wrote, "where all sense of hope had vanished, and with it any idea of a future."

The truth is that our will to live is not remotely stable. It fluctuates with how we feel—day to day, even hour to hour. In a remarkable study, psychiatrist Harvey Chochinov and colleagues administered periodic surveys to terminal cancer patients in palliative care, measuring, among other things, their "will to live." They found dramatic changes over intervals as short as twelve hours. As the researchers concluded, "These large fluctuations suggest that will to live is highly unstable."

Although empirical research on suicide is difficult, in part because suicide so often goes unreported, and in part because those who attempt it and are successful are not around to discuss their motives, the limited research that has been done suggests that many if not most suicides are not the product of stable, calculated, appraisals of one's prospects for future happiness. Rather, they're impulsive. They tend to occur during the intense emotional down periods that many people experience from time to time. Such fluctuations in moods would rarely result in suicide—if only people could recognize them as such.

But depression, like all emotional states we've discussed in this chapter, distorts perspective. Both personal accounts of depression and more rigorous empirical research find that when people are unhappy, they tend to remember and think about their lives differently. They more readily recall moments of having felt similarly unhappy in the past and they anticipate feeling similarly unhappy in the future. Research by the psychiatrist J. John Mann shows that people who are prone to impulsive behavior are especially likely to attempt suicide, again suggesting that suicide is often an impulsive, rather than carefully thought out, act.

Finally, and perhaps most sensationally, studies have found that those who do attempt suicide and fail are, in retrospect, often relieved. Of course, some of these survivors of suicide attempts may not truly have wanted to commit suicide in the first place; their attempt may have been a "cry for help," but this seems unlikely for the many people who jump from the Golden Gate Bridge—a method that is successful in the great majority of cases. In a profile of survivors of Golden Gate Bridge jumps, *The New Yorker* writer Tad Friend wrote that "survivors often regret their decision in midair." A particularly dramatic, though seemingly not unusual, example was that of Ken Baldwin, who

> hurdled over the railing, afraid that if [he] stood on the chord [he] might lose courage. Baldwin was twenty-eight and severely depressed on the August day in 1985 when he told his wife not to

> expect him home till late. "I wanted to disappear," he said. "So the Golden Gate was the spot. I'd heard that the water just sweeps you under." On the bridge, Baldwin counted to ten and stayed frozen. He counted to ten again, then vaulted over. "I still see my hands coming off the railing," he said. As he crossed the chord in flight, Baldwin recalls, "I instantly realized that everything in my life that I'd thought was unfixable was totally fixable—except for having just jumped."

In a study titled "Where Are They Now?" Richard H. Seiden tracked the fate of 515 people who were prevented from jumping from the bridge between 1937 and 1971. When Seiden followed up—on average, about twenty-six years after the initial attempt—94 percent were either still alive or had died of natural causes. As Seiden concluded, "the findings confirm previous observations that suicidal behavior is crisis-oriented and acute in nature." Yet the decision, for all but the fortunate few who manage to survive the fall, is permanent. As Proust wrote, "It is always thus, impelled by a state of mind which is destined not to last, that we make our irrevocable decisions."

When I present my empathy gap research to young audiences, I often try to connect these observations to their own lives, in the hope of possibly averting such a calamity. I talk about how, when you fail an important exam or get dumped by a boyfriend or girlfriend, it can feel like the end of the world—like you will never feel better again. What you learn as an adult is that you almost always will end up feeling better; but you can never outgrow the feeling, in the moment, that you won't.

3

Because Our Self-Worth Is Shaped by Others

> Nature, when she formed man for society, endowed him with an original desire to please, and an original aversion to offend his brethren. She taught him to feel pleasure in their favourable, and pain in their unfavourable regard. She rendered their approbation most flattering and most agreeable to him for its own sake; and their disapprobation most mortifying and most offensive.
>
> —Adam Smith, *The Theory of Moral Sentiments*

Big Brain, Thin Skin

By the mid-1980s, Thomas Schelling had attained a status in academia that few others could ever hope to achieve. A distinguished economist, he used game theory to revolutionize strategic thinking during the Cold War and developed models—like "tipping points"—that explained how individual behavior could shape large-scale social phenomena such as racial segregation. He held a professorship at Harvard, published widely and influentially, and would go on to win the Nobel Prize in Economics. By any reasonable standard, his reputation should have been secure.

And yet Schelling did not feel secure.

This was especially striking if you ever saw him speak. I once shared a stage with him at a conference in Bergen, Norway, where he gave a keynote that left the audience spellbound. At one point, he told a story—if memory serves, about a time when one of his children had fallen ill—that had me so tense with emotion that, when the child turned out to be fine, I burst into tears. I then had to collect myself before delivering my own, far less eloquent and emotionally evocative remarks.

So I was startled to discover, in a 1988 essay, that this same preeminent intellect confessed to being deeply sensitive to criticism. His mood, he wrote, could shift dramatically depending on how an audience received him. "I have observed in myself," he noted, "so often that it no longer surprises me, that if I give a performance before some audience, I am jollier at dinner, and eat more, if I am pleased with my performance. Disagreeable feedback spoils the evening."

What puzzled Schelling was not just the intensity of his reaction, but the irrationality of it. He knew that, statistically speaking, one bad moment shouldn't outweigh decades of success. "At my age," he wrote, the "record of my performance ought to reflect so many observations that one more experience . . . could hardly affect a rational self-assessment." And yet it did. He was, as he put it, committing a "rudimentary statistical error": allowing the salience of the latest feedback to cloud a lifetime's worth of experience.

Even with this insight, he remained vulnerable, his sense of himself swayed by the fleeting judgments of others. Schelling's struggle underscores a paradox of self-esteem: its inherent fragility. How is it possible to amass a mountain of evidence affirming our worth, only to have it shaken by the smallest setback?

Why can't we just ignore the little whispers of self-doubt we hear in our heads? The answer has to do with the architecture of our self-esteem system. As we'll see in the pages ahead, that system is deeply implicated in almost every form of psychic misery. It makes us hesitant to ask for help when we desperately need it, quick to take offense (sometimes with violent results), and painfully sensitive to slights others barely notice. It can distort our memories, fuel overweening ambition or crippling insecurity, and lock us into feedback loops that are as destructive as they are difficult to escape.

Self-Esteem Is a Group Project

Schelling's surprisingly delicate ego would hardly surprise the psychologist Mark Leary. Now an emeritus professor at Duke University, Leary began his career by studying social anxiety and the fear of rejection. He noticed in his experiments that research subjects were profoundly concerned with how they were perceived by others and would go to great lengths to avoid social injury. And, much like Schelling, they had a surprisingly unstable opinion of themselves. If they felt momentarily accepted by someone else, their self-esteem would blossom; if they faced an instance of rejection, it would wilt.

Alain de Botton, in his book *Status Anxiety*, compared self-esteem to a leaky balloon "forever requiring the helium of external love to remain inflated, and ever vulnerable to the smallest pinpricks of neglect." Botton claimed that there was something "absurd" in our ego's hypersensitivity: "Our mood may blacken because a colleague greets us distractedly or our telephone calls go unreturned. And we are capable of thinking life worth living because someone remembers our name or sends us a fruit basket."

In our common, everyday understanding, we tend to think of self-esteem as something distinct from how other people judge us. The way we are perceived by others may be a *contributor* to self-esteem, according to this view, but people can and should be able to achieve high self-esteem even when the world is not flooding them with love and admiration. Indeed, it is sometimes argued that "true" or "mature" self-esteem is not affected by other people's opinions. Yet, according to Leary, this is really an illusion. Our self-esteem can't be independent of our perceptions of how other people see us because self-esteem is entirely *based* on those perceptions. As he puts it, what we usually call self-esteem is just an individual's assessment of their "relational value" to other people.

We are a social species. We evolved to form cooperative groups to pool our resources and provide protection and support in times of need. Such mutual aid often made the difference between life and death. Because of the immense survival value in being a well-regarded member of such groups, humans evolved automatic mechanisms to ensure they would behave in ways that foster social acceptance—without having to spend our limited brainpower calculating, in each situation, whether a specific person's approval might be advantageous.

Leary's theory conceptualizes self-esteem not as some independent, relatively stable internal sense of how much we may like or dislike ourselves, but rather a dynamic, hyperresponsive gauge of how other people are perceiving us moment to moment. Leary calls this gauge "the sociometer." As soon as the sociometer detects that we are the recipient of even mild social disapproval—such as frowns, disinterest, physical distancing, or as Schelling sometimes experienced after public speaking, negative feedback—it pulls out its stick and administers a beating. Admittedly, the sociometer doesn't *only* administer beatings; we do feel good when our self-esteem is high. But the system displays the same marked asymmetry we saw with emotions: the stick that accompanies social rejection or devaluation is far more potent than the meager carrot of social acceptance.

Perhaps because the self-esteem system evolved in small, tight-knit social circles in which nearly every person we encountered was important for survival, the sociometer responds automatically and often disproportionately to social feedback from almost anyone, even those who objectively don't matter to us. This is why the rude honk of a horn from a stranger at a traffic light or a dismissive gesture from a store clerk in a city far from home can evoke an instant and visceral emotional response. The system acts, in effect, as if *anyone* we encounter matters to us, prompting an automatic emotional reaction to even trivial instances of perceived rejection. While we can later rationalize these situations—telling ourselves, for instance, that we'll never see that rude driver again—the initial sting of rejection often occurs too quickly for reason to intervene, reflecting how deeply entrenched these emotional responses are in our evolutionary makeup.

It Hurts to Ask

As indispensable as the sociometer has been to the survival of our species, there are times when it would be better for us as individuals if we could just switch the damn thing off. This is not only because it feels awful to experience low self-esteem—that much is obvious. But there's a deeper, less appreciated issue: we often go to self-destructive lengths to avoid experiencing those very feelings. A particularly vivid example is when we hesitate to ask other people for much-needed help.

Surely you've heard the advice: *It doesn't hurt to ask.*

Actually, it does. That's precisely why the saying exists—not because it's true, but because we need reassurance to overcome our deep reluctance to ask for help. In a recent paper I wrote with Ania Jaroszewicz and Roland Bénabou, we found that asking for help is often so uncomfortable that people will forgo significant benefits—sometimes even life-or-death benefits—to avoid the emotional risk involved.

Take an extreme case like end-stage kidney disease. A transplant from a compatible friend or relative might offer a chance at survival, yet many patients struggle to bring themselves to ask. The same basic dynamic shows up in more mundane situations. Perhaps you are struggling financially, and friends or family might be able to provide a critical lifeline, but reaching out for that help feels worse than being broke. Or you need your neighbor to watch your kids so you can work a crucial shift—but the idea of asking feels too awkward. Why, when the benefits of help are so clear, do we so often avoid the simple act of requesting it?

The answer we propose lies in how the sociometer shapes our decisions. When we receive help, we don't just get the practical value of the help itself—the money, the kidney, the babysitting. We also get a self-esteem boost, a "carrot," in the form of an emotional reward: the feeling that the person who is helping us values and cares about us, viewing our relationship as important and close.

But if receiving help feels mildly good, getting turned down feels *incomparably* worse. The rejection stings not just because we needed the help, but because asking required overcoming our own hesitations, making ourselves vulnerable in the hope that the other person would come through. When they don't, the pain is amplified by the knowledge that they *know* how much it matters—and still refuse. Rejection hurts whether the request is big or small. A small request denied feels insulting because it would have been so easy to grant. A desperate plea denied is devastating because the other person *could* have made a life-changing difference—but didn't. Knowing all this, at least implicitly, many people in many situations struggle in silence rather than face the potential blow to their self-esteem.

What we truly want when we are in need isn't to ask for help and have someone come through—it's for them to offer *without having to ask*. An unsolicited offer of help signals three critical things: (1) the helper is aware of the need, showing they "see" us in our moment of vulnerability; (2) the helper understands the discomfort and potential rejection involved in asking for help and wants to spare us from that anxiety; and (3) the helper values us enough to offer assistance without requiring a request, showing that the relationship is important to them.

But there are many reasons why someone who can help won't offer and needs to be asked. They might assume our silence means that we're okay. They could fear offending us, since an unsolicited offer might imply that they think we can't handle our own problems. They might worry about overstepping boundaries, especially if the situation feels personal. In such cases, it would serve us far better to reach out and face any uncertainty head-on. But the sociometer, ever vigilant and protective, makes us hesitate. At such moments we are being sabotaged by our own evolutionary wiring. A system designed to keep us alert to social threats also makes us too afraid to ask for help, even when it's right in front of us.

Insecurity, Aggression, and Ambition

The sociometer's hypersensitivity to perceived social threats doesn't just affect our willingness to seek help—it can also fuel more destructive behaviors, such as violence and aggression.

Social scientists once believed that certain marginalized groups, particularly in low-income, underserved areas, had developed cultural norms that not only tolerated but *encouraged* aggression and violence. The idea, widely embraced in mid-twentieth-century criminology, was called the *subculture of violence* theory. According to this view, certain "subcultures" were conditioned to see violence as a normal way of resolving conflicts, defending one's honor, or maintaining respect. The theory had the unfortunate effect of reinforcing stereotypes about specific communities, casting their members as inherently more violent due to their cultural backgrounds.

But when social psychologist Leonard Berkowitz actually spent time interviewing incarcerated violent criminals, he found no real evidence to support this theory. What he discovered instead was that much of the violence committed by these men was a response to perceived insults—*ego threats*—rather than an adherence to their group's cultural code. These men didn't turn to violence because it was normalized within their communities; they did so because they felt their self-worth was under attack. When writing up his findings, Berkowitz observed that these aggression-prone men were "quick to see themselves as challenged and frequently interpreted someone else's remarks as belittling them," which "often infuriated" them and "stimulated them to lash out impulsively."

When it came to violence and self-esteem, psychologists had assumed that people who acted aggressively suffered from *low* self-esteem, and attributed their aggression to deep feelings of inadequacy and self-loathing. Such ideas have filtered into our culture. In portrayals of supervillains—whether from the pages of comic books or the annals of history—violent tendencies are often ascribed to a low sense of self-worth. How many times have we encountered the familiar claim that, if only Adolf Hitler had been accepted by the Viennese Academy of Fine Arts, he might have channeled his energy into painting rather than becoming a mass murderer? In fiction, characters like these abound—individuals who commit acts of violence, all seemingly driven by inner turmoil, rejection, and a *lack* of self-esteem.

But when psychologists have actually studied aggressive people, the results revealed something surprising: people with violent tendencies actually have *high* self-esteem. At an intuitive level, this seems to make no sense. If those given to violence have such high self-esteem, why do they react so intensely when they feel they're being disrespected?

This remained an open question until the early 1990s, when the psychologist Roy Baumeister got his hands on the seemingly contradictory data. Baumeister's resolution of the paradox was brilliant. Maybe, he proposed, people who are aggressive actually do have a very high opinion of themselves, but it's incredibly fragile, even by the hypersensitive standards of the sociometer.

It's as if they're walking a narrow wall, constantly on guard against anything that might knock them off their lofty but precarious position. For these people, Baumeister explains, "that miserable sinking feeling that goes with a drop in self-esteem is all too familiar, and they are on guard to avoid it. Even a slight hint or mild implication that questions their personal worth may elicit a strong response."

Baumeister built his theory on a variety of earlier studies, including Berkowitz's, that showed a link between insecurity and aggression. In a 1989 study, for example, the psychologist Michael Kernis and his colleagues gave subjects paging devices for a week, which prompted them periodically to answer questions about how they felt about themselves. A week later, subjects completed four scales designed to measure their levels of anger and hostility. The results revealed that *fluctuations* in self-esteem—rather than low self-esteem itself—predicted aggression. Specifically, those with *high but unstable* self-esteem were the most prone to violence. As the authors noted, such people have the most to lose from an ego threat: "Although they possess a positive self-concept, it is fragile and sensitive to evaluative information. Unless they react with anger and hostility to a self-esteem threat, they may be compelled to negatively revise their self-concept in line with information provided in the threat."

As Baumeister explains, this fragile self-esteem is why those with high but unstable self-worth are often the most aggressive: their self-image is too easily destabilized by criticism or rejection. When faced with ego threats, they react violently, not out of self-loathing, but out of fear of losing their inflated, fragile sense of superiority.

It's no coincidence that all sixty-five violent offenders in Berkowitz's study were men, as are the vast majority of subjects in aggression research. The fact that men are far more violent than women is so obvious it's often taken for granted. The prevailing explanation is that men are simply "hardwired" to be more aggressive—a view that might now be framed in terms of *toxic masculinity*. But clever and intriguing research by Jennifer Bosson, Joseph Vandello, and colleagues on what they call "precarious masculinity" suggests that men's delicate self-esteem system might also play a role in the gender gap.

These researchers document the phenomenon of precarious masculinity in a number of different ways, including presenting people with statements such as "Manhood is hard won and easily lost"—or in contrast, "Womanhood is hard won and easily lost"—and then asking them whether the statement makes sense to them. The manhood statement is easy for most people to understand, but the parallel statement about womanhood leaves many scratching their heads.

They then examine the impact of such fragility on a variety of different behaviors, including aggression, by having men braid some cords of fabric, and informing some of them that it is a rope-braiding task (a framing that might evoke, for example, images of sailors preparing their ship for a voyage) while telling others that it is a hair-braiding task (chosen to be quintessentially female). Men whose manhood had been threatened by being told they were braiding hair were more likely to choose to hit a punching bag instead of solving a puzzle, and they punched it more aggressively. They were also more likely to gamble and to opt for a smaller, but more immediate, payoff.

Fragile self-esteem has been linked not only to aggression but also to poor health behaviors, gender disparities in education, and support for extremist politicians. The pattern is clear: when faced with a threat to their shaky sense of masculinity, some men would rather make reckless, even violent, choices than risk feeling weak.

But insecurity doesn't always lead to destructiveness. Sometimes it leads to ambition. The same hair-trigger sensitivity that makes people lash out can also drive them to prove themselves—relentlessly, obsessively, sometimes brilliantly.

That's why so many biographies of powerful men dwell on their deep insecurity. Robert Caro's *Years of Lyndon Johnson* is a case in point. "What was it he wanted—attention? sympathy? respect? dominance?" Caro asks of LBJ. "Whatever it was, he was desperate to have it." A colleague from Johnson's early years described him as having "some kind of inferiority complex. You could see that right away." Alexander Hamilton, writes Ron Chernow, was "a mass of insecurities that he usually kept well hidden." Walter Isaacson calls Henry Kissinger an "odd mixture of ego and insecurity." These men accomplished extraordinary things—but their insecurity didn't just fuel their ambition. It also made them domineering, vindictive, and sometimes ethically indifferent. Johnson's quest for power helped pass landmark civil rights legislation—but it also played a role in the catastrophic quagmire of Vietnam. Kissinger's need to outmaneuver his rivals may have sharpened his geopolitical thinking—but it also led him to treat human lives as pawns on a global chessboard.

In my own (far less consequential) case, I think a measure of insecurity has been essential to whatever success I've achieved as an academic. I have colleagues and collaborators who are brilliant—but who have been much less productive. My theory about several of these people is that their brilliance was evident from an early age, so that success came easily and they became very secure in the veracity of the world's appraisal of them. Basically, they have nothing to prove. The insecure types, like me, in contrast, feel the need to prove ourselves in all tasks and at all points in time, and, for whatever level of success we do achieve, often fear "falling on our face" if we don't maintain our performance.

My mother, Sophie Freud, once told me about a friend of hers from Vienna, a certain psychiatrist, who gave an absolutely dreadful public lecture. Despite his dismal performance, he stepped down from the podium utterly convinced that his lecture had been the embodiment of perfection. He was, in a sense, the anti-Schelling—blissfully immune to self-doubt. While I sometimes envy such people, I can't say I would trade my own insecurity for their high self-esteem.

Why It Hurts to Look Up

As we've seen, sometimes the self-esteem system is reliably triggered by ego threats such as bad feedback or perceived social rejection. But often, the threat is simply the presence of other people—people who seem better than us in some way, and whose very existence makes us feel worse about ourselves.

This reflexive tendency to compare ourselves to others was the subject of Leon Festinger's social comparison theory, developed in the 1950s. Festinger argued that in the absence of objective benchmarks, we turn to the people around us as reference points for understanding who we are and how we're doing. His most important insight wasn't that people compare themselves to others—that much is obvious—but that we compare ourselves most intensely to those who are *personally relevant*: people similar to us in age, background, ability, or status. The coworker who was hired at the same time but is promoted earlier. The grad school classmate who goes on to outshine us. The friend whose kids seem to vault over every childhood hurdle, while ours stumble. These are the comparisons that sting.

Because people have many dimensions—height, charm, salary, intellect, fitness, popularity, and so on—there's usually some axis on which we come out ahead. But in classic asymmetric fashion, the dimensions where we're "up" tend to give us little joy. They're neutral, sometimes embarrassing, other times guilt-inducing. The traits we lack, meanwhile, *gnaw* at us—a subject I'll delve into deeper in the chapter on envy.

I recently got to thinking about the way social comparison influences self-esteem after a former colleague of mine, Alex, made an offhand comment about being short. I'm reasonably tall, but I never noticed the height difference between us (partly because he has a giant wall of curly hair). I had, however, very much noticed the difference between myself and Peter, another colleague who is taller than me. That contrast stuck in my mind. So did another: On a visit to a large internet company (the largest, in fact), I was told by the head of HR that the organizational structure was completely flat—everyone treated everyone else as peers. This, I was assured, was their culture. But in every meeting we attended, that same HR executive was treated with extraordinary deference, and people seemed far more relaxed when he wasn't present.

These observations led to a hypothesis: status differences seem larger when looking up than when looking down—the opposite of the swimming pool "high-dive illusion," where the height seems negligible from below but terrifying from above.

That conversation with Alex ended up sparking a research project. Together with a graduate student, Jae Yeon (Jenny) Chang, we ran a series of studies exploring how people think they stack up against others across various dimensions. We started literally—with height. We asked everyone in a department of our university to estimate the height of their colleagues. Then we expanded to mass surveys on other dimensions people care about: status, attractiveness, body mass, education, humor, and so on. Participants were asked to think of a friend, judge how they compared on each dimension, and assess the magnitude and emotional impact of the difference.

Surprisingly and disappointingly, we didn't find evidence that differences seem greater when looking up. But we did find something else: people looking up *thought about* those differences much more often than those looking down. Like moths to a flame, we are drawn to upward comparisons—comparing ourselves to those better off in some way—which of course are the very kinds that make us miserable.

The Friendship Paradox

If you wanted to design a technology to maximize the misery caused by social comparison, it would be hard to do better than social media. Platforms like Instagram, TikTok, and X (Twitter) provide constant cues of popularity—likes, views, reposts—and most make it easy to compare your metrics to others'. Alas, thanks to a perverse logic known as the "friendship paradox," those comparisons are usually unfavorable.

First observed by the sociologist Scott Feld, the friendship paradox is the odd fact that most people's friends, on average, have more friends than they do. It sounds illogical, but it's just a quirk of how social networks work. People with lots of friends appear in more people's social circles, so you're more likely to bump into them than you are to bump into people with just one or two friends. Even in a small group, this creates a lopsided view: when you look around, you're statistically more likely to see people who are more connected than you are.

The same logic applies with a particular vengeance online. Your friends will, on average, get more likes than you do, because they have more friends. And, for the same reason, the people you follow will have more followers than you. Algorithms that prioritize the most liked and shared content only magnify this imbalance. The result is a distorted social mirror, in which everyone else seems more admired, more included, and more connected than you.

This would be bad enough, but social media doesn't just show us other people's numbers; it also shows us their best moments, which are often posed, filtered, photoshopped, and curated. I once watched a table of glum-looking young women in Brillobox, a Pittsburgh bar named after one of the iconic silk screens by Andy Warhol (a Pittsburgh native we claim despite his lifetime efforts to disavow his hometown). They sat in near silence for almost an hour, each one absorbed in her phone. Then one of them lifted her phone to take a selfie. Suddenly, the table transformed: everyone smiled, laughed, leaned in. It was an explosion of joy—entirely for the camera. The photo, I have no doubt, was a hit. It probably made dozens of acquaintances feel like they were missing out on a moment of perfect friendship. But it didn't make the people in the photo any happier—and may have done the opposite.

Indeed, a mountain of evidence supports the idea that upward social comparisons—the constant exposure to gorgeous models, social influencers with seemingly perfect lives, and even the curated feeds of one's friends—make people, and especially adolescent girls, feel worse about their own bodies, faces, and lives. For example, a systematic review found that online social comparison was strongly linked to negative body image and harmful attitudes toward food and weight that may lead to eating disorders. And, a study by economists Luca Braghieri, Ro'ee Levy, and Alexey Makarin that measured the mental health consequences of the staggered introduction of Facebook across US colleges during the platform's initial rollout, found that the rollout of Facebook at a college had a negative impact on student mental health and concluded that these negative impacts resulted from "Facebook fostering unfavorable social comparisons."

I often wonder, however, whether these studies only tell half of the story. Could it be that projecting a good life on social media doesn't just make people on the receiving end feel bad, but also makes the poster feel bad—when they compare their real life to the one they display online? Their own imperfect body they see when they look in the mirror compared to the one shot from flattering angles and perhaps edited with AI tools? The face they wake up to in the morning compared to the unblemished, perfectly made-up face on their Instagram feed? Is it possible that we aren't looking up only at others, but also at the idealized image of ourselves that we created for them?

Feedback Effects

I've spent most of this chapter arguing that the self-esteem system is fragile by design—that a hint of criticism or an unflattering comparison can send it tumbling. The problem is that recovery comes much more slowly. Self-esteem drops in an instant but drags its feet on the way back up, because our feelings of worth—high or low—have a tendency to feed on themselves.

Like many other psychic miseries, those associated with negative self-esteem are intensified by *feedback effects*: self-reinforcing loops that intensify whatever state we're in. How does this work? One well-documented mechanism is *mood-dependent cognition*: when we're in a good mood, we're more likely to recall positive, ego-reinforcing memories; when we're in a bad mood, our mind retrieves failures, rejections, and embarrassments. This cycle is captured in the figure below: high self-esteem brings to mind confidence-boosting memories, while low self-esteem triggers mortifying ones.

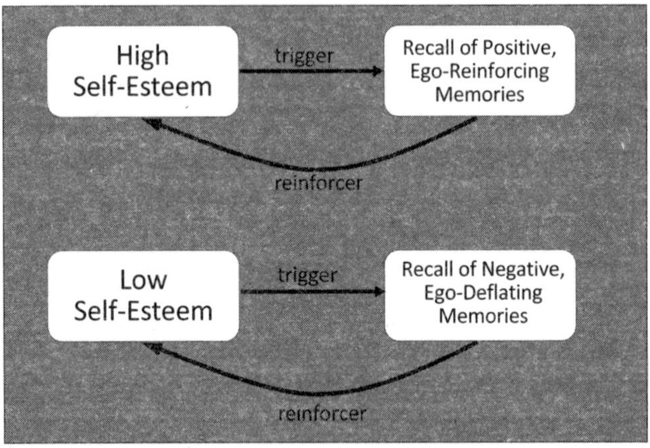

This is great when we're riding high, because positive thoughts tend to lock that mood in place. But when the mood is low, the same mechanism can make us wallow—unable to recall evidence to the contrary, or imagine that we might ever feel differently. That state is almost a kind of emotional amnesia in which we forget our own history of success and worth, as Schelling experienced.

The effect is compounded by interpersonal factors. When we're self-assured, the world tends to reflect that confidence back. People trust us more. They defer, approve, buy what we're selling—including, crucially, when what we're selling is ourselves. But when our self-esteem falters, we come across as tentative, needy, or downcast—because we are—and people react accordingly. As we sense their hesitation, skepticism, or even avoidance, our mood and self-esteem plunge.

These loops help explain why "average" self-esteem is so rare. If we feel confident, feedback effects push us toward overconfidence. If we start to doubt ourselves, they ensure the doubt deepens. I suspect that many of us are aware on some level that there is very little middle ground when it comes to self-esteem, and so if we happen to be riding high, like Berkowitz's violent felons, we have a well-founded horror of falling into a low state—because we know it's a long way down.

Feedback effects are a misery multiplier. And—spoiler alert—nearly every negative emotion in the second half of this book is made worse by them. A fear of rejection makes people paranoid and suspicious, leading them to sabotage relationships and trigger the very outcome they dread. Anxiety sharpens our focus on potential threats, which heightens our vigilance, inflates the sense of danger, and leaves us feeling ever more on edge. Loneliness distorts our social instincts, pushing others away and deepening the isolation we're desperate to escape.

Not long after I started noticing this pattern, I was at a small interdisciplinary meeting filled with some of the smartest economists and psychologists I know. I used the opportunity to ask the group why feedback effects exist—in other words, what possible evolutionary advantage could there be to having so many psychological mechanisms that make bad feelings worse? In coffee breaks and meals during the remainder of the meeting, several people told me they found my question provocative and intriguing. Alas, none provided anything close to a persuasive answer. I'll offer my own before this book ends.

4

Because We Have Feelings About Feelings

> For a moment he felt good about this. A moment or two later he felt bad about feeling good about it. Then he felt good about feeling bad about feeling good about it and, satisfied, drove on into the night.
>
> —Douglas Adams, *So Long, and Thanks for All the Fish*

Getting Meta

In 1993, during a sabbatical in Berlin, I arranged to meet my mother in Castillonnès, a small village in southwestern France. During World War II, she had spent a few anxious months there after fleeing Nazi-controlled Vienna and then Paris. Despite the harrowing circumstances, she remembered the town fondly. She and her mother had been taken in by a kind local family who owned a brick factory, and the mayor, a gentle, bookish man, lent her volumes from his private library and later arranged the *sauf-conduit*—the safe-conduct papers—that allowed them to travel onward to Nice and, eventually, the United States. Visiting the village for the first time in fifty-three years was deeply moving for her.

That evening, we had a choice between two restaurants, one clearly superior to the other in food, ambiance, and general charm. I begged my mother to let us go to the better restaurant. Given the time and expense of meeting there, and the significance of the event, it made sense to cap off the day with a memorable meal, and both of us could easily afford it.

But I knew my pleas were useless. Right up until her death in 2022, my mother remained an inveterate tightwad. She had trouble spending money even when, as in this situation, it made perfect sense. She was not uniformly cheap; she could be quite generous in funding big-ticket items, such as down payments on her children's houses or a quality cello for her musical granddaughter—but she simply couldn't bring herself to pay for certain types of expenses. Taxis, flowers, and restaurants all fit into this category.

Interestingly, it didn't matter who was paying; she would never take a cab even if it could be expensed, and it made no difference to her that I would be paying for the dinner in France. Her horror at the extravagance of flowers was so extreme that she alienated any number of houseguests by aggressively rejecting bouquets that they arrived (and ended up leaving) with.

What always struck me as so remarkable about her tightwad tendencies was how at peace she was with them. She never cared what others thought. She experienced no inner conflict. She had simply accepted that certain things weren't worth spending money on.

Unfortunately, I inherited her stinginess but not her self-acceptance. For me, spending money is often painful—but so is noticing my own reluctance to spend. That conflict came into sharp relief one summer in Croatia, when, in the ripeness of middle age, I found myself sharing a bed with an adult male friend in a sticky, cramped budget Airbnb. Listening to him breathe as I lay wide awake and vaguely resentful, I remember thinking: *This is so ridiculous. What is wrong with me? Couldn't I just pay for my own room, like a normal person?* It was a two-tiered kind of problem: I disliked spending money, but I also disliked that I disliked it.

We all have preferences, tastes, things that we do and don't like. But sometimes, we don't like what we like. We wish we were the kind of person who wasn't so hungry for praise, or who appreciated opera, or who liked to wake up early, or who wanted sex less—or more.

Classical economic theory typically assumes that people want what they want, and that happiness comes from getting it. But when your desires are out of step with your values, your identity, or some better version of yourself that you're always aspiring toward, getting what you want often makes you feel not better—but worse.

The economist and philosopher Amartya Sen coined the term *meta-preference* to describe this dissonance: situations when we wish we wanted something other than what we actually want. Consider, again, social media. It satisfies desires—to be distracted, to feel engaged, to not be alone with your own thoughts. But many people hate how often they reach for their phones. They find themselves scrolling at red lights, on the toilet, while walking down the street—half aware, the whole time, that they're going to feel a little worse afterward. The algorithm gives us what we want, but not, as the philosopher Harry Frankfurt might have put it, what we *want to want.*

Frankfurt referred to these as "second-order desires"—desires about our desires—and argued that the capacity to form them is what sets humans apart from other animals. While other species may act on impulses and even deliberate in some rudimentary sense, only humans reflect on what they wish they wanted—and judge themselves accordingly. For Frankfurt, this capacity defines us as persons. It is also a major source of misery.

The Cost of Being at War with Yourself

For much of his life, the writer John Cheever had two serious problems. The first was a legendary case of vodka-for-breakfast alcoholism, which he finally managed to kick after a stint in rehab in the 1970s. The second was more complicated. Famous for his short stories and novels like *The Wapshot Chronicle*, Cheever was the bard of mid-century suburban malaise—an ambitious writer who dreamed of seeing his face on a US postage stamp. He was also a committed husband and father, a self-mythologized lover of women who nevertheless was privately tormented by an erotic desire for men. In a piece in the *London Review of Books*, Colm Tóibín describes his predicament, quoting from Cheever's own journals, which are a lacerating record of shame and self-loathing:

> On the one hand, he wanted to be a happily married man and a devoted father, the man whom his friends and readers believed him

to be. "It is my wife's body that I most wish to gentle, it is into her that I most wish to pour myself," he wrote. But, on the other hand, his thoughts had a habit of turning, as they did in that same diary entry, to his sexual interest in men, this time to a male figure he had seen by a swimming-pool. "His soft gaze follows me, settles on me, and I have a deadly itchiness in my crotch." He thought about having sex in the shower with the young man; he contemplated "the murderous checks and balances of a flirtation." But then he realised that he was, in fact, a respectable married man with three children who dreamed of having his face on a stamp.

Cheever lived at a time when he could not safely give in to his desires, and, more to the point, he had so fully internalized mid-century mores about homosexuality that he did not *want to want* to give in to them. "If I followed my instincts," he wrote in another entry, "I would be strangled by some hairy sailor in a public urinal. Every comely man, every bank clerk and delivery boy, was aimed at my life like a loaded pistol." The result was that his inner life was deformed by a "terrifying erotic chaos." In one reflective entry, he gestures toward a more general truth about this kind of inner conflict: "we obscure our self-knowledge with anxiety . . . it is not what we desire but what *we fear and dread we may desire* that impedes us" (emphasis added).

Such inner conflicts constantly play out in quieter ways in everyday life. I saw just how common they are when my colleagues Linda Thunström, Andrea Mannberg, Benjamin Gilbert, and I conducted a series of studies on risk-taking preferences. When people think of risk, they typically think of financial speculation, fast cars, extreme sports—anything with speed, high stakes, and potential for disaster. But, in most people's lives, risk doesn't look like this. It can be risky to tell someone how you really feel. Or to voice an unpopular opinion. Or to ask for help.

According to most decision-making models, people choose whatever level of risk suits them. Some are risk-averse, others are daredevils—but either way, the assumption is that people are broadly acting in accordance with their own preferences. We wanted to test that assumption.

Across three surveys, we asked nearly 1,200 people how they felt about the risks they take in life—whether their choices reflected the kind of person they wanted to be. The results were striking: about half of all respondents said they were dissatisfied with their overall risk-taking. And of those, a large majority—around six to one—wished they took *more* risks in life, not fewer.

This dissatisfaction wasn't about thrill-seeking or reckless behavior. When we asked people what domains of life they felt misaligned in, they pointed to everyday social and emotional vulnerabilities: speaking up, meeting new people, being open in their relationships with loved ones. These weren't people regretting that they never went skydiving.

In most cases, what held them back wasn't their circumstances. It was their emotions: fear, anxiety, self-doubt. Conversely, the smaller group who felt they took too many risks often blamed impulsivity or thrill-seeking—again, internal forces that overpowered them. In both directions, the same pattern emerged: a split between the self that feels and acts, and the self that reflects.

Crucially, this misalignment seemed to have real consequences for people's well-being. Those who were dissatisfied with their level of risk-taking—whether they saw themselves as too cautious or too impulsive—reported significantly lower life satisfaction. The size of the gap was striking. On standard well-being measures, the difference between satisfied and dissatisfied participants was about as large as the difference between someone earning $37,500 a year and someone earning $75,000. Of course, money is only a crude proxy for well-being, yet it gives us a hint at just how costly these inner conflicts can be.

The Impartial Spectator

Adam Smith was one of the earliest thinkers to examine this tension between our preferences and our meta-preferences. He viewed human nature as a battleground of conflicting desires, a continuous tug-of-war between our immediate urges—what Smith called "the passions"—and our higher aspirations.

In *The Theory of Moral Sentiments*, Smith introduces the idea of the "impartial spectator," a powerful internal force that acts as a detached moral judge, observing and evaluating our impulses and actions. This inner voice isn't just a conscience—it's a mechanism of self-regulation that allows us to see ourselves as others might, making us both the actor and the audience of our own lives. By enabling us to step outside ourselves, the impartial spectator guides us to form judgments about our behavior and, ideally, strive toward a higher standard of conduct.

However, Smith was keenly aware of human frailty. While the impartial spectator sets exacting standards, even "the most perfect knowledge of those rules" cannot stop us from breaking them. As he puts it, the passions are "very apt to mislead" us—sometimes driving, sometimes seducing us into violating the very principles we uphold in our cooler, more rational moments. Even when we know what's right, the pull of our emotions and appetites can lead us astray.

In moments of intense desire, our passions often overpower our principles, leaving the impartial spectator temporarily sidelined. Only after the passion is satisfied do we confront the inner judge. Smith describes the result as "mortification"—a deep sense of guilt and self-reproach. This moral whiplash can be jarring: we find ourselves regretting or even despising the very thing or person we so intensely desired just moments before.

This sometimes happens when we eat too much cheese. It also sometimes happens after sex.

In one memorable passage, Smith seems to describe, in veiled terms, the aftermath of a visit to a prostitute—or at least that's how I've always read it. As soon as the "bodily appetites are gratified," he writes, "the object that excited them ceases to be agreeable: even its presence often becomes offensive to him; he looks round to no purpose for the charm which transported him the moment before, and he can now as little enter into his own passion as another person."

Even if, in the main, the impartial spectator succeeds at keeping us in line, Smith recognized that the constant clash between our better angels and our baser passions is a recipe for frequent misery. "The individual, by a great effort, may behave perfectly well; but the contest between the two principles, the warfare within the breast, may be too violent to be at all consistent with internal tranquility and happiness."

Many later thinkers took Adam Smith's concept of internal moral judgment and pushed it further, exploring the psychological costs of our relentless inner critic. For instance, Karen Horney, the German American psychoanalyst, saw the impartial spectator as a kind of personal oppressor. Horney coined the term *tyranny of the shoulds* to describe the endless demands people impose on themselves to be someone they're not. In extreme cases, such pressure can turn the psyche into a kind of "police state," one that suppresses "the spontaneity of feelings, wishes, thoughts, and beliefs." The result is that we can hardly feel anything without wondering whether we should.

Emotions, Squared

One of my best friends—let's call him Tom here, to protect his privacy—has an almost saintly character. He's generous, patient, and quietly self-sacrificing. But he's still human. One day, Tom confided in me that he found it painful when close friends of his—a very humble, unassuming couple—shared good news about their two children. This couple's pride was so understated, so charmingly devoid of arrogance, that it only made Tom feel worse about his own feelings of annoyance. He wanted to feel pure, unadulterated joy for them, but instead, he felt a pang of envy—maybe wishing his own children's talents received more recognition. The fact that such feelings arose at all troubled him deeply. Did they reveal a defect in his character?

I assured him, as any good friend would, that mixed feelings are just part of being human. Feeling envy doesn't negate the genuine happiness he also felt for his friends. Still, the moment was a perfect illustration of how we don't only judge our emotions intellectually—we also have visceral feelings about our feelings.

Throughout this chapter, I've explored the inner conflicts between how we feel and how we *think* we should feel. But these judgments often trigger a second wave of emotions, as they did for Tom—creating *emotions about emotions*. Sometimes, it's an excess of emotion that troubles us, like feeling embarrassed or ashamed after we lose our temper. Other times, it's a lack of feeling that bothers us—like guilt over not experiencing enough grief after the death of a loved one.

Joan Didion experienced a version of this unease in the midst of devastating loss. In the year both her husband and her daughter died, she found herself chastising her own grief, reproaching herself for focusing too much on her own feelings and not enough on what those who died may have felt.

"We remind ourselves repeatedly that our own loss is nothing compared to the loss experienced (or, the even worse thought, not experienced) by he or she who died."

These judgments may start merely as thoughts and self-reflections, but they quickly acquire an emotional charge of their own. The effort to feel somehow better or differently usually only makes us feel worse, as Didion observed. "This attempt at corrective thinking serves only to plunge us deeper into the self-regarding deep. (*Why didn't I see that? Why am I so selfish?*) The very language we use when we think about self-pity betrays the deep abhorrence in which we hold it."

The psychologist John Gottman—an expert on relationships and marriage—originally coined the term *meta-emotion* in the 1990s to describe how one person responds to another's emotions—especially in close relationships like those between romantic partners or parents and children. In his research, people tended to adopt a consistent *meta-emotional philosophy*—either accepting or dismissive—which shaped how they reacted to others' feelings and how they managed their own in the context of the relationship. These emotional stances, he discovered, played a crucial role in the health of marriages and the development of children. Children whose parents encouraged them to express all emotions, even the uncomfortable ones, showed greater resilience and emotional intelligence. Similarly, couples who acknowledged both positive and negative feelings with curiosity and acceptance tended to build stronger bonds and communicate more openly.

Of course, meta-emotions don't only affect our relationships with others; they also shape how we relate to ourselves. People who react negatively to their own emotions—who feel guilty or ashamed about being angry or sad—can trap themselves in a self-perpetuating spiral. John Teasdale, a clinical psychologist, argues that what sustains serious depression is not just sadness or despair but the self-critical feedback loop that follows—what he calls "depression about depression."

There haven't been many empirical studies about the role of meta-emotions in perpetuating misery. One exception is a recent experience-sampling study by Natasha Bailen, Haijing Wu, and Renee Thompson, who asked seventy-nine adults to report on their emotional states in real time over the course of a week. They found that people with higher levels of depressive symptoms were significantly more likely to experience "negative-negative" meta-emotions—like guilt about feeling sad or shame about feeling anxious. An earlier study by the Austrian psychologist Horst Mitmansgruber and colleagues used a Meta-Emotion Scale in a sample of over three hundred medical students to assess people's emotional reactions to their own emotions. They found that negative meta-emotions—especially shame—were robustly linked to lower psychological well-being. The authors speculate that "to maintain well-being, it might be as rewarding to minimize negative meta-emotions . . . as to minimize negative emotions [themselves]."

Of course, much of the wellness and mental health industry is devoted to resolving exactly such inner conflicts. There's a whole menu to choose from, depending on temperament and tastes: cognitive behavioral therapy for the rationalists, meditation for the spiritualists, pharmaceuticals for the biologically inclined. All promise, in their own way, to quiet the inner critic, to make peace between the passions and the impartial spectator. They can help—sometimes a lot. But at the end of the day, I doubt we can control our meta-emotions and meta-preferences any better than we can control our first-order ones. Treating any of our feelings as if they're illegitimate or unworthy probably just makes them—and us!—that much harder to live with.

5

Because We Crack Under Pressure

While gambling at checkers with some shipmates, [Benjamin Franklin] formulated an "infallible rule," which was that "if two persons equal in judgment play for a considerable sum, he that loves money most shall lose."

—Walter Isaacson, *Benjamin Franklin: An American Life*

One Night in Glasgow

I spent my junior year of college in Scotland. My university's clueless foreign office had spun tales of quaint harbors and fishermen with weathered faces. Instead I landed in the grimy splendor of Glasgow—then one of the poorest, unhealthiest, and most crime-ridden cities in Europe. It ended up being a great year, although my memory of it is smudgy, probably because of the number of brain cells I killed drinking in pubs. But somewhere in that haze of cheap pints, I met *her*.

She lived across the landing of my fifth-floor tenement, a schoolteacher with golden hair and enchanting blue eyes. To me, she seemed totally unattainable—older, more experienced in every way, and locked in a torrid love affair with a guy named Chip, a seedy, pathetic drug dealer who always left me wondering, *Why him?* My fascination with her was not subtle, and one day her roommate offered a word of advice (imagine, if you can, a strong Glaswegian accent): "Mind how you go. She's an elusive butterfly."

Partly to win her over, I bought a ridiculous hardtop convertible—completely impractical for Glasgow, where it rains almost every day. But one rare sunny afternoon, I took a chance, ditched the roof, and somehow persuaded her to drive into the countryside with me, all the while praying the weather would hold. Of course, it didn't; but she didn't seem to care. We arrived back sodden, and me more smitten than ever.

Then one night we ran into each other on Sauchiehall Street, and she stayed by my side all evening. When we finally stumbled into bed together, I could not believe my luck. I had fantasized about this very moment a hundred thousand times. But as my excitement soared, my body mutinied. Was it the alcohol? Possibly. My nerves? Almost certainly. Whatever the reason, I had never felt so betrayed by myself. She was right there, and I . . . couldn't. In the days that followed, I was suffocated by disappointment and longing, replaying the *what-ifs*, marinating in regret and shame. I've come to think of that night as a crowning example of one of life's cruelest truths: The moments that matter the most to us are often the ones we are least equipped to handle. Just when we need to keep it together, we begin to fall apart.

When Trying Hurts

Self-sabotage takes many forms. In the last chapter, I explored how people become their own worst enemy—abhorring themselves for how they feel, judging themselves for what they want, wishing they could be different than they are. Our meta-preferences and meta-emotions, shaped by the stern impartial spectator in our heads, often create inner conflicts that make us miserable. In this chapter, I shift from self-judgment to another insidious form of self-sabotage: the betrayal of our own best efforts, precisely when they matter most.

When we care deeply about succeeding, we push ourselves, focus more intensely, and give it everything we've got. Sometimes, that's exactly what's required. But in high-stakes moments, those same efforts can backfire. The harder we try, the *worse* we perform.

Take my Glasgow misadventure: a painfully vivid case of *choking under pressure.* Psychologists and economists, myself included, have studied this phenomenon in detail. From a purely economic perspective, choking makes no sense. The greater the incentive, the more it should theoretically motivate us to sharpen our focus and perform better. But as most of us have learned the hard way, trying desperately to succeed can sabotage our ability to do so.

During a crucial presentation, your voice cracks, your mouth goes dry, and your thoughts scatter. You feel yourself faltering, which makes you panic—and the panic worsens your performance, locking you into a vicious cycle. Beneath the surface, your body is mounting the same stress response that once helped our ancestors escape predators: the adrenal glands flood your system with adrenaline, your muscles tense, your heart pounds, your throat tightens. In a memorable *New Yorker* piece on stage fright, Joan Acocella described how even the most seasoned performing artists can be unraveled by this primal overreaction: "What Cro-Magnon man needed upon finding a bear in his cave is not what a modern person needs in order to play King Lear."

For me, the most visceral example of choking happens while mountain climbing. Having taken inadequate precautions against falling (almost all of the many risks I've taken in my life result from laziness, incompetence, or their close relative, hubris), I've found myself in precarious spots on rock faces, gripping handholds with nothing but air and a long drop beneath me. In such moments, every climber knows that the key is to stay calm and keep moving. I tell myself this, but my body doesn't listen. My palms sweat, my arms shake uncontrollably, my legs go into "sewing machine mode"—an uncontrolled twitching of the foot that resembles the action required to operate an antique foot-powered sewing machine. At such moments, it feels like my body is betraying me, taking me farther from safety when I most need control.

Choking under pressure is a particularly vivid example of a "feedback effect," a concept I first introduced in the discussion of self-esteem (Chapter 3), which will be a recurring theme throughout this book. A feedback effect happens when one's attempt to solve a mental or physical problem only makes that problem worse. Dry mouth degrades the quality of your performance, and awareness that it's not going well increases the tension and worsens the dry mouth. Sewing machine leg increases your chance of falling off a cliff, which naturally increases your level of fear, and so on. These loops seem to be not only perverse but also antithetical to our survival and reproduction. So why are we so susceptible to them?

Part of the answer is that emotions are only useful within a certain range. Like most evolved systems, they are blunt instruments—designed to activate in response to rough environmental cues. The mechanisms that regulate fear, jealousy, sadness, or anger don't rely on your conscious deliberation; you can't just *decide* to start or stop feeling them, just as you can't decide to slow your heart rate or stop your hands from shaking. Nor do these emotions respond precisely to the particulars of a given situation. This means they often overshoot or undershoot. Too much emotion is of course dangerous, but too little emotion also carries serious risks: people with abnormally low anxiety (a condition called *hypophobia*) are more likely to take reckless, sometimes fatal risks; people who don't feel jealousy may lose romantic partners; people who don't experience much sadness or regret may keep making the same harmful mistakes.

Most emotions serve us well only within a certain bandwidth—like a car that handles beautifully up to eighty miles per hour, but starts to spin out of control at higher speeds. When it comes to performance, the trick is to stay within the speed limit.

Psychologists have long tried to quantify what that optimal range looks like. One of the earliest and most influential attempts came in 1908, when Robert Yerkes and John Dodson set out to test how varying levels of arousal affected learning. They used Japanese dancing mice as their subjects and placed them in an enclosure with two passageways. One passageway, marked with a white card, concealed a punishing surprise—a mild electric shock. The other passageway, marked with a black card, was neutral and provided no shock. The researchers sought to determine how quickly the mice could learn to avoid the passageway with the white card and therefore escape the electric shock.

First, to avoid confusion, it's worth clarifying what it means when a psychologist uses the word *arousal.* In this context, arousal refers not to sexual excitement, but to a general state of physiological and mental alertness. It's how activated the mind and body are—which can usually be measured through changes like an increased heart rate, heightened sensory awareness, and energy levels.

Yerkes and Dodson wanted to see how arousal levels affected learning, so they manipulated the intensity of the shocks given to the mice if they went down the passageway marked by the white card: low (a mild buzz), medium (a forceful jolt), or high (a ferocious zap). What they discovered, which is now enshrined as the "Yerkes-Dodson Law," is that there is an inverted U-shaped relationship between performance and arousal.

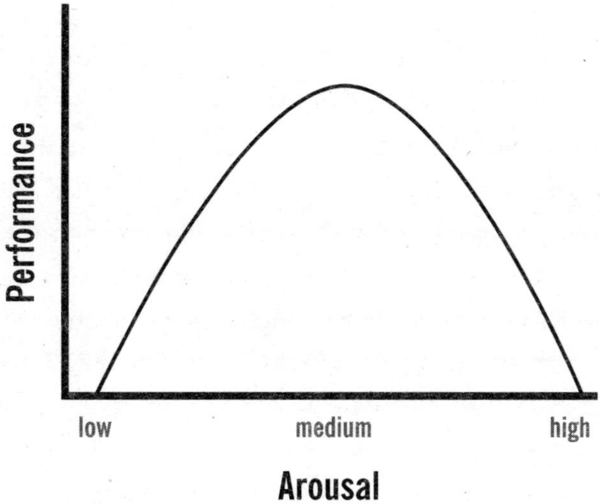

Performance improves with increased arousal up to an optimal point, but beyond that, further arousal hinders performance. In other words, the mice learned most quickly when they received shocks of intermediate intensity. Low-intensity shocks didn't give the mice the motivation they needed to make the effort to learn; high-intensity shocks were so overwhelming and stress-making that the mice couldn't learn from the experience and often tragically repeated their mistakes. The general tendency to perform best at medium levels of motivation has been observed across species, from monkeys to birds to fish to humans.

Tolstoy intuited the same law in *Anna Karenina*, when Vronsky, dabbling at painting, steps away from his canvas because he suddenly feels "too agitated": "He could work neither when he was too indifferent nor when he was too highly roused and saw everything too distinctly. There was only one stage between calmness and inspiration, at which work was possible, and to-day he was too excited."

You might think the lesson of Yerkes-Dodson is that, whatever the task, we need to train ourselves to stay in the Goldilocks zone of medium arousal—and that practice and experience are critical for keeping us there when the stakes are high. In many cases, that's true. But choking isn't just about pressure pushing us out of the optimal zone. It's also about how *awareness* of that pressure warps our attention, sometimes causing even the most practiced performances to unravel.

The Putting Green

On the sixteenth hole of the 1989 Masters Golf Tournament, Scott Hoch appeared to be on the brink of victory. A fan called out that he needed "just two pars to win the Masters!"—one of professional golf's most prestigious contests. He later told ESPN that the comment broke his concentration. He tried to shake it off and stay "in the zone," but he ended up driving his next shot far off the course, slipping into a tie. In the sudden-death playoff, Hoch seemed to recover, and soon he found himself on the green with just two feet standing between him and triumph. For a professional golfer, this putt was as close to a sure thing as it gets. He decided to take his time. He paced, replaced his ball, examined the line for what felt like an eternity.

"I wasn't nervous," he insisted later.

But then he sent the putt skimming past the hole, a miss so astonishing it stunned the crowd, which groaned in sympathetic agony. Hoch chucked his putter into the air, disgusted with himself. He lost the championship on the next hole.

At the press conference afterward, he said: "Well, I'm glad I don't carry a gun with me"—a thought I confess to having not infrequently in the course of everyday life, especially in the middle of the night (more on that later).

The curse of that fateful miss lingered, overshadowing the rest of his career. He never came close to winning another Masters. Other players on the tour avoided him, overwhelmed by pity and social awkwardness. "Some guys would see me and feel so bad they wouldn't know what to say," he said. From then on, the nickname "Hoch the Choke" followed him wherever he went.

What makes choking under pressure so fascinating—and cruel—is how it defies logic. How can an expert golfer miss a putt he's practiced and perfected a thousand times?

In the early 1990s, the psychologist Richard Masters set out to answer this very question, using the game of golf to study why people choke. He described how skills are learned and automated, beginning with explicit, rule-based knowledge before progressing to an effortless, almost unconscious mastery. As athletes move from the attentional phase—where performance is "slow, erratic, and requires much effort"—to the automatic phase, their actions become "smooth, effortless, and fast," relying less on conscious thought.

But under extreme pressure, Masters found, experts often "reinvest" their actions with explicit knowledge. It's like their brain thinks: *This is important; I'd better pay attention!* But paying attention is the last thing they need to do. They "overthink" a task that has become second nature, disrupting its natural flow.

To test this theory, Masters conducted an experiment involving participants who had never played golf before. He divided these novices into groups that would be trained under different learning conditions. Some players learned the skill explicitly, receiving verbal feedback and written instructions to focus on the mechanics of putting. Others trained implicitly, practicing their putts while distracted—an experimenter asked them to recite random letters of the alphabet. This prevented them from consciously focusing on their movements.

After practice, Masters tested both groups under pressure—making them believe that their putts would be closely scrutinized, that there was money on the line (twelve pounds), and that they could earn more or lose almost all of it based on their performance. All participants attempted the same putt—from 150 centimeters away, twice the length of Hoch's infamous miss.

The results were striking. When pressure was introduced, participants who had learned to putt explicitly—focusing on rules and deliberate thought—suffered a clear and reliable drop in performance, holing substantially fewer putts than they had in practice sessions. By contrast, those who had learned the same skill implicitly showed no comparable decline under pressure.

This experiment reminds me of a story involving the son of a friend, a college grad who, for several years, pursued his dream of becoming a professional golfer. Catching up about our children, my friend noted that his son had a tendency to play extremely well going into tournaments, but to choke if he started strong and the tournament was "his to lose." Since I had done research on the subject, he asked me if I had any advice for his son, and I came up with what I thought was a clever idea.

Anticipating that he would inevitably become deliberative—pay (too much) attention to his shot—when the stakes were high, I advised him to practice under exactly those conditions—to deliberately overthink his swing when he was practicing, essentially creating the state of mind that he would inevitably experience in a tournament.

Although I thought (and still do think) that, logically, such a strategy makes perfect sense, I was then unaware of Masters's research showing that this was the *worst* way to prepare for a high-pressure performance. I doubt my bad advice played any role in it, but my friend's son ultimately gave up on his dream and went to law school (which, not being a golf lover, is what I thought he should have done all along).

Large Stakes and Big Mistakes

Studying how high stakes affect performance is harder than you might think. Today, many experiments in psychology and economics rely on platforms like Amazon's Mechanical Turk, where participants earn about a dollar for completing a ten-minute study. While useful for many purposes, it's hard to believe that winning or losing such a meager sum could genuinely induce the feelings that arise in high-stakes situations. Dramatically increasing incentives is an obvious solution, but even the most generous research budgets won't enable researchers to hand out life-changing amounts of money.

However, in some of the world's poorest regions, relatively modest payouts *are* life-changing. Taking dubious advantage of the situation, my colleagues and I conducted an experiment in a rural Indian village to explore how monetary pressure influences performance across different types of tasks.

The study involved six games, each testing a different skill: creativity, memory, or motor coordination. Participants solved a complex nine-piece metal puzzle, repeated sequences of flashing lights, memorized spoken digits, guided a ball through a maze, threw tennis balls at a target, and used rods to drop balls into precise slots. The stakes were significant. Reaching a "very good" performance level on any task earned participants four hundred rupees (roughly ten dollars at the time), equivalent to a month's living expenses in the village. Those achieving a "good" level earned half as much, while those falling short received nothing.

We designed the study to answer a simple question: How does the magnitude of incentives affect performance on different types of tasks? On motor and creative tasks—where flexibility and focus are key—we expected performance to deteriorate under pressure. But on memory-based tasks, which rely more on recall than creativity, we predicted performance might improve, as pressure could help sharpen attention.

The results surprised us: participants choked across *all* tasks. Whether solving puzzles, recalling sequences, or completing physical challenges, their performance worsened in the high-stakes condition. What was going on? We concluded that the culprit was attention misallocation. Instead of focusing on the task at hand, participants' attention was diverted to the consequences of succeeding or failing. High stakes drew their minds away from the puzzle or maze and toward the potential reward—or the disappointment of falling short. In this sense, choking under high stakes isn't about the nature or complexity of the task—it's about how the pressure itself hijacks our attention, pulling us away from what matters most.

The Hidden Costs of Attention

Why does pressure, which ideally would sharpen focus and elevate performance, so often have the opposite effect? The answer lies in how the brain manages its most limited and valuable resource: attention. We like to think our attention is under our control, but most of the time it's steered by fast, automatic, and unconscious processes. We can see this very clearly in the digital age, where notifications, endless feeds, and irresistible "clickbait" headlines hijack our attention by exploiting basic drives for novelty, curiosity, and social comparison—while algorithms personalize what we see to keep us from looking away.

Because attention is such a precious resource, our brains are wired to conserve it. One of the most efficient strategies is *automation*: once we've practiced a task enough times, we no longer need to consciously think about it. This frees up attention for other things. Learning to drive a car is a useful example. When we first learn to drive, every action demands focus. But once driving becomes second nature, we can navigate traffic while bickering with our partner or getting absorbed in a true-crime podcast. However, if something unexpected happens—a dog darts into the road, a collision appears ahead—we instantly stop talking and redirect our attention to the road. (Our conversational companion usually stops talking, too, for the same reason.) This is normal and adaptive. The brain is hardwired to deploy its attentional "superpower" when circumstances demand it—and in many situations, that leads to better performance.

The problem is that in many high-pressured performances—hitting a golf ball, playing a piano in front of an audience, having sex with a new partner—we would actually be better off if the brain did *not* treat the situation as especially important. Here, paying attention often breaks the flow and backfires. In the athletic arena, "Hoch the Choke" is by no means the only victim. In a study of NBA free-throw performance, economist Zheng Cao and colleagues analyzed data from eight seasons (2002–2010) and found a measurable drop in accuracy during high-pressure moments. Free-throw percentages fell by about 4 percent when players shot in the final minute while trailing by one or two points. The decline became steeper in the final fifteen seconds—dropping 6.3 percent when the team was losing by two points and 8.8 percent when down by one. Even players whose teams were ahead by one or two points showed signs of choking, especially on the second of two free-throw shots, when pressure tends to peak.

If paying too much (or the wrong kind) of attention is the reason we choke under pressure, then maybe the solution is *redirecting* attention. Indeed, some studies show that subtle distractions can help high-level performers stay in the flow. Surgeons, according to some studies, are less likely to make errors when operating while listening to music. And skilled baseball players perform significantly better at batting practice when prompted to focus on subtle cues in the environment (either an auditory tone or the direction of the ball coming off their bat) instead of the mechanics of their swing. As the influential sports psychologist Bob Rotella once put it, "The best swing thought is no thought."

•••

So far, we've seen how pressure causes failure by making performers too aware of tasks that should run on autopilot. But raising the stakes can also backfire in a different way—by *narrowing* attention at the exact moment when success requires flexible, open-ended thinking.

In one 1979 study, representative of a larger body of research documenting the negative impact of rewards on creativity, the psychologists Kenneth McGraw and John McCullers showed that even a small monetary reward could hinder performance on tasks requiring creative problem solving. They asked two groups of college students to solve ten water-jar problems—puzzles that involve measuring out a precise amount of water using three jars of different sizes. One group was offered no incentive; the other stood to earn a monetary reward for each problem they solved. The first nine problems could all be solved using the same slightly convoluted method, and repetition trained participants to rely on it. But the tenth problem was different: the old method no longer worked. The only solution was to abandon the familiar strategy and discover a different—and, in fact, simpler—one. That's where things went wrong. The students working for money took nearly 60 percent longer to solve the final puzzle than those in the no-reward group. While both groups did equally well when sticking to the established pattern, the reward group began to choke precisely when a shift in thinking was required.

The Attention of Others

Raising the stakes, even slightly, can scramble your attention in ways that make you falter. Sometimes your attention shifts to the stakes themselves—what you might win or lose. Other times your attention interferes with skills that should run on autopilot. And when success requires flexible, creative thought, your attention can narrow so intensely to the task that you lose the ability to think outside the box. In all these cases, it is *your* attention that undoes you. But there is a kind of attention that can be even more disabling to performance: the attention of others.

Sports psychologists Ken Harb-Wu and Alex Krumer, for instance, identified a surprising "home disadvantage" among professional biathletes: athletes were more likely to miss shots when competing in their home countries than when abroad. The likely culprit? The pressure of performing in front of a home crowd, and the heightened desire to make local fans proud.

This dynamic showed up again in one of the companion studies to our field experiment conducted in India. Uri Gneezy, then a professor at the University of Chicago, ran a simple classroom experiment in which students solved anagrams—jumbled-letter word puzzles—under two conditions: either alone at their desks, or at the front of the room, on an overhead projector, with everyone watching. Students were clearly more motivated while under scrutiny, and, consistent with the idea that too much motivation can hurt performance, they solved substantially fewer anagrams.

Artistic performances are another realm in which the attention of others cripples even highly practiced performers. Daniel Day-Lewis famously walked off the stage in the middle of a performance of *Hamlet* in 1989, and has not performed live theater ever since. One night in 1967, Barbra Streisand, singing in front of more than one hundred thousand people in

Central Park, forgot the lyrics to her own songs—and for nearly thirty years after would only do the occasional charity concert. In her *New Yorker* article, Acocella mentioned that a 1987 survey by a group of fifty-two major orchestras in the United States found that 27 percent of its members had used beta-blockers to manage their performance anxiety. "Today," she writes, "the figure is no doubt considerably higher."

Unlike professional athletes and artists, whose lives really are conducted under intense scrutiny, for most of us the pressure of being watched is compounded by something else: the *spotlight effect*, a concept introduced by psychologist Thomas Gilovich and colleagues. In one memorable study, students asked to wear embarrassing Barry Manilow T-shirts wildly overestimated how many of their classmates noticed. In another, people assumed that far more of their peers noticed their bad hair day than those who actually did. We chronically overestimate how closely others are paying attention—and this distorted belief ramps up the pressure even further.

Finally, as we saw in the last chapter, it's not just others' attention we fear. The "impartial spectator" in each of us is often far harsher than any external critic. Even when no one else is watching, we're watching ourselves—scrutinizing, second-guessing, turning up the heat from the inside.

Super Freaks!

One thing that's tough about high-stakes performances is that, as much as we may try to prepare ourselves for them mentally, we can never really experience the heat of the moment until we're in it. Thus we are, in effect, perpetually surprised by our emotions—how nervous or afraid we end up feeling—and by how these emotions inevitably affect our abilities. The difference between the two states is a classic cold-to-hot empathy gap (see Chapter 2) and is key to understanding not just choking but also another performance-related defect: *chickening out.*

For a 2005 article, Leaf Van Boven, David Dunning, Ned Welch, and I ran a set of studies in which students were offered a chance to do something embarrassing—like telling a joke, miming, or dancing in front of a classroom full of their peers—in exchange for a payment. In one study, students were asked whether they'd be willing to tell a joke in front of the class a week later for two dollars (it was quite a long time ago; two dollars still meant something!). At the time when they made the commitment, 32 percent agreed and rated their anticipated fear at 6.1 on a scale of 10. But when the "moment of truth" arrived, and they had a chance to reconsider, the majority backed out—and not a single student who had initially declined changed their mind in favor of performing.

Next, we tried to close the empathy gap that we suspected was causing such bad predictions. Just before deciding whether they would tell a joke in front of the class a week later, some students were shown a short clip from *The Shining*—chosen to induce a flash of genuine fear. The intervention had its intended effect. Only 10 percent in this group agreed to perform, and those who did reported much higher levels of anticipated fear—7.3 out of 10. Yet we hadn't managed to entirely close the gap: those few students who were spooked by the clip but nevertheless said yes to telling a joke in front of their class a week later still chickened out when the moment of truth arrived.

Interestingly, the empathy gap doesn't just warp how we predict our own reactions—it also distorts how we imagine other people will behave. In a follow-up study, we again asked students whether they'd perform in front of their peers—but this time we made the scenario far more embarrassing. For a payment of five dollars would they be willing to dance, onstage, in front of their classmates, to Rick James's funk anthem "Super Freak"? Students were asked not only to consider this hypothetical choice for themselves, but also to predict how many of their classmates would accept the same challenge. Meanwhile, a second group of students faced the *real choice*: Would any of them actually dance to "Super Freak" onstage in front of their classmates for a cash reward?

The results were striking. A full third of the hypothetical group said sure, they'd get up and dance. But when we presented the second group with the real choice of taking the stage, only 8 percent agreed to. Predictions about the bravery of others facing this same choice were just as delusional: students safely in their seats guessed that 36 percent of their classmates would dance—more than four times the actual rate. The experiment provides a dramatic illustration of how empathy gaps distort our understanding of emotional reactions—both our own and others'.

Chickening out and choking under pressure, while distinct phenomena, underline a common truth: We often break down in the moments that matter most. The first problem keeps us from stepping onstage, the second strikes mid-performance, but both reveal how decisive moments can twist our emotions and undermine our best efforts—and how much misery can be packed into a few short seconds.

6

Because Our Thoughts Have a Mind of Their Own

The devil! . . . what beastly incidents our memories insist on cherishing! . . . the ugly and disgusting . . . [T]he beautiful things we have to keep diaries to remember!

—Eugene O'Neill, *Strange Interlude*

A Gaffe That Keeps On Giving

In Marcel Proust's *Swann's Way,* the eponymous Swann is obsessed with Odette, a woman depicted as mediocre in all ways, perhaps to highlight the arbitrariness of passion. Swann not only falls for the unworthy Odette, but manages to completely debase himself as doubts about her love for him lead him to engage in a series of humiliating and self-defeating acts. In one of these, succumbing to a jealous compulsion to check the truth of her excuse for sending him home—that she was feeling ill—he returns to her street several hours later, and, as feared, finds her bedroom light illuminated. Angry and determined to expose her perfidy, he knocks on her window—or what he thought was her window—and disturbs a social gathering at her next-door neighbor's. Swann never tells Odette about the episode, but he cannot help but recall it himself:

> Now and then his thoughts in their wandering course would come upon this memory where it lay unobserved, would startle it into life, thrust it forward into his consciousness, and leave him with a sharp, deep-rooted pain. As though it were a bodily pain, Swann's mind was powerless to alleviate it; but at least, in the case of bodily pain, since it is independent of the mind, the mind can dwell upon it, can note that it has diminished, that is has momentarily ceased. But in this case the mind, merely by recalling the pain, created it afresh.

Who cannot relate to Swann's misery? Who has not been attacked by intrusive thoughts, or forced to relive through memory the humiliation of social blunders, the regret of having made a terrible life-changing decision, the mortification of a shameful moment we can't seem to forget? To recall physical pain is not to reexperience it at all, but only to remember the vague idea of that pain. But, because emotions often begin as the product of our thoughts, recalling the events that generated them often reignites the original emotions. Which is why we do everything in our power to avoid such thoughts.

Alas, everything in our power is not nearly enough. And, as Dan Wegner's famous research on ironic thought processes shows, attempts to suppress certain thoughts often make them more persistent and intrusive. He demonstrated this phenomenon vividly with his classic "white bear" experiment, in which participants instructed not to think of a white bear found themselves almost unable to think of anything else. This tendency becomes particularly excruciating when it involves traumatic memories. As Proust observes, "To determine not to think of it was to think of it still, to suffer from it still."

Psychological research shows that memories of facts and life experiences tend to be organized in clusters that we forage over, much like bees forage for pollen-laden flowers. Bees concentrate their search in one cluster until it's depleted, only moving to a new cluster when necessary. Humans do something similar with information, organizing it in locations—libraries, databases—so we can find what we need according to some scheme. Our memory works in an analogous way: related items are stored in close connection to one another, so recalling one item tends to "prime" the recall of others in the same cluster.

Asked to generate a list of animals, for example, people typically begin with pets—dog, cat, rabbit, parrot—then, once that cluster becomes depleted, shift to a new one: farm animals, safari animals, or birds and insects. Although research on memory foraging usually involves emotionally neutral items, the same dynamics apply to emotionally charged ones. The problem is that, in the emotional landscape of memory, not every patch is safe. Some contain hidden hazards—associations we'd rather not stir up.

Most of us learn, consciously or not, to tread carefully around these volatile spots. But despite our best efforts, we sometimes stumble onto those "beastly incidents," as Eugene O'Neill called them. Sometimes they occur at the worst possible moment, like when the memory of a failed talk resurfaces just as you're about to walk up to the podium. At other times, the trigger seems random: Why did that memory pop into my head *now*?

Neuroscientists have identified a likely culprit: the brain's *default network*, a system that kicks into gear when we're at rest, unfocused, or daydreaming. Research by Matthew Lieberman and colleagues shows that, in this state, much of our mental energy goes to replaying social interactions—a territory strewn, for many people, with humiliations and regrets. And because our defenses are down when we drift into default mode, we're especially vulnerable to sudden, involuntary recollections—turning over memory-rocks we'd have preferred to leave undisturbed.

While intrusive thoughts seem to appear out of nowhere, others have more obvious triggers—a scent, a song, a turn of phrase—that inexorably drag unwanted thoughts into consciousness. Karl Ove Knausgaard describes one such moment when he comes across a pair of black Wrangler shoes with yellow laces. He remembers buying them in Copenhagen, while attending a book fair—an occasion now inseparable, for him, from a particularly mortifying episode onstage, "when I had been incapable of answering sensibly a single question the enthusiastic and insightful interviewer had asked me."

Research by Craig Steel and Emily Holmes on involuntary memory in post-traumatic stress disorder (PTSD) offers a useful window into how people typically try to protect themselves from distressing thoughts—and why those protections fail. When our thoughts stray too close to what Steel and Holmes call a "hotspot"—a raw, upsetting memory—the brain sends up a warning flare. This is the cognitive equivalent of detecting the smell of a rotting animal and instinctively changing course to avoid the carcass. It might result in a woozy feeling or a tightening in the chest, a sudden urge to change the subject or distract oneself.

But this system is hardly perfect. Sometimes the warning comes too late. And other times—like when Knausgaard stumbles upon his old shoes—there is no warning at all, because the trigger instantaneously summons the memory. The culmination of the passage from *Swann's Way* about his attempts to avoid thinking about the "window incident" concludes, "when, in conversation with friends, he forgot about it, suddenly a word casually uttered would make him change countenance like a wounded man when a clumsy hand has touched his aching limb."

Tailspins

An intrusive thought doesn't just sting in the moment—it can set off a cycle of escalating negativity, pulling us deeper into a kind of mental undertow. During my sabbatical at the Russell Sage Foundation in New York City, I got to know a historian from Cornell, a man determined to take full advantage of his newfound proximity to the city's fine dining. At lunch, after an excursion to the Four Seasons or another acclaimed restaurant the previous evening, he would regale us with tales of the exquisite food he had consumed. Yet I never got the impression he truly enjoyed these outings. Instead, they seemed to follow a predictable pattern.

He would sit down to dinner and start to enjoy the food, but it rarely seemed to justify the exorbitant prices. *Am I getting my money's worth?* That question soured his mood, which made him enjoy the food less, and made its price feel even more outrageous—for a dinner he wasn't even enjoying. Around it went, each lap robbing him of a bit more pleasure until nothing remained but the check. This is yet another classic feedback loop, in which small disruptions set off a self-reinforcing cycle—in this case, spiraling thoughts about value and disappointment. One hopes that such spirals eventually bottom out, hitting a kind of floor—a minimum level of enjoyment, or rather, a maximum level of misery.

I've experienced something similar while traveling to a conference where I know no one, or where the talks are uniformly dull. At some point, I'll ask myself: *Why the fuck did I travel so far, leave my family and friends, for this?* That thought alone is enough to cast a pall over everything. And once I start tallying up the personal costs—lost time, disrupted sleep, the sheer inconvenience of airports—it makes the trip seem even less worthwhile. Which makes the costs feel even steeper. Which makes my mood dip further. Which makes the trip seem even *more* pointless. And so on.

Perhaps this is why I love the film *Lost in Translation* so much—not just because Bill Murray and Scarlett Johansson are two of my favorite actors, but because it so perfectly captures that quiet, nagging malaise of being stranded in a soulless hotel, far from home, wondering what exactly you're doing with your life. What's striking about these experiences—whether they're triggered by a disappointing meal, a lonely conference, or a sad hotel room—is how easily they prime further thoughts and feelings in the same emotional register.

Given how often our experiences are hijacked by uninvited thoughts and moods, one might wonder why the Cornell historian kept making his culinary pilgrimages, and why I keep going to conferences. That probably has to do with the power of what B. F. Skinner called "intermittent" reinforcement. Every once in a while, a conference does turn out to be well worth the trip. Likewise (perhaps because of a negative bias in my own memory) I have likely forgotten the few, but disproportionately reinforcing, times when the Cornell historian returned with rave reviews of his evening out.

Demons, Distractions, and the Witching Hour

One thing that protects us from intrusive thoughts is sheer activity. The busier we are, the less time we have for our minds to wander, and the less likely we are to stumble over a memory mine or let a train of thought take us to a dark place. Routines, obligations, and simple pleasures provide a kind of armor, keeping us focused on the here and now rather than letting our minds drift to where we'd rather not go. Asked when I'll retire, my common response is "when I die," followed by the explanation that I don't think I'd last a month after retirement before sinking into the quicksand of depression. One of my biggest motivations for working all the time is to keep the demons at bay.

Of course, not everyone relies on work to fend off unwanted thoughts. Many people seek refuge in more passive forms of distraction—those that demand little effort but effectively occupy the mind, a specialty of the modern economy. In her masterful book about the slot machine industry *Addiction by Design*, the anthropologist Natasha Schüll argues that the real draw of slot machines isn't the hope of a jackpot but the promise of mental escape—a brief reprieve from the misery of one's own thoughts. Schüll documents stories of gamblers who aren't chasing riches so much as relief: one man describes himself as being "after nothingness," a woman says she plays to stay in a zone "where nothing else matters," and another woman calls the slots a welcome hideout from a "human world" she experiences as "capricious, discontinuous, and insecure."

Slot machines are big business—around $35 billion in annual revenue. But electronic games such as *Fortnite*, *Call of Duty*, and *Minecraft*—which together generate roughly twice as much—serve a similar purpose, especially for adolescent males. One study found that the strongest predictor of gaming addiction was a decline in happiness, suggesting that people use games at least in part to take refuge from misery. The same goes for social media platforms like TikTok and Instagram, which dominate the waking hours of adolescent girls. Both are engineered to induce a state of "flow," in which users lose track of time. Features like infinite scroll and autoplay ensure there's no natural stopping point, keeping the mind numbly and pleasantly occupied. Rare is the modern consumer who hasn't, at some point, discovered the mercy of these thought-dampening pastimes.

But there are times when no amount of activity or distraction can protect us from upsetting thoughts. One of these occurs, at least for me, pretty much daily—or more accurately, nightly. When I wake up in the middle of the night (which means pretty much every night), I feel like a naked mole rat exposed to daylight—completely defenseless against intrusive thoughts. There's no one, or nothing, to divert you from rooms of your brain you would be better off steering clear of—lost relationships, guilts, regrets, worries. *Did I talk too much at dinner? Will my daughter get into the program she applied to? Will this book attract savage reviews, especially from experts who have spent their lives carefully studying various topics—like intrusive thoughts—that I've only just parachuted into?*

In an insightful essay titled "Why Do We Wake Up at 3am and Dwell on Our Fears and Shortcomings?" Greg Murray, an Australian clinical psychologist, explains the neurobiology behind this phenomenon. Around 3 or 4 a.m., our sleep drive starts to wane. Our body temperature rises, and the secretion of melatonin tapers off while cortisol levels begin to spike. The body is preparing to face the day. It is at this moment when many people report what I call "the witching hour" and Murray calls (in my opinion less evocatively) "barbed-wire thinking" ("because you can get caught in it"). Physiologically and cognitively, we're at our most vulnerable. We're also cut off from the external resources—friends, routines, distractions—that help us cope during the day. As Murray puts it:

> With none of our human skills and capital, we are left alone in the dark with our thoughts. So the mind is partly right when it concludes that the problems it's generated are unsolvable—at 3 a.m., most problems literally would be. Once the sun's up, we're listening to the radio, chewing our Vegemite toast and pushing the cat off the bench, and our 3 a.m. problems are put in perspective. We can't believe the solution of just ringing this person, postponing that thing, or checking such-and-such was overlooked in the wee hours.

A mountain of research has uncovered what is sometimes called *the U-shaped function* of happiness: that happiness peaks early in life and late in life, and reaches its nadir in midlife—e.g., between about thirty-five and fifty. (I personally would relabel it the inverted-U-shaped curve of misery.) Though I believe the main finding of this research, I have some quibbles with the research focusing on the two age extremes. For one, these studies typically start measuring happiness in early adulthood, thereby skipping what I and many others I have exchanged notes with would consider *the* most objectively miserable phase of life: middle school. But perhaps more relevant here, none of these investigations take into account middle-of-the-night happiness levels. Old people tend to wake up much more often in the middle of the night, but happiness researchers almost never measure their happiness during these episodes. I wonder if doing so would substantially change the conclusions that researchers reach about happiness in old age.

While for most of us most of the time, our worst thoughts arrive in the dead of night, sometimes, when our circumstances are truly dire, it's the morning that delivers the real gut-punch. Sleep, for all its disturbances, provides at least some respite (or so we assume—few of us know what we actually think about when we sleep). But when the pain is real—when you've lost a loved one, when your child is struggling, when you've been fired, when the wrong person has been elected president—morning doesn't bring perspective. It brings the awful onslaught of awareness.

The Counterfactual

Some intrusive thoughts are based on reality. But others emerge not from what did happen, but from what didn't. As discussed earlier, painful memories can resurface without warning, dragging the original emotions back with them. But just as often, our minds dwell not on the past itself but on imagined alternatives to it—on things that almost happened, or could have happened, but didn't. These *counterfactual* thoughts can be just as intrusive, and just as emotionally powerful, as real memories. And they, too, often arrive uninvited.

Let me give you an example.

In the summer of 2025, while putting the finishing touches on the first draft of this book, I was anticipating a momentous event—a celebration of my seventieth birthday, to which I invited all the former PhD students I had mentored over the course of my career. Three students had taken me up on the hint (well, a bit more than a hint) that this would be extremely meaningful to me, and took on the burden of organizing it. They had proposed holding it in Pittsburgh, which is fairly accessible to people on both sides of the Atlantic, but, having some "control freak" tendencies, I had asked for it instead to happen in Bellingham, Washington, where my wife and I have spent summers since our son and his family moved there.

As the date drew near, and people were pressured to commit, I started to receive "regret" emails from several students who had been meaningful to me. Their reasons for missing the occasion were all completely understandable—unavoidable scheduling conflicts, long-planned family events, the recent birth of a child. And yet I began to have involuntary images of the achingly sad scene in Charlie Chaplin's *The Gold Rush*, in which, after striking it rich, Chaplin prepares an extravagant feast only to find himself alone at the table. Plenty of students still planned to attend. But I couldn't help fixating on those who would be missing, and imagining how much greater the event would be if only they were there. These imagined versions weren't far-fetched, which made them all the harder to shake.

That's the cruel power of counterfactual thought: it generates suffering not from reality, but from alternatives to reality. We imagine a world where things went differently, and feel worse in the one we actually inhabit.

Many of the miseries we'll examine in detail in Part 2 of this book can be filed under "counterfactual emotions," and all of them tend to produce unpleasant thoughts that we can't keep out of our heads. Impatience stings in part because while we wait for something, we imagine all the better ways we could be spending our time. Boredom arises when the present moment fails to measure up to some imagined experience that would be richer, funnier, more absorbing. Envy draws its venom from the imagined life we'd be living, if only we had what someone else does. And the true horror of regret is not that we made a costly mistake but that it could have been avoided—if only . . .

As the psychologist Neal Roese writes in his review of academic research on counterfactual thinking, "The defining feature of a counterfactual is the falsity of its antecedent." That is, the scenario we're imagining is explicitly unreal—a fantasy—but imagining it carries a very real emotional cost.

In the same way that it feels bad to compare ourselves to people who are better off than we are—a point that you might remember from the discussion on self-esteem—it feels bad to compare what actually happened to something better that *almost* happened. And, once again, fitting the general bad-is-stronger-than-good pattern, our emotional reactions to these comparisons are not symmetrical.

Upward comparisons—to alternative realities that are superior to what we are actually living—are reliably immiserating: they make us feel worse. But downward comparisons, while theoretically comforting, often don't make us feel that much better. Who experiences glee when passing a gruesome wreck on the highway—triggering an almost automatic downward counterfactual: "It could have been me!" If you are like me, this is not a pleasurable thought; instead of celebrating my good fortune, I am more likely to feel bad for the victims and worried that next time it *will* be me.

The evolutionary utility of counterfactual thinking is that it helps us learn. Humans are uniquely gifted at imagining what might have happened, and that capacity—for simulating unrealized outcomes—likely contributed to our intelligence and problem-solving abilities. Of the two main types of counterfactuals, upward (how things could have gone better) and downward (how they could have gone worse), it's the upward ones—the ones that hurt—that tend to teach us more.

If something better could have happened, we very likely can and should change our behavior to make it happen in the future. If something worse could have happened, we should probably stick with what we're doing. The greater practical usefulness of upward counterfactual comparisons may help to explain why empirical research has consistently found that they not only evoke more intense emotions, but are also much more common than downward ones. Neal Roese and James Olson noted that when people spontaneously generate counterfactual thoughts in everyday life, more than 90 percent tend to be upward rather than downward. In other words, when our minds drift to what might have been, they almost always drift toward something better. Which, of course, only makes us feel worse.

7

Because Pain Is Stickier Than Pleasure

There is neither happiness nor misery in this world; there is merely the comparison between one state and another, nothing more.

—Alexandre Dumas, *The Count of Monte Cristo*

Peter and the Canoe

I first met Peter Ubel in the early 1990s when he took my graduate class in behavioral economics in Pittsburgh. At the time, he was juggling a demanding medical internship but somehow still found time for outdoor adventures, which we often pursued together—until one trip went so disastrously wrong that his wife insisted he never go on another with me.

That trip began on a dreary January day, when I was restless from a winter that already felt too long. A week of rain and flooding had transformed a usually unnavigable tributary of the Cheat River in West Virginia into navigable rapids. I proposed to Peter that we brave the river by canoe. We dropped the boat at the riverbank, drove miles downstream to leave the car so it would be waiting for us, then biked back to the launch point, locking our bikes to a tree before setting off.

At first, it was exhilarating. The flood conditions made the river's flow both incredibly powerful and thrillingly treacherous. Dodging obstacles and navigating rapids, we had to keep pulling over to bail out the canoe as water sloshed over its sides. The surge of adrenaline brought me back to the carefree adventures I'd enjoyed before my son—then two years old—was born. Since his birth, I'd resolved to take fewer risks.

But after several miles of thrills, the river started to widen out, and the rapids grew less frequent. Though the current was still swift, the water had calmed. By the time I saw the top of a dam approaching about a hundred feet away, I was experiencing a kind of adrenaline withdrawal. I had *adapted* to the level of excitement we'd been experiencing, and now I wanted more.

Peter and I pulled the canoe to the side of the river, and I reconnoitered before returning to tell him what I'd seen. The dam was about three feet high and the water flowing over it was plentiful and rapid. In the past I'd enjoyed shooting dams in canoes, never successfully making it over without capsizing, but always without injury, given that these earlier experiences had been in the warmth of the summer and not in flood conditions. Unfortunately, I wasn't adjusting for these factors when I proposed to Peter that we attempt to shoot the dam.

To understand what happened next, it helps to know a bit about hydraulics. When water pours over a dam, it cuts into the riverbed just below, creating a powerful downward flow beneath the surface. This, in turn, generates an upward flow at the surface and a backward suction, which is why one can often see debris stacked up and bobbing just below dams, held in place by a hydraulic.

Not surprisingly, our attempt to shoot the dam was a dismal failure. The front of the canoe teetered over the edge for a brief, thrilling moment before nosediving straight into the hydraulic. In an instant, we were treading water, pounded by thousands of gallons spilling over the dam and crashing down from above. My brand-new canoe—purchased only weeks earlier for over a thousand dollars, a fortune at the time—was now caught in the current, spinning like a crazed waterwheel.

Peter was a weaker swimmer than I was, and although he had a life jacket, he was showing every textbook sign of distress that one learns about in junior life-saving class. He drifted past me, struggling against the churning water, as I desperately tried to kick him out of the hydraulic. But the suction was too strong. I watched helplessly as he was pulled past me by the current to a position under the most violent part of the downpour, which slammed him under the surface. I waited—but he did not come back up. He was gone.

This was perhaps the single worst moment of my life.

At that point I faced a horrible dilemma. I had killed Peter, and it was completely my fault. I rapidly imagined having to inform his wife (whom I was also friends with), and his parents (whom I had met), of his death and of my responsibility for it. Still supremely confident that I could get out of the situation if I chose to (based on earlier instances of cheating death), I wasn't at all sure that I *wanted* to survive, only to face the horrible reality of what I had done. It must have only been a fraction of a minute, but it felt like I spent a long time weighing the options: leave my two-year-old son without a father or live with the burden of having killed Peter. Finally, I decided, perhaps self-servingly, that it was more important to live and face the consequences. Dying would be the selfish way out.

The problem was that escaping from the hydraulic wasn't as easy as I had assumed. It was winter, the water was freezing cold, and I'd drunk gallons of it by that point. My life vest had gotten waterlogged, and I was exhausted just trying to keep my head above the surface. After several minutes of futile struggle, I finally lost the will to fight. I stopped treading water, and, like Peter before me, I was slammed under by the force of the falling water.

Once submerged, I remember looking up through the water to the gray winter sky, realizing, with great sadness, that this was the last light I would ever see, and that I would never see my son grow up. Then, to my surprise, I popped up, downstream of the hydraulic. I gasped for breath and got pulled through a set of rapids (which resumed a few yards below the dam). I was too exhausted to do anything but passively float in a daze of relief and dread, because I quickly remembered: I had killed Peter.

If watching my friend disappear under the water was the worst moment of my life, then the best came a few seconds later. As I bobbed downstream, too weak to resist the current of the rapids, I heard the bleating sound of my name being called by a shriveled, wet figure standing on the shore of the river.

Having had a couple of minutes to recover, Peter waded into the river to pull me to shore. As he dragged me up on the river's bank, I went into shock, and his skills as a physician came in handy. My heart started beating erratically and at high speed. Taking my pulse, he spent the next several minutes calming me down. When he had succeeded, we made our way up the riverbank to a farmhouse, where the inhabitants took us in and put us in front of a fire. It took many hours for our body temperatures to recover from severe hypothermia. As we sat there, looking out the window, I saw the canoe, which had finally come free from the hydraulic, floating down the river.

"I don't care if I never see that fucking boat again," I told Peter.

But four hours later, as hypothermia waned, I *did* start to care. Peter and I ran along the riverbank, racing against the early onset of winter darkness, in search of the canoe. Remarkably, we found it—rescued by a Good Samaritan and dragged safely onto shore.

The Biology of Adaptation

It's strange how quickly the mind resets. One moment, you're grateful merely to be alive; the next, you're worried about a piece of expensive plastic floating downriver. The intensity of an experience—whether joy, fear, or relief—fades, making way for the next concern.

So far in the first half of this book I have argued that misery is our evolutionary fate—the dark force that helped our species survive, even as it embedded suffering deep into the human condition. But now I want to step back and consider what might seem, at least briefly, like some much-needed good news: Misery isn't built to last. No matter how intense a feeling is at the outset, it will inevitably level off. This tendency is called *hedonic adaptation*: as we experience something over time, our emotional (or hedonic) response to it weakens.

But now for the bad news: Hedonic adaptation isn't always a relief. Just as it helps us recover from pain, it also robs us of sustained pleasure. The highs fade, leaving us wanting more. On the Cheat River, I experienced both sides of adaptation. The rapids that thrilled me at the start became less exciting as I adjusted to the level of stimulation. My foolish decision to shoot the dam was a direct result of this craving for more. Later, after surviving the dam and renouncing my expensive canoe, I felt that the only thing that mattered was getting home safely—until those emotions, too, leveled off, leaving me wanting my canoe back.

This tendency isn't unique to humans. Adaptation is a deep biological feature of all organisms with nervous systems. The reason for this is simple: adaptation solves a fundamental problem. Most neurons that monitor stimuli—whether visual, auditory, or tactile—transmit information by firing electrical signals at a specific rate. However, neurons can't fire at infinitely variable speeds. The range of possible firing rates is narrow, even though the range of stimuli we encounter is vast. Take brightness, for example: our eyes must function across conditions as different as full daylight and near-total darkness, a difference of thousands of times in luminance. Yet neurons in the visual system can only fire at a maximum of about five hundred spikes per second, which is nowhere near enough range to map the full spectrum of light intensity directly.

Max Bennett, in his masterful book *A Brief History of Intelligence*, refers to this as the "squishing problem": "Neurons have to squish this huge range of natural variables into a comparably minuscule range of firing rates."

Humans and other animals with nervous systems have evolved an extremely clever solution to the problem: they are *adaptive*. Instead of responding to raw levels of brightness, pain, or pressure, they adapt to a baseline and then respond to deviations. This is why, whether you're reading this on the beach in bright sunlight or at night in a dimly lit bedroom, the black letters appear black and the white spaces appear white. Your visual system constantly resets its reference point.

This same dynamic is at play with our emotions. They measure deviations from a baseline that resets itself over time. The result is that we can get used to almost anything, as our old friend Adam Smith once observed:

> Some people faint and grow sick at the sight of a chirurgical operation; and that bodily pain which is occasioned by tearing the flesh, seems, in them, to excite the most excessive sympathy.

But, he continues,

> The chief cause, however, why such objects produce such violent effects upon us, is their novelty. One who has been witness to a dozen dissections, and as many amputations, sees, ever after, all operations of this kind with great indifference, and often with perfect insensibility.

The same principle governs our experience of happiness. Remember that happiness and unhappiness, like sensory perceptions, are evolved signals—tools our brains use to get us to act in certain ways. And just like sensory neurons, our emotional systems don't encode absolute happiness; they encode change. That's why we can exist in an astonishing range of circumstances—from dire poverty, disease, and oppression to unimaginable luxury—without experiencing unrelenting misery on one end or permanent bliss on the other.

Regardless of our starting point, we tend to return to our happiness "set point." This set point varies by individual—some people are naturally more cheerful, others more melancholic—but the general tendency is the same: we adapt. This kind of adaptation makes sense—especially for positive experiences. If we never adjusted to good things, we'd become complacent as soon as our situation improved, losing the motivation to achieve more.

My early career provides a good example. When I finished graduate school, my department failed to promote me on the academic job market. At the economics meetings, my classmates had ten to twenty interviews with different departments. I had none. Well—almost none. I had a lunchtime chat with some curious professors at a small university and an actual interview with a recruiter from Quaker Oats, who (if I recall correctly) was looking for someone to be a brand manager for dog food.

By a total fluke, however, I managed to land my dream job with a quirky department at the University of Chicago Business School. Though the early years were a slog (as I clawed my way toward academic legitimacy in a nascent field), my work situation eventually brightened considerably. Even so, as my circumstances improved, my emotions did what emotions do: they adapted. I tried to hold on to the satisfaction of having realized my earlier goals, to be grateful for all that I had. I often told myself: "YOU SHOULD BE THRILLED! YOU COULD BE SELLING *DOG FOOD*" (with no disrespect intended toward those who are). But such attempts proved futile, as they always do. Shortly after some achievement or milestone, I'm always looking toward the next thing, and envious of those who already have it.

In a review of hedonic adaptation research I coauthored with Shane Frederick, we cataloged the many things people chase—money, status, possessions—hoping for lasting happiness, only to adapt. The one exception we were able to find was cosmetic surgery; people who get it report that whatever emotional benefits they've received from the procedure persist over time.

What could account for this strange exception? Based on my own experience (albeit not with cosmetic surgery), my guess is that the pleasure is lasting because the wrinkles or other perceived imperfections that the surgery corrected were persistent irritants. My own version of this experience happened when the woman who used to cut my hair at Supercuts suggested that I try dyeing my gray hair black. I took her up on the offer, and was pleased with the results. When my dismayed children asked me if it didn't seem strange when I looked at myself in the mirror, I responded, "Not at all"—that it *had* felt strange when I looked in the mirror for decades and saw a gray-haired man looking back at me. My children got the last laugh, and teased me mercilessly, when the dye faded and my hair turned from black to a hideous orange color that extinguished my taste for appearance enhancement.

Exceptions That Prove the Rule

Most of us can recognize—at least in hindsight—our capacity to get used to good things. A long-coveted promotion eventually becomes just a job. A thrilling romance settles into routine. We grow accustomed to good fortune, no matter how extraordinary it once seemed. Yet when it comes to bad things, we resist this logic. It's hard to imagine that we could ever stop grieving a profound loss, adjust to a major disability, or resume ordinary life after a catastrophe. And sometimes, we don't. I have known people who have faced terminal illness or near-death experiences and emerged transformed in ways that defied adaptation.

The first was Stephanie Byram, a young graduate student in our PhD program. She was diagnosed with breast cancer and given a five-year survival prognosis. She outlived that estimate, but only by three years. Before her diagnosis, she had always struck me as a bit overly formal and self-contained. But after the diagnosis, it was as if something unlocked inside her. She started putting her true self out there—not just in her work, but in her relationships. She was bolder, looser, more open. She dated actively and, in a short time, met the man she would marry. She traveled. She documented her experiences with unflinching honesty in *Knowing Stephanie*, a book she coauthored with Charlee Brodsky and Jennifer Matesa.

Another case was Steve Klepper, a longtime colleague from my department. He was diagnosed with melanoma and lived only one more year after his diagnosis. He and I had been cordial colleagues up until then (I always found him extremely intimidating), but, after I proposed taking a walk, we became fast friends. The illness had changed him almost instantly. He spent his last year basking in the love of his family, who, he told me on our walks, were there for him in both spirit and presence. Steve's colleagues also honored him at an event that, because it was in the late stages of his illness, the university generously flew him to, horizontal, in a private plane. His wife—a beautiful, accomplished woman—was by his side, watching him be celebrated. I know—because he told me—that it was immensely meaningful to him.

In one of our early walks, Steve told me that he had been bedeviled during his life by his own tendency to be judgmental (which, he reported, he had picked up from his mother), but that he had almost instantly managed to cast off the mindset when he got sick—and that he felt liberated as a result. As an academic, being judgmental comes naturally—it's practically a job requirement. But being judgmental can also be a burden. It can interfere with friendships, and (as I discussed in the chapter on meta-preferences) it's hard to shield oneself from the harsh glare of one's own judgments.

A happier story is the case of Kevin Volpp, a close colleague and friend. He had a massive heart attack while traveling to a squash meet in Cincinnati with his daughter, Daphne. Only about 10 percent of people survive such an event if it occurs outside of a hospital, but Kevin was incredibly lucky: paramedics arrived within a few minutes and resuscitated him. Recently, I asked him how the experience had affected him, and he said that it radically improved his quality of life. Each morning, he wakes up feeling incredibly lucky to be alive and appreciates every day, hour, and minute. He told me he believes the experience even made him a kinder person, which I told him was impossible because he was already in the ninety-ninth percentile of kindness (an opinion that is ubiquitous among those who know him).

These are dramatic stories—the kinds of transformations we want to believe in. But the reason I bring up these uplifting cases in a book about misery is because they are the *exception*, not the rule. In 1978, Philip Brickman, Dan Coates, and Ronnie Janoff-Bulman published a paper that spawned decades of follow-up research. Titled "Lottery Winners and Accident Victims: Is Happiness Relative?" it presented two studies suggesting that lottery winners were no happier—and accident victims (specifically, paraplegics) no less happy—than a control group of people who had experienced neither extreme. Subsequent research has refined their methods and, in some cases, challenged specific details of their study, but their central claim has held up: humans are astonishingly adaptable creatures, able to adjust emotionally to most anything that life throws at us.

I myself have had numerous near-death experiences, but I don't believe that any of them—including the incident with Peter—have been transformative or had a lasting impact on my outlook on life. In reviewing the psychology of mountaineering, I found the same pattern among climbers who, after barely surviving harrowing expeditions, believed earnestly that they would call it quits—only to return to the mountains again.

You might think that the effect of almost losing your life is to make you realize that if you don't spend time with your family now you may not have a chance to do so in the future; that today may in fact be your last opportunity to go out to dinner with your spouse, call your parents, or take your child to the zoo. As Peter Potterfield, who suffered a devastating accident during his ascent of Chimney Rock in the Cascade Mountains, commented, "After Chimney Rock, there was a strong sense that life is uncertain, highly so." But how long does that feeling last?

During the worst moments of his Antarctic trek, Mike Stroud (who appeared earlier in the chapter on empathy gaps) lamented his detachment from his children and vowed, on his return, to become a model father and cease his quest for "firsts." In the epilogue to his book, however, he reports that he never quite got around to building the dollhouse he had promised his daughter and that, within weeks of his return to daily life, the wanderlust had him in its grip once again.

The Eternal Error

One of the most mysterious things about hedonic adaptation is that we seem incapable of learning from it—let alone "pricing in" its effects. We persist in believing that the next promotion, the next million dollars, the next romantic conquest, or the next publication will finally deliver lasting satisfaction. This tendency has been most extensively documented by the psychologists Dan Gilbert and Timothy Wilson. In one of their studies, they surveyed assistant professors who were being considered for tenure—perhaps the defining moment in an academic career—and asked them to predict how the outcome would affect their long-term happiness. Those expecting tenure believed it would bring them lasting satisfaction, while those fearing rejection anticipated lingering devastation. Yet when the researchers followed up after the decision was made, the professors who were denied tenure were no less happy than those who received it. Their initial devastation faded far more quickly than they had imagined, as life adjusted, new paths emerged, and their attention shifted to other concerns.

This pattern holds across an astonishing range of experiences. In my own research, I've observed the same effects in people receiving positive or negative HIV test results, and in those imagining versus experiencing paraplegia, below-the-knee amputation, colostomies, and end-stage renal disease. Whether we compare people's predictions to the actual self-reports of those living with these conditions or track the same individuals before and after a major life change, the pattern is unmistakable: people underestimate their ability to adapt.

This failure to anticipate adaptation basically means that the pursuit of happiness is self-defeating. Whatever we desire—health if we are sick, money if we are strapped, a nicer house, a better title, more time, a different lover—seems to promise a measure of lasting satisfaction. But once we have that thing, the promise is quickly broken.

Seven years before he published his famous study on lottery winners and paraplegics, Philip Brickman, along with his colleague Donald Campbell, wrote that adaptation "condemns men to live on a hedonic treadmill, to seek new levels of stimulation merely to maintain old levels of subjective pleasure, to never achieve any kind of permanent happiness or satisfaction." Tolstoy had already captured this sorry cycle in *Anna Karenina*. Vronsky, after seven hundred pages of longing and struggle, finally succeeds in his quest to be with Anna. And yet—almost immediately—he is restless, discontent:

> In spite of the complete fulfillment of what he had so long desired, he was not completely happy. He soon felt that the realization of his longing gave him only one grain of the mountain of bliss he had anticipated. That realization showed him the eternal error men make by imagining that happiness consists in the gratification of their wishes. When first he united his life with hers and donned civilian clothes, he felt the delight of freedom in general, such as he had not before known, and also the freedom of love—he was contented then, but not for long. Soon he felt rising in his soul a desire for desires—boredom.

The delusion that getting what we want will actually make us happy not only leads to dissatisfaction once we attain our goal but also causes us to suffer *while we pursue it.* This is because of that great engine of misery we introduced before—the counterfactual, the imagined future in which we already possess that which we desire. Because we believe (falsely) that achieving a long-sought-after goal will bring lasting happiness, the fact that we have not *yet* achieved it makes our present state feel profoundly lacking by comparison. And so a shadow is cast over the present, making everything now feel inadequate. Tom Wolfe effectively captured this Sisyphean cycle in *A Man in Full*, his novel about an Atlanta real estate magnate named Charlie Croker.

> I've been a real estate developer for most of my life, and I can tell you that a developer lives with the opposite of tranquility, which is perturbation. You're perturbed about something all the time. You build your first development, and right away you want to build a bigger one,

> and you want a bigger house to live in, and if it ain't in Buckhead, you might as well cut your wrists. Soon's you got that, you want a plantation, tens of thousands of acres devoted solely to shooting quail, because you know of four or five developers who've already got that. And soon's you get *that* you want a place on Sea Island and a Hatteras cruiser and a spread northwest of Buckhead, near the Chattahoochee, where you can ride a horse during the week, when you're not down at the plantation, plus a ranch in Wyoming, Colorado, or Montana, because *truly* successful men in Atlanta and New York all got their ranches, and of course now you need a private plane, a big one, too, a jet, a Gulfstream Five, because who's got the patience and the time and the humility to fly commercially, even to the plantation, much less out West to a ranch? What is it you're looking for in this endless quest? Tranquility. You think if only you can acquire *enough* worldly goods, *enough* recognition, *enough* eminence, you will be free, there'll be nothing more to worry about, and instead you become a bigger and bigger slave to how others are judging you.

If we were better at predicting adaptation, we might suffer less from "the eternal error." Recognizing how fleeting our pleasures and satisfactions are might steer us away from the endless pursuit of happiness for its own sake. Likewise, understanding just how quickly we adjust to adversity could help us face hardship with greater resilience, knowing that our suffering will soon fade. But alas, human beings are terrible at exactly this kind of foresight. Why can't we predict hedonic adaptation, despite having a lifetime of evidence that should enable us to do so? My guess is that adaptation is an automatic process that occurs outside of consciousness, unfolding gradually, like the slow movement of a glacier. Because we don't understand how it happens, and can't perceive it happening, we constantly underestimate its speed and impact.

The Asymmetry of Adaptation

While we possess a remarkable ability to adapt to both good and bad outcomes, a careful reader will not be surprised to discover that negative events are harder for us to bounce back from. In earlier chapters, I discussed some of the fundamental ways in which negative emotions hold an edge over our psyche. First, we experience a greater number of negative emotions than positive ones. Second, bad feelings are stronger, more distinct, and better remembered than good feelings. Third, people tend to make upward social comparisons, focusing on what they lack or could improve rather than on what they already have. Fourth, losses have a greater psychological impact than equivalent gains. This same "negative bias" also applies when it comes to adaptation: we do not get over bad events as quickly, or as completely, as we do good ones.

An intriguing demonstration of this asymmetry came from a longitudinal study by Richard Lucas and his colleagues, which followed more than twenty-four thousand Germans over fifteen years. The researchers tracked changes in life satisfaction before and after two major (but wholly incommensurate) life events: marriage and the death of one's spouse.

On average, newly married people experienced a modest but reliable rise in well-being of about a quarter of a point on a 0–10 point scale. But notably, this "honeymoon effect" lasted just two years before it entirely disappeared. Widowhood told a different story: a sharp drop of nearly a full point, followed by a slow and only partial recovery. Even after eight years, most participants had not fully adapted to the loss of their partner.

The use of marriage as a "good event" and widowhood as a "bad event" is of course imperfect. However much we may love our spouse, marriage is a choice, a milestone in a relationship that predated the nuptials; emotionally, it's always a mixed bag. Widowhood is not a choice and, for the vast majority of people, it's an entirely unwelcome experience. But still, the study captures a truth we intuitively feel: it's often easier to adjust to a gain than a loss. And subsequent research has generally supported its findings, showing that certain negative events (like persistent unemployment) resist the typically indomitable forces of adaptation.

Tuning Out the Apocalypse

Ultimately, adaptation is about efficiency. The nervous system doesn't waste resources responding to things that don't change. Just as sensory neurons stop registering the hum of a refrigerator or the feeling of a shirt against your skin, the brain dampens emotional responses to persistent distress. Our emotions exist to spur action, but if such action proves impossible, the brain eventually shifts tactics—it tunes out. We can see this process in a stark, exaggerated form in some of our most distant biological relatives. Take the nematode—small roundworms found in a wide range of environments. Deferring again to Max Bennett, the author of *A Brief History of Intelligence*:

> If a nematode is exposed to thirty minutes of a negative stimulus (such as dangerous heat, freezing cold, or toxic chemicals), at first, it will exhibit the hallmarks of the acute stress response—it will try to escape, and stress hormones will pause bodily functions. But after just two minutes of no relief from this inescapable stressor, nematodes do something surprising: they give up. The worm stops moving; it stops trying to escape and just lies there. This behavior might seem like learned helplessness, but it's actually quite clever: spending energy escaping is worth the cost only if the stimulus is in fact escapable.

A similar kind of numbing process occurs in humans, though with far graver consequences for the species and the planet. Just as our nervous system adapts to physical sensations—growing numb to a persistent smell, tuning out background noise—our emotional system adapts to suffering, injustice, and existential threats. If a problem emerges suddenly, like an earthquake or a terrorist attack, it triggers an immediate, intense emotional response, motivating us to act. But if a problem grows gradually—climate change, creeping authoritarianism, the normalization of mass shootings or deaths from car accidents—our emotional response fails to keep pace.

This is one of the most insidious consequences of adaptation: we fail to sustain the emotions necessary to address long-term existential threats. Studies on emotional motivation confirm what we all intuitively recognize: outrage, sadness, and fear can spur people to action, but only briefly. In research I conducted with Daniel Schwartz, we found that emotionally powerful videos about climate-related animal suffering initially increased charitable giving and engagement with information about energy use. But when we followed up one day, and even just one hour later, the effects had disappeared. Without sustained emotion, action withers.

The same phenomenon plays out on a massive scale. The first images of climate disaster—starving polar bears stranded on melting ice floes—were shocking. Now, the destruction is background noise. We still see it, but we no longer react. In the early days of mass shootings in America, they were national tragedies, covered in exhaustive detail. Now, they flash across the news for an evening, maybe two, before fading into the churn of other stories. Adaptation helps us to move forward, but it also helps us to move on, even when, individually and collectively, we'd be better off fixing our attention and effort on a chronic problem. Many of the ills that plague society—climate change, obesity, and gun violence—have gradually climbed to levels which, if we experienced them abruptly, would horrify us and likely trigger action.

As Adam Smith observed earlier, sometimes it doesn't take that much exposure for the numbing effect of adaptation to sink in. Jon Krakauer, in *Into Thin Air*, describes his reaction to encountering dead bodies on his ascent of Mount Everest. "The first body had left me badly shaken for several hours; the shock of encountering the second wore off almost immediately."

Moral decay often follows this same creeping trajectory. Few people wake up one morning and decide to commit atrocities. Instead, they adjust, step by step, to new moral baselines. The psychologist Stanley Milgram demonstrated this process with chilling precision in his famous obedience experiments. Participants were not asked to immediately administer potentially lethal shocks, but were given a series of requests to increase the voltage marginally. Having given someone a 100-volt shock, the prospect of administering a 110-volt shock seemed much less horrifying than it would if one had not already witnessed, and adapted to, the victim's reaction to the 100-volt shock. Over time, the subjects in Milgram's experiments adapted, until they found themselves doing what, at the outset, they would have sworn they were incapable of. Unfortunately, such reasoning is not confined to laboratory settings. Miroslav Bajramovic, a member of the Croat special police who took responsibility for the deaths of eighty-six Serbs during the Yugoslav Wars, reported that "the most difficult thing is to ignite a house or kill a man for the first time; but afterwards, everything becomes routine."

Yet it's rare for moral erosion to be traced to a single decisive moment. Usually, it occurs as a gradual forgetting of what once felt unthinkable. The psychiatrist Robert Jay Lifton documented a similar process in his study of Nazi doctors. These men, many of whom had taken the Hippocratic oath, did not start as killers. First they were only asked to be present when euthanasia took place. Then they were asked to add their signature to a document approving euthanasia. Later they were asked to supervise a mercy killing. And so on until the point where many of them were routinely administering lethal injections to eugenically "undesirable" persons.

Given the stakes, we should not allow ourselves to adapt to a world in which school shootings are routine, in which democracies backslide into authoritarianism, in which scores of species vanish from the earth each year. And yet here we are. If our emotional systems had been designed differently—if we were capable of sustaining alarm rather than acclimating to crisis—perhaps we would be better equipped to meet the great challenges of our time. Instead, we are designed to get used to things.

Maybe adaptation is how the world will end—not with a bang, nor a whimper, but with a shrug. The scientist René Dubos seemed to suggest as much in his prophetic 1965 book *Man Adapting*: "This very adaptability enables [us] to become adjusted to conditions and habits that will eventually destroy the values most characteristic to human life."

8

Because Hope Refuses to Die

Any parent who has had to confront a child's drug abuse is familiar with the drawn-out agony of despair, impotence, fear, grief and, while there is still a chance for recovery, hope. That last is perhaps the most ravaging of all.

—From Dominique Browning's *New York Times* book review of *The Lost Child: A Mother's Story* by Julie Myerson

A Jar of Poison

Years ago, on a family vacation in the Florida Panhandle, I was walking on the beach with my daughter, Rosa, when a nostalgic idea popped into my head. She was just entering middle school then, and I thought it would be fun to re-create something we used to enjoy when she was a little girl. I persuaded her to accept a piggyback ride. She got up on my shoulders successfully, but then started to fall forward, and I used the full strength of my neck muscles in an unsuccessful attempt to halt her fall. Though she landed on the beach a bit shook up, Rosa was fine. But a loud crack emanating from my neck signaled the beginning of a long medical ordeal for me. Over the next several months, muscles started to disappear from my neck and back, and those that remained would form painful golf-ball-sized knots, which, mysteriously, produced excruciating headaches.

Every doctor I visited seemed to believe that my problem emanated from whichever part of the body they specialized in, and that whatever procedure they specialized in was the cure. A spinal surgeon, whose specialty was vertebrae replacements, concluded that I had cracked my sixth vertebra, which he needed to replace. I asked him, or actually his assistant—since he disappeared almost instantly after confidently suggesting that I schedule the operation on my way out of the clinic—about possible adverse effects of such a procedure. I was informed that, because the incision was made in the front rather than the back of the neck, some fraction of patients (though he couldn't even give me a ballpark number) suffer damage to their vocal cords, and permanently lose their voices. Only in part because my occupation depends on being able to speak to people, including classrooms of students, even a small risk of losing my ability to speak appeared more serious to me than the doctor seemed to view it. I declined to schedule the operation, and instead visited another specialist who gave me a nerve test that consisted of simultaneously stabbing two electrodes into different parts of my body, then sending an electrical current from one to the other, causing my arms and legs to convulse in pain.

After several years of fruitless visits to specialists whose advice I fortunately never followed, I finally found a neurosurgeon whom I trusted, mostly on the basis that he didn't want to operate on me. He told me that my muscle atrophy clearly indicated a tear of the cranial accessory nerve, which runs entirely outside of the spinal column (hence, replacing a vertebra would have been worse than senseless), and that there was nothing I could do about it. I would simply have to live with it. That might seem like bad news, but it was actually liberating. It gave me license to stop searching for a solution to a problem that didn't have one, and I set about finding ways to live with my disability, both physically and psychologically. Paradoxically, it was only when I abandoned all hope of recovery that I experienced genuine relief—an insight that made me question whether hope is truly the ally our culture insists it is.

Countless adages like "The darkest hour is just before the dawn" reinforce the notion that hope is essential, especially during hard times. Meanwhile, the opposite of hope—hopelessness—is a synonym for extreme despair. From an evolutionary perspective, hope likely emerged as an adaptive response to uncertainty, helping our ancestors persevere through adversity and motivating them to pursue long-term goals. Decades of empirical research has consistently affirmed the value of hope, linking it to improved mental and physical health. Hopeful people manage pain and stress better, face lower risks of suicide, depression, and early death, and experience fewer chronic illnesses and even higher survival rates from certain cancers. Few emotions enjoy such a sterling reputation.

And yet, if you look into the deep literary origins of hope, a more ambiguous—and troubling—portrait emerges. Nearly three millennia ago, Hesiod, among the earliest poets in the Western canon, depicted hope not as comfort but as a strange, perhaps even sinister force. In *Works and Days*, Hesiod recounts the original myth of Pandora, the first woman, who was sent to Earth by Zeus as punishment for Prometheus's theft of fire. Pandora carried with her a sealed jar (often mistranslated as a "box") containing every imaginable sorrow—disease, war, toil, as well as psychological torments—and famously scattered all these evils upon humanity.

All, that is, except one:

> Only hope remained there inside in her secure dwelling, under the lip of the jar, and did not fly out because the woman [Pandora] put the lid back in time by the providence of Zeus the cloud-gatherer who bears the aegis.

Hesiod never explains why hope is treated differently than the other evils. This has left generations of readers with a profound puzzle: If hope is confined to the jar, why are humans so prone to experiencing it?

Nietzsche, a keen reader of ancient Greek, resolved this ambiguity by arguing that Zeus didn't deny hope to humanity by trapping it in the jar—after all, we feel hope all the time, for better or for worse. Instead, by placing hope in the jar, just out of our reach, Zeus gave humans the false impression that our salvation is always close at hand. In this sense, hope *was* the final evil—a cruel joke, a curse disguised as a gift.

As Nietzsche wrote, "Zeus did not wish man, however much he might be tormented by the other evils, to fling away his life, but to go on letting himself be tormented again and again. Therefore, he gives man hope—in reality, it is the worst of all evils, because it prolongs the torments of man."

A Lesson from "The Disappeared"

My father didn't need to read Nietzsche to be wary of hope. Like my mother, he was a German-speaking Jewish immigrant to the United States who had only narrowly escaped the Nazis. He spent part of the war hiding with his family in rural France, and nearly died in an internment camp. He spoke English with a thick accent—he sounded exactly like Henry Kissinger—and his catchphrase in our family was "This will end badly."

I once asked him if it was his experience in the war that explained why he was so unremittingly pessimistic.

"No," he said. "The reason is because my father never believed in me."

The war did, however, profoundly shape his worldview. He became an avowed pacifist, and throughout his career as a metallurgic engineer, he sought to create inventions that would be beneficial for humanity. Late in life, he helped develop an exceptionally hard metal alloy that incorporated depleted uranium, which initially seemed promising for various peaceful applications. To his profound dismay, however, his alloy was soon adapted for use in military technology—specifically, depleted uranium anti-tank shells, weapons that not only proved lethal on the battlefield but also left dangerous radioactive contamination behind. I guess my father's story reminds us that expecting the worst doesn't shield us from bitter disappointments.

Maybe my father planted in me a seed of doubt about the value of hope, but I didn't seriously begin to reflect on the downside of this usually uplifting emotion until graduate school at Yale. Around that time, my wife and I became close with a couple from the law school, Sam Issacharoff and Cindy Estlund, who remain good friends. They had just come back from Buenos Aires, where they'd worked on a fascinating legal project. Following Argentina's humiliating defeat in the Falklands War, the military dictatorship collapsed and a new democratic government came to power. That government sought justice for atrocities committed during the previous regime—particularly the mass disappearances of dissidents (*los desaparecidos*). Sam and Cindy had traveled to Argentina to help the fledgling government confront this terrible legacy.

They met with several mothers of children who had "been disappeared." These women were all traumatized, and they picketed the central government building each day, imploring the country's leaders for information and justice. At a dinner after they returned to Yale, Sam and Cindy shared an interesting observation: the mothers who had seen tangible evidence of their child's death seemed to fare much better psychologically than those who could reasonably assume their child was dead (since none of the disappeared ever reappeared) but who had no proof. The faint yet persistent possibility—the hope—that somewhere, somehow, their child was still alive inflicted an emotional pain far greater than even grief.

The writer Kyleigh Leddy, whose sister was presumed dead after jumping off a suspension bridge in Philadelphia (although her body was never found), eloquently captured the misery that arises in such a situation:

> When someone you love disappears, there's no finality of an autopsy report or the closure of a funeral. All you have is a lack of presence. You can piece together the mystery like in the Nancy Drew books you used to devour, but there's no memorial service to confirm the truth. And that's the problem: the promise of possibility. Such misery is by no means limited to family members who are unable to grieve their missing (and likely deceased) loved ones.

Randolph Nesse, in *Good Reasons for Bad Feelings*, recounts a striking finding from German psychologist Jutta Heckhausen: middle-aged women who were still hoping to give birth to a child experienced growing emotional distress as they approached menopause. But once menopause passed—and they relinquished that hope—their depressive symptoms often disappeared. The pain was in the unresolved possibility. As Nesse puts it, "The irony is deep: hope is often at the root of depression."

The journalist Michael Scott Moore learned this lesson in one of the hardest ways imaginable, after he was kidnapped by Somali pirates in 2012 and held hostage for 977 excruciating days. During his ordeal, one of the pirates, Bashko, kept Moore's hopes alive by feeding him rumors about ongoing ransom negotiations.

"He made it sound as if I would go free in a matter of days," Moore said in an NPR interview. "Of course, I was happy to believe him." Over time, however, crushed by continual disappointment, Moore decided to give up. What he realized then was that his state of mind, if not his lot in life, improved. "It turns out you can live without hope. Any Hallmark-like quotes to the contrary are wrong . . . And if you would recognize that, and simply don't think forward toward the future, and don't insist on a rosy outlook for the next couple of weeks or months or years, then you can live in the moment. And that's what I had to learn to do. I would have snapped if I had done it any other way."

In his book *The Desert and the Sea*, he put it more starkly: "Hope is like heroin for a hostage, and it can be just as destructive."

In each of these cases—the families of the disappeared, a hostage waiting for a release that might never come, women clinging to the last possibility of motherhood—hope itself became a source of suffering. The idea yields a kind of irony: people who are *objectively* better off, because there remains a real, if remote, chance that their situation might improve, are often *subjectively* worse off, because that very chance prevents them from adjusting to their present circumstances. They are essentially unable to reap the rewards of hedonic adaptation that we discussed in the last chapter. Unable to fully accept the loss, they are trapped in the misery of their own hope.

The Disability Paradox

One thing that's important to understand about hedonic adaptation is that, when it comes to truly catastrophic setbacks, people refuse to believe, even when they are presented with evidence, that it's possible to adjust to them. They assume that after a devastating injury or a profound loss they will never be as happy as they were before.

Since the pioneering work of Philip Brickman and his colleagues in the late 1970s, researchers have documented what's known as the *disability paradox*—the finding that severely disabled people typically report happiness levels comparable to their nondisabled peers. Despite its robustness, the finding remains hard for people to accept. In one recent survey, 82 percent of physicians reported that they believed patients with significant disabilities have a lower quality of life than their nondisabled peers.

Even researchers who study quality of life doubted whether disabled people could really be "so happy"—they theorized that perhaps disabled people were misrepresenting their emotional state to avoid pity, or even fooling themselves, unable or unwilling to confront the true extent of their own suffering. To investigate these possibilities, my colleagues and I designed a study focusing on people with end-stage renal disease undergoing dialysis. Patients on dialysis face painful, tedious treatments lasting several hours, multiple times per week, with no possibility of a cure, only life extension and symptom relief. If these patients truly were miserable but hiding it (even from themselves), we reasoned, their moment-to-moment emotions—reported spontaneously during daily life—should reveal that hidden suffering clearly.

Remarkably, when prompted at random times to report their emotional state (using a technique called *experience sampling*), dialysis patients rated their momentary happiness slightly *higher* than a control group of healthy participants. Moreover, the healthy group, just as in earlier research, significantly overestimated how unhappy the dialysis patients would be. The disability paradox was neither a result of some mass delusion among disabled people nor a methodological fluke. Instead, it turned out to be one of the clearest demonstrations of hedonic adaptation in action: people genuinely adjust to seemingly intolerable circumstances.

Yet here's the crucial caveat: virtually every example of successful hedonic adaptation involves conditions that are, to a large extent, *permanent.* What happens when circumstances remain uncertain—when there is a real possibility that one's condition could improve or be reversed? Could hope itself, perversely, become the obstacle to psychological adjustment, trapping people in ongoing suffering precisely because it leaves open the possibility that things might get better?

Happily Hopeless

In 2009, for a project with my longtime collaborator Peter Ubel—yes, the same Peter who once braved the Cheat River in a canoe with me—I was able to test whether hope might actually do us more harm than good. Peter and his team recruited 107 patients at the University of Michigan Medical Center who had just received a colostomy, a surgical operation in which the colon is shortened to remove a damaged part and the cut end is then diverted to an opening in the abdomen, where a pouch is usually placed to collect waste.

The composition of our experimental groups was the key to testing whether hope might be a negative factor. About half of the patients had undergone an *irreversible* procedure. The remainder faced the potential to have their colostomies reversed and normal bowel function restored at some point in the future.*

Recruitment of patients into the study was done while patients were still in the hospital recovering from surgery. Patients who agreed to participate were mailed surveys at three intervals: one week after being released from the hospital, one month after, and six months after.

Research participants were asked to rate their life satisfaction. They were given five statements, such as "In most ways my life is close to my ideal" and "So far I have gotten the important things I want in life." They indicated how strongly they agreed or disagreed with these statements on a scale of 1 (strongly disagree) to 7 (strongly agree). There was also a "ladder scale" asking respondents to position themselves somewhere between 0 and 10. The bottom, 0, represented the worst possible life; the top, 10, was the best possible life.

It was astonishing to see the trajectory of the results over time. Patients with reversible colostomies, surveyed one week after their procedure, initially reported higher life satisfaction, and almost equivalent levels on the quality-of-life scale. Roughly speaking, they were happier than their counterparts who knew their condition was hopeless. But one month after the procedure, those with a permanent colostomy were experiencing relatively higher levels of life satisfaction and quality of life. By six months, there was a yawning gap between the two groups: those without hope for recovery were doing

---

* Unlike a randomized experiment (which would not have allowed us to answer our research question), the study design was not perfectly "clean": there were potential confounds—factors other than the permanence of the procedure that may have caused the differences between the two groups. One issue is whether people with potentially reversible colostomies might suffer from more severe conditions. Although intuition points in the opposite direction, we did attempt to control for factors such as what caused the patient to need a colostomy. As it turned out, permanent colostomy patients were more likely to have had cancer, while temporary colostomy patients were more likely to have had inflammatory bowel disease (IBD).

much better on both measures, while the patients who were holding out hope were miserable.

There are several possible explanations for why hope impedes our natural ability to adapt to a difficult situation. First, those with hope may differ in motivation from those who lack it. Because acknowledging loss can be momentarily but intensely painful, people may not be willing to "take the hit," and therefore may fail to engage in conscious and/or unconscious adaptation until and unless they have no alternative. People may also be conserving their emotional resources—they may not want to expend the mental or physical effort required to adapt if there is some possibility that such measures might later prove to have been unnecessary. For example, it may require mental effort to find a silver lining in a calamity, and people may not be sufficiently motivated to put in the effort if there is some prospect that the effort will turn out to be unneeded. Finally, knowledge of a potentially better future could remind people that their current circumstances are less than ideal, serving as an upward point of comparison that causes one's present circumstances to be viewed in a more negative light.

After presenting these results at conferences, I always ask my audience: "Now that you've seen these results, if faced with a choice between a potentially reversible or permanent colostomy, which would you prefer?"

If we were living in a world in which the goal was increasing subjective measures of happiness, then everyone should choose a permanent colostomy. And yet I can't recall any member of my audience choosing the irreversible procedure. This yields an important lesson about human nature: we prefer to have a shred of hope, even when we know that hope will make us miserable.

Doctors might learn something from these results about how a prognosis should be delivered to a patient. Generally speaking, health professionals find it easier to deliver optimistic news to patients even when they believe the prognosis is unfavorable. It is, of course, easier to give good instead of bad news. But physicians justify this practice because they think it is in the interests of the patient and his or her friends and family to provide some hope, even in cases that are relatively hopeless.

The colostomy results suggest, however, that while hopeful news may be easier to deliver and, initially, more pleasant to receive, it may not be in the best interest of the recipients because it may hinder emotional adaptation. A doctor's natural (and self-serving) tendency to provide hope, even when a condition is hopeless, may actually do more long-term harm than good. And, though even a worthless medication might still provide some benefit in the form of a placebo effect, the downside may be far greater, since such treatments keep patients psychologically oriented toward recovery, postponing adaptation and setting them up for bitter disappointment. As Adam Smith put it, "The medicines of the physician are often the greatest torment of the incurable patient."

Obviously, hope isn't always a bad thing, but instead of valorizing hope in all contexts it's worth considering when it is helpful and when it might be harmful. I acquired one of my favorite adages about this from a fortune cookie: "Hope makes a good breakfast but a bad supper." The obvious interpretation is that hope is beneficial when you are young, but perhaps foolish or unsatisfying when old.

Now, well into the "supper" (or perhaps dessert) phase of life, I'm not as taken with the adage as I was when I was young. I still find things to hope for (and, alas, even more things to worry about). At my stage in life, an even more popular adage springs to mind: "hope springs eternal." After conducting this research, my own view is that hope is still a good thing—except in very bleak situations that are not likely to improve. In such situations, hope impedes the relief arising from adaptation, and people are, if not "happily hopeless," then at the very least "*happier* hopeless."

PART 2

What We Suffer From

9

Impatience

She was waiting for something to happen. Like a sailor in distress, she kept scanning the solitude of her life with anxious eyes, straining to sight some far-off white sail in the mists of the horizon. She did not know how it would come to her, what wind would bring it to her, to what shores it would carry her, whether it would be a launch or a towering three-decker, laden with sorrow or filled to the gunwales with bliss. But every morning when she awoke she expected it to arrive that day; she listened to every sound, periodically leapt to her feet with a start and was surprised when she saw it had not come; then, at sundown, sadder than ever, she longed for the next day.

—Gustave Flaubert, *Madame Bovary*

Stretched on the Rack of Time

My earliest memory of the misery of waiting was waiting for my older sister, Andrea, to get invited to the prom. It was the middle of the 1960s, a decade we now romanticize as rebellious, full of free love and drugs. But in the sleepy suburbs not that much had changed since the 1950s: prom was still a monumental event. As the date drew near, and one by one her friends secured their invitations, Andrea's remained conspicuously absent. Soon the whole family was on tenterhooks. Dinners, which we ate on tall chairs around an island at one end of the kitchen, were funereal. The phone was mounted against the wall at one end of the island, and we all studiously avoided looking at it.

Finally, only a few nights before the prom, when we had pretty much given up all hope, the phone rang. True, the invitation came from a very inferior representative of the male gender, who had probably already been turned down by virtually every prospective date he had asked; but an invitation from anyone was infinitely better than no invitation at all. My mother flew into action and sewed a dress out of Marimekko cloth from Finland, which was then all the rage, and my sister was ready to go at the appointed time.

Alas, the boy never showed up.

When I asked Andrea for permission to share this story, she agreed—then confessed she had no memory of it whatsoever. My younger sister, Dania, corroborated the basic outline while disputing nearly every detail. Our phone, she reminded me, sat on the countertop, not on the wall. And our mother, then in the midst of finishing her PhD, "would never have sewn Andrea a dress, especially not a prom dress out of Marimekko." (My mother and I had shared the memory of the prom incident shortly before she died in 2022, and it was she who provided the detail about the Marimekko.)

So maybe some of the details are wrong. But what stuck with me was that excruciating wait, the sense that time itself had stalled, and that a single phone call could change everything for the better, and yet it refused to come.

Waiting for the phone to ring may be one of the most exquisitely miserable forms of waiting ever invented. Unlike the days of the knock on the door or the afternoon mail delivery, which offered only a narrow window for hope and disappointment, the telephone expanded the waiting window to nearly the entire day. Outside of sleeping hours, the call could come at any moment—or not at all. And so one waited, suspended between hope and despair, trapped in a state of constant vigilance.

Lena Andersson captures this perfectly in her superb novel *Willful*

Disregard, about a woman obsessed with a man who shows no reciprocal interest. "Friday limped on," she writes. "The most common question since the invention of the telephone could very well be: *Why doesn't he ring?*" Like Proust's Swann, who cannot let go of the mediocre Odette, Andersson's heroine grows increasingly deranged by her own anticipation that he *might* call at any time.

Technology, rather than easing our impatience, has only stretched it thinner. The return calls we used to wait for have become replies to text message and emails or comments and "likes" to various posts on social media—greatly expanding the time range in which we could receive possible gratifications, or disappointments. As Andersson puts it, "What she must definitely not do now was to expose herself to the anguish of sending a text message that would go unanswered. The anguish generated by the nonappearance of an answer was something the creators of texts and e-mails could not have anticipated."

Needless to say, she breaks her resolution within moments of making it.

Present Versus Future

In economics, the question of whether it's worth it to wait for something or not—what in the field is called *intertemporal choice*—is an important area of study. In fact, this was the focus of my first research project as a graduate student. Intertemporal choice refers to trade-offs between sooner and later options—the choice between spending your money now or saving it, pursuing further education or entering the workforce, devouring a plate of loaded nachos tonight or enjoying greater health and a better physique in the future.

The standard economic theory of intertemporal choice assumes that when people make impatient choices they are "discounting"—or putting less value on—the future as compared with the present. People, according to this view, don't save enough and eat too much because they are placing greater value on the immediate pleasures of spending and eating than the delayed gratifications of accumulating a nest egg or being healthy or attractive. But this perspective entirely misses the subjective *feeling* of waiting. It's not that people, as a general rule, don't value the future; most of us do, enormously. But putting off an immediate pleasure for a distant and uncertain one requires a long interval of miserable waiting. And many of us can't bear it.

Because it gets the psychology wrong, the standard economic model of waiting—what is known as the "discounted utility model" (DU)—mispredicts people's behavior in a wide range of important situations. For example, one of DU's most straightforward predictions is that we should always want to delay negative things as much as possible—move them to a time we discount more (and so care about less)—while prioritizing positive experiences. I'll eat my ice cream *now*, but schedule my dental procedure *later*.

This may be true for some people, some of the time. My own tendency, however, is to want to get most unpleasant things over with quickly—to eliminate the miserable period of dread when I'm waiting for them to happen. And when it comes to positive things, I once again behave contrary to the economic model. I often find myself saving the best for last—leaving, for instance, the tastiest morsel on my dinner plate until everything else is consumed. While my behavior may be anomalous by economic standards, it is by no means uncommon. A number of studies have found, for example, that given a choice between immediate and delayed electric shock, most people opt for the former, and will even pay—or accept a higher voltage shock—just to get their shock *sooner*.

It (Almost) Always Hurts to Wait

Consider two scenarios: waiting for something bad versus waiting for something good.

Waiting for something bad pretty much always feels bad. Some of the most anguished responses to the Misery Survey that I conducted for this book—the survey that invited people to describe, in their own words, the experiences they found most psychologically painful—involved the slow vigil of waiting for a loved one to die. One female respondent in her seventies described watching both her mother and her husband slip away in hospice: "There's no way of knowing how your loved one is feeling, whether they're in pain, physically or mentally, or how long they will hang on. You're simply waiting for them to pass away with no other outcome possible."

Of course, the looming bad thing doesn't need to be quite so bad for the wait to make us miserable. Much of our lives are filled with unpleasant tasks we dread in advance. For me, it's grading student papers, knowing that many will be painful to read (apologies to past, present, and future students!). For someone else, it might be a difficult conversation—like knowing you need to break up with someone and enduring the excruciating interval before finally having "the talk."

Then there's the misery of waiting to face the consequences of your own stupid mistakes. I can think of two recent examples from my life: standing in line to leave a country, knowing I'd lost the vital entry certificate they explicitly warned me not to misplace; and watching the police approach my car on the highway, knowing they'd ask for my license—which I'd left at home. All these predictably awful things are predictably miserable to wait for.

The writer Elizabeth Strout—through the voice of her fictional alter ego in *My Name Is Lucy Barton*—captured the torment of waiting for something unpleasant when she described a childhood experience: visiting the dentist. This particular dentist was generous in providing free care to poor people like Barton's family, but he did so only begrudgingly and treated his pro bono patients with hostility. Because Lucy and her siblings didn't visit the dentist regularly, their dental issues accumulated between visits, and most visits entailed not only the humiliation of getting free care, but excruciatingly painful procedures.

As she waited anxiously for her appointment, Lucy began to grasp a profound truth: the anticipation of a bad event multiplies its pain. In her case, she had to endure psychological distress in the lead-up to the dentist and then physical pain when the moment finally arrived. What dawned on her was how emotionally inefficient waiting could be: "You are wasting time by suffering twice." Yet this insight did little to free Lucy from her dread. This reflects an emerging, and recurrent, theme in this book: understanding the mechanics of suffering does little to soften its sting.

Oddly, as already touched upon in the chapter on hope, uncertainty about a future event often makes the subjective experience of waiting worse, even though that same uncertainty might mean you're objectively better off: after all, there's always the possibility that the bad event might not happen. But ambiguity about whether a bad event will in fact happen doesn't ease the dread; if anything, it makes it harder to bear. *How bad will it be? Is there any way out?* The mind seizes on these questions, spinning out endless scenarios that amplify the misery of waiting. In fact, research shows that when we experience dread we tend to think about not the most likely negative outcome but the worst possible one.

Perhaps the worst kind of uncertainty is knowing that a bad thing will happen but not knowing exactly *when*, so it is always possible that the proverbial shoe is about to drop. There can be no better embodiment of such misery than the Japanese practice of executing death row prisoners (by hanging) with little or no warning. The rationale for this convention, according to the Justice Ministry, is that providing advance notice "might cause serious harm to [condemned prisoners'] mental states," presumably based on the assumption that a prisoner's distress would only increase as they approached the date of their execution.

But it's difficult to imagine a system that could produce more psychic harm than one in which the axe could fall at any moment. Lawyers for two death row inmates who filed an unsuccessful lawsuit to provide advance notice described the effect: "Death row prisoners live in fear every morning that that day will be their last. It's extremely inhumane." Amnesty International echoed this sentiment in a 2009 report, which condemned the practice as "cruel, inhuman and degrading," noting that it leads prisoners to develop "significant mental illness." (In defending its no-warning policy, the Japanese Justice Ministry cited the case of a prisoner who, under the previous policy of alerting them to their impending death, committed suicide rather than wait for his execution. Apparently, it is important to the Justice Ministry that *they* be the ones who do the killing.)

It's hard to top the misery of waiting on death row, but waiting for potentially bad medical news might come close. One respondent to the Misery Survey described the agony of going to sonogram appointments after enduring multiple miscarriages:

The visits to wait for sonograms to check for a heartbeat and viable pregnancy were hellish, particularly sitting in the waiting room, waiting to be called back for the exam. This was before smart phones. I would read *People* magazine and grit my teeth. Waiting to be called back was harder than having the exam itself. I had so many adverse events that I ran out of people to go with me and usually went alone. I could talk later about the result with my spouse and friends, but the waiting room was just me.

Clearly, waiting for potentially bad outcomes is bad. But what about waiting for good things? You might assume that anticipating a positive event would be an equal and opposite experience as waiting for a negative event—that it would result in a serene, satisfying lull before the good thing arrives, like watching a gorgeous soufflé rise in the oven or inhaling the scent of lavender bath salts as the tub fills with warm water. Yet notice that there is no precise word in English that describes the feeling of waiting for something good; our language lacks a perfect antonym for *dread*. No greater expert than the author A. A. Milne noted this in his classic, *The House at Pooh Corner*.

Christopher Robin said: "What do you like doing best in the world, Pooh?"

"Well," said Pooh, "what I like best—" and then he had to stop and think. Because although Eating Honey was a very good thing to do, there was a moment just before you began to eat it which was better than when you were, but he didn't know what that was called.

In fact, the more you think about it, the more you realize that even if the thing you're waiting for is good—a vacation, a family reunion, a dreamed-of promotion—the wait itself is very often not good at all. The reasons why are complicated, but they intersect with a whole range of psychological mechanisms discussed in the first half of the book.

The first reason is that thinking about a future good thing often triggers immediate appetites—like hunger or sexual desire—leading to a craving for the thing one expects to consume, but isn't consuming *yet*. Such cravings can sometimes enhance the pleasure we feel when our desires are finally satisfied—as in the phrase "hunger is the best spice," which applies as much to sex as to food—but hunger doesn't make the waiting itself pleasant so much as it enhances the pleasure of finally eating. In fact, the real purpose of the appetites is to make you feel bad, so you do something that evolution has determined is good for you, or, in the case of the sex drive, good for the species.

The second reason that waiting for something good is rarely pleasurable is that there's usually a degree of uncertainty about whether the good thing will actually happen. When the outcome feels secure, you can savor the wait—like Pooh with his honey in hand. But if there's even a sliver of doubt, the pleasure evaporates. Waiting for a date, a vacation, or a wedding may seem delightful at first, but add the tiniest uncertainty—*What if they cancel? What if I'm disappointed?*—and it becomes a source of stress.

If a tiny bit of uncertainty can rob us of the pleasure of waiting for a good event, substantial uncertainty can make waiting for good things downright miserable. Consider awards, which in a very wide range of fields tend to be announced about once a year. For those eligible for a coveted prize, or the undoubtedly far larger population of people who *consider themselves* eligible, the entire year is spent waiting for the announcement, after which, for the vast majority of those in the latter, larger, group, there is likely a period of intense disappointment punctuated by the knowledge that getting over the disappointment will only usher in a new period of painful waiting. One economist I knew personally, who had led an exceptionally full life, filled with adventure, professional successes, and a wide array of close friends and family, confessed on his deathbed that he was bitter that he had not won the Nobel Prize. I have always wondered whether such prizes cause a lot more misery than the pleasure they (hopefully) bring to those who win.

In the unusual event that a good thing is certain, how it feels to wait depends in large part on how long the good thing will last. Waiting for something that will last a long time—such as a pay raise, the arrival of a much-longed-for child, permanent relief from a medical condition—is always miserable because the brain naturally asks: If things are going to get better in the future, why can't they get better *now*? It is, therefore, not a coincidence that almost all the things that are pleasurable to wait for—a dinner, a date, a vacation, a celebration—are short-lived.

But short-lived things have their own downside; by nature of being short-lived they are going to come to an end, and the aftermath of a good thing is often a feeling of deflation—of being let down. Which, for the pessimistically inclined, may provide yet another source of dread. Exactly such a perverse pattern can be seen in the novelist Annie Ernaux's thinly disguised autobiographical essay about her passion for a married man:

> When he rang to arrange a meeting, his long-awaited call had no effect on me and I remained locked in the same state of anxiety as before. My condition was such that not even the sound of his voice could make me happy. It was all infinite emptiness, except when we were together making love. And even then I dreaded the moments to come, when he would be gone. I experienced pleasure like a future pain.

Pass-Fail

The worst wait of my young life came after I flunked my comprehensive exam in grad school. For those fortunate enough to live outside the ivory tower, the comprehensive or qualifying exam ("quals" to the initiated) is a brutal, make-or-break test for fledgling academics. Imagine being grilled on everything you're supposed to know by a committee of professors who will judge whether you're worthy of continuing your academic journey.

Shortly after failing, I started a summer job on Wall Street (at Salomon Brothers); it was a very easy job, and paid well, so I should have enjoyed it. But I didn't, because most of what I thought about wasn't the valuation of bonds (which is what I was supposed to be thinking about), but the retake of the exam at the end of summer, and the dire consequences of failing it a second time—basically, all my life plans collapsing around me. My misery was so great that, though I was only twenty-seven at the time, my hair started to turn gray—decades younger than my father's had.

At the end of the summer, when the job was over but before the semester began, I holed up with all my course notes in a cottage owned by my grandparents deep in the woods. Far from any other human habitation, I was immersed each night in a sea of sinister-sounding animal and insect noises. To drown them out—and distract myself—I turned to the cabin's old black-and-white TV, which received only one fuzzy channel. I vividly remember one particularly bad night, after trying to unwind after a long day of studying, when I watched the program shown on that channel, about a woman who—perhaps in isolated circumstances not too dissimilar from my own—had murdered her children.

Waiting to take the exam was bad enough, but then there was a second waiting period after I'd retaken the exam but before the results became available, possibly even more intolerable because there was nothing I could do at that point—except *wait*! In the end, I did pass on my second try, and there turned out to be a silver lining to my suffering: the misery of waiting ended up giving me the idea for my dissertation—about the pleasure, and more often pain, of waiting.

Part of what made waiting for the qualifier so miserable was its binary nature. These either-or outcomes torture us because there's no middle ground. Pass or fail. Pregnant or not. Malignant tumor or benign lump. The psychological distance between good news and bad is immense—and we live suspended between them, dreading the worst.

These binary outcome situations are especially torturous when getting the good outcome requires an investment of time and effort, like studying for an exam. Putting in that time and effort is painful, because it's difficult not to think about the fact that if you end up failing you know it will be wasted, and all your work will have been for nothing. But focusing on the prospect of success doesn't help much, because even if you do succeed, you will most likely end up having worked more than you needed to: any effort invested beyond the point of securing the positive outcome is, again, wasted.

What's the Holdup?

When it comes to waiting, *why* you're waiting matters almost as much as how long. Think, for example, how eminently tolerable it is to wait for a friend you're supposed to meet—*when you arrive early*. There is, however, an abrupt change in the experience of waiting when the appointed time comes and goes and your friend hasn't shown up. Now the delay becomes a signal of how much—or actually, how *little*—they care about you—about the low value they place on your time. As the minutes tick by, the signal gets stronger, and the discomfort morphs into indignation.

But the later it gets, the more complicated the feelings. On the one hand, indignation is likely to escalate into outrage. On the other hand, fear might creep in: *What if something bad has happened to them?* The mind then goes into contortions, vacillating from one of these unpleasant thoughts and the emotions it generates to the other thought and the very different emotions *it* evokes. Then, unpleasant meta-emotions enter into the emotional whiplash: Guilt that you are angry when something terrible might—*must!*—have happened to them. Resentment that they are making you *this* worried while simultaneously displaying an almost unfathomable disregard for you.

A long wait can also produce self-blame; it can be a signal that you made a stupid decision. Consider a typical consumer experience: paying for your food at the supermarket. In most stores, a shopper must line up behind one of several cashiers. Though it's made quickly, this decision can incorporate a remarkably wide range of potential considerations: How many people are waiting at each line? Do they have many items? Do any of them seem like the type who will try to use an expired coupon or pay for their groceries with a personal check? Does the cashier seem like a novice who will need to look up the QR code for each item in a folding plastic booklet?

Many stores now offer another option: self-checkout. On the surface, it promises the freedom to skip the line and handle your purchases independently. In reality, it often leads to a different kind of wait—standing awkwardly by the machine, hoping a roving employee will eventually appear after you've inevitably misread the prompts or triggered an error.

In a brilliant 1984 essay, Lance Morrow captured the important role of meaning—one's interpretation of *why* one is waiting—in creating the feeling of impatience:

> Waiting is a form of imprisonment. One is doing time—but why? One is being punished not for an offense of one's own but often for the inefficiencies of those who impose the wait. Hence the peculiar rage that waits engender, the sense of injustice. Aside from boredom and physical discomfort, the subtler misery of waiting is the knowledge that one's most precious resource, time, a fraction of one's life, is being stolen away, irrecoverably lost.

That essay came to mind during a weekend conference I once cohosted for a well-funded government agency. I'd dragged a few friends along, thinking it might be worthwhile. It wasn't. Two days of drudgery later, the organizer rose to bid adieu to the departing participants: "This has been a wonderful two days. And I'm so grateful you generously gave your time. As we all know, time is the one resource you can never recover." The truth landed like a gut-punch. If I alone had wasted time it might have been bearable, but the fact that I inflicted this tedium on my friends made the misery ten times worse.

(Of course, I may have been judging the event more harshly because I was worried about whether my friends would think it worthwhile. In a similar vein, I've noticed that when I persuade a friend to accompany me to my favorite restaurant, the food always seems to be *off*. And, when I sway a group to go see the latest film of my favorite director, I always have the feeling that the movie I've dragged my friends to is "not one of his best." The reason is, I think, that I am especially focused on evaluating the meal's or film's quality, and academic studies find that such a focus tends to produce negative evaluations. It surprises me that so many service providers, including hotels that leave little questionnaires in the room about one's experience, don't seem to be familiar with this research.)

Some of the best research on the misery of waiting comes from studies examining the experience of consumers waiting in line. The MIT operations research scientist Richard Larson distinguished between *slips* (when someone else joins a line after you but gets served before you) and *skips* (when you get served first even if someone else had been waiting longer). Consistent with the asymmetry between bad and good that has arisen in virtually every chapter, it feels much worse to be the victim of a slip than it feels good to be a beneficiary of a skip. In fact, skips may only make you feel guilty toward whomever you inadvertently cut in line.

Revolutions of Rising Expectations

Perhaps you've noticed when taking a long-haul flight that waiting for a connecting flight feels much worse if your layover is close to your final destination. For example, suppose I'm traveling from Toulouse, France, (a hotbed of behavioral economics) to Pittsburgh (my hometown). That trip requires two layovers, one likely in Paris, the other in a hub near Pittsburgh—say Newark, Philadelphia, or Atlanta. Waiting at the airport in Paris feels relatively tolerable, even rather civilized if I manage to have a croque monsieur and a glass of wine. By contrast, waiting in a nearby domestic hub feels almost intolerable, because at that point my brain is screaming, *You're almost there! You should be there already!*

This irrational surge of impatience as the finish line nears was first documented in the 1930s by psychologist Clark Hull. In his research on the *goal-gradient hypothesis*, Hull found that animals became increasingly motivated as they approached a reward. Mice navigating a maze, for instance, moved faster (and, if outfitted in a harness, pulled harder) the closer they got to the food at the end. Their effort—and, by implication, their impatience—seemed to rise in tandem with proximity to the goal. Humans, it turns out, are no different. At a connecting airport just a short flight away from home, every delay takes on outsized significance, making it feel as if time itself is slowing down. The principle is as simple as it is maddening: the closer we are to our destination, the harder it becomes to wait.

The same principle helps explain the irritation we often feel with real-time tracking apps, which are supposed to soothe our impatience. Companies like Uber and DoorDash allow you to follow your meal or ride inching toward you on a map. These features are meant to give users reassurance that their food or ride is on its way—but they often backfire. Watching your driver pause at a red light or your food getting cold as it takes a detour can provoke far more frustration than if it had simply arrived without warning.

This psychological dynamic—that waiting becomes harder the closer we are to relief—doesn't just affect travelers and takeout customers. As already touched upon, one of the most miserable venues for waiting—by design—is prison.

Waiting behind bars is often most agonizing at two distinct points. The first is at the beginning of a sentence: the memory of freedom is still painfully vivid, and acclimating to life behind bars can be brutal, especially for first-time inmates. The second low point occurs near the end—when the prospect of release looms large. Logically, if one had the means to escape, the optimal time to do so would be early in the sentence, when the reward of regained freedom is greatest. And yet, paradoxically, researchers have found that a surprising number of prison escapes occur late in sentences. Why? Unlike future bad events, which we resist adapting to because of our stubborn hope that they might not happen, we readily adapt to *good* events before they even happen. This makes incarceration less tolerable because, having mentally adjusted to the expected improvement, the prisoner becomes more acutely aware of what he (since most prisoners are male) doesn't yet have. He feels, in effect, *already entitled* to freedom—and the wait becomes unbearable.

The same pattern emerges on a societal scale. The J-curve theory of revolution, first proposed in 1962 by the political scientist James C. Davies, argues that political revolutions don't erupt when conditions are at their worst, or even when they're deteriorating. Instead, they happen when things start to improve—just not fast enough to satisfy rising expectations.

Davies showed how this dynamic could explain the French and Russian Revolutions, which both occurred after periods of economic and social progress. Similar patterns have appeared elsewhere. After independence, many nations in Africa and Latin America saw hopes for prosperity and equality soar, only to collide with the slow realities of nation-building; stalled progress often bred unrest or civil war. In the United States, the civil rights movement likewise gathered force not during the most repressive decades of segregation, but after mid-century gains began to make genuine equality seem within reach. When progress stalled, the disappointment of rising expectations turned into widespread protest.

More recently, the Arab Spring uprisings followed a similar emotional arc, with less positive results. Early victories in Tunisia and Egypt sparked optimism across the region, but when meaningful reforms proved slow or elusive, impatience led to unrest and, in many places, renewed authoritarianism. In all these cases, it wasn't the *absence* of progress that pushed people into the streets but the unbearable frustration of waiting—triggered by the apparent prospect of relief. As Alexis de Tocqueville observed, "The most perilous moment for a bad government is one when it seeks to mend its ways."

A Sliver of a Silver Lining

Though the news about waiting is not good, there may be two small consolations.

The first is that the pain of waiting can, in some cases, counteract a common human failing: the tendency to defer pleasure. Adam Smith observed that, in the pursuit of wealth and greatness, people often "sacrifice a real tranquility that is at all times in [their] power" for some distant goal—only to discover, if they finally get what they wanted, that it's no better than "the humble security and contentment" they sacrificed to achieve it. In this light, the discomfort of waiting might serve a modest purpose: pushing us to enjoy what we can now, rather than postponing pleasures already within our grasp for the sake of rewards we mistakenly believe will make us happier.

The second consolation is simpler: the misery of waiting tends to disappear once the wait is over. Unlike regret or rejection, which linger in memory, the pain of waiting is often hard to reconstruct. Like physical pain or "hot" emotional states (as discussed in Chapter 1), impatience is tightly bound to immediate circumstances. Once those circumstances pass, the emotion vanishes—a mercy that is not granted by many of the miseries to come.

10

Boredom

> In between the periods of sexual excitement came agonizing crises of boredom. Boredom seemed to swell like a balloon inside the head; it became a pressure inside the skull: sometimes I feared the balloon would burst and I would lose my reason.
>
> —Graham Greene, *A Sort of Life*

A Feeling You Can't Control

Decades ago, I went to an academic talk given by a Swedish psychologist. Titled "Ramsey Said It All," the presentation went through the career of Frank Plumpton Ramsey, a British polymath genius who, before his untimely death at the age of twenty-six, made seminal contributions to philosophy, mathematics, and economics. The talk was unbearably dull—just a chronological listing of Ramsey's accomplishments with no narrative arc, no big-picture analysis, no dramatic turns. By the end, I felt I had wasted an hour of my life. The only redeeming factor was the pleasure of the postmortem discussion with colleagues about the seminar, which I snidely referred to as "the most boring talk in the world."

The joke was on me. Years later, having written a series of papers in which I made the poorly researched claim that Paul Samuelson, a Nobel Prize–winning economist, had come up with an important framework called the *discounted utility* model, I got an email from a colleague at Harvard forwarding a complaint from another economist that Samuelson was not in fact the progenitor of the discounted utility model.

Perhaps you guessed it? It was Frank Ramsey.

At that moment, I wished I had paid closer to attention to the talk. Then again, I know from my own research how difficult it is to pay attention when one is bored. For very good evolutionary reasons, we can't control whether we feel boredom, just as we can't control whether we feel hunger or pain. Hunger, pain, and boredom are all signals designed by evolution: the first motivates us to eat, the second minimizes bodily injury, and the third—the topic of this chapter—pushes us to shift our attention.

Despite its universality, boredom has remained surprisingly under-explored in scientific research. For years, theories of boredom tended to be descriptive rather than explanatory, merely predicting when it occurs rather than addressing what function it serves or why it evolved. Worse, those predictions were often wrong. The most common explanation—that boredom arises from under-stimulation—sounds plausible but doesn't hold up to scrutiny. Some of life's least stimulating moments—like lying in bed before sleep—are not particularly boring. Conversely, some things that are technically very stimulating—children's television, small talk, PowerPoint presentations with unnecessary animations—are intolerably boring.

When I think about boredom in the abstract, I picture a smoky, existentialist café. Sartre, Camus, and their ilk helped shape the modern understanding of boredom—or perhaps I should say *ennui*—as a low-energy, melancholic state, a kind of existential vacuum. This is also the world of Alberto Moravia's novel *Boredom*, which follows Dino, a wealthy painter who feels utterly disconnected from life: "My boredom might be described as a malady affecting external objects and consisting of a withering process; an almost instantaneous loss of vitality—just as though one saw a flower change in a few seconds from a bud to decay and dust."

For Dino, boredom is not just a private affliction but a force that drains the world of meaning, making everything seem lifeless, inert. This aligns, somewhat, with the traditional psychological model of boredom as a "low-arousal emotion," often contrasted with high-arousal negative states like anger or anxiety. But is that really how people experience boredom? When we're bored, do we feel merely empty and listless, or do we feel something more urgent?

I have been bored many times in my life, and it rarely feels like a hollow stillness. More often, it feels like a blunt instrument being slowly bored into my head, a sense that almost anything would be better than *this*. The hero of Joshua Ferris's novel *To Rise Again at a Decent Hour* definitely shares my perspective, describing "the boredom that overtakes me inside a church" as "not a passive boredom. It's an active, gnawing restlessness." As did Graham Greene (see this chapter's opening quote), judging from the drastic measure he took to relieve the agonizing pressure in his skull:

> Once on my free day I walked over the hills to Chesterfield and found a dentist. I described to him the symptoms, which I knew well, of an abscess. He tapped a perfectly good tooth with his little mirror and I reacted in the correct way. "Better have it out," he advised.
>
> "Yes," I said, "but with ether."
>
> A few minutes' unconsciousness was like a holiday from the world. I had lost a good tooth, but the boredom was for the time being dispersed.

Bored in the USA

My research colleagues and I wanted to understand the function of boredom—what purpose it had evolved to serve. But first, we realized, we needed to take a step back. Before we could determine what boredom is *for*, we first had to understand when and how people actually experience it. What kinds of situations bore people? And, when people feel boredom, what other emotions do they experience at the same time?

The only way to find this out was to capture boredom as it was happening, not in retrospect, when our fallible memory could distort it. So, in 2017, my colleagues Alycia Chin, Amanda Markey, Saurabh Bhargava, Karim Kassam, and I analyzed the data from one of the largest studies of boredom ever attempted. Using a custom iPhone app, the daily experiences of 3,867 US adults were tracked over a period of about one week. Every thirty minutes, participants logged what they were doing, where they were, who they were with, and how they felt, selecting "yes" or "no" for boredom along with sixteen other emotions.

Once we crunched the data from 1.1 million time-use and emotional reports, we received our first major surprise: boredom was far less common than we expected. Even though there is compelling evidence that people are more bored now than ever before (more on that later), those in our study reported boredom in only 2.8 percent of all half-hour reports. More than a third of participants never reported being bored at all. Even among those who did occasionally report feeling bored, it was a relatively small part of their waking lives, appearing in just 4.6 percent of reports.

Yet boredom wasn't distributed randomly. Some groups were far more prone to it than others. Younger people experienced boredom at much higher rates—twenty-five-year-olds were four times as likely to report boredom as forty-five-year-olds. Men were more susceptible than women, reporting boredom 33 percent more often. At first glance, this might suggest that boredom is an affliction of youth or masculinity, but a closer look at the data revealed that these differences were largely a function of how different groups spent their time.

Men and younger people spent more time in situations that all people tended to rate as boring—working, studying, and being alone—whereas women and older individuals spent more time in social or active settings, which were less likely to elicit boredom. A similar pattern emerged with socioeconomic status: people with lower income and lower education levels were more likely to report boredom, and again this difference was largely explained by how they spent their time. Those with lower socioeconomic status were more likely to engage in solitary or monotonous activities, such as repetitive work or extended periods alone, while those with higher education or income reported less boredom—but only up to a point.

Interestingly, college graduates did not report significantly lower boredom than high school graduates, suggesting that boredom's relationship with socioeconomic status is not straightforward. Meanwhile, married individuals were significantly less likely to report boredom than their unmarried peers, though whether this reflected differences in social engagement, life structure, or other factors remained unclear.

Certain activities reliably induced boredom. Studying was the most boring, followed closely by "doing nothing" and then working. By contrast, sports and exercise were the least boring activities, along with a wildcard entry in the low-boredom category: personal grooming. Consonant with our previous chapter on the hell of waiting, airports and medical facilities were among the most boring places to be, sharing the top spots with schools and workplaces, while restaurants, bars, gyms, and even fast-food establishments ranked among the least boring locations.

For me, the most striking revelation came from boredom's emotional profile. As I mentioned, the prevailing view, both in psychology and in everyday conversation, is that boredom is a low-energy state, a kind of emotional limbo between the heaven of positive emotions and the hell of negative ones. But our data conformed more closely to the perspectives of authors Joshua Ferris and Graham Greene, and to my own experience: boredom wasn't just passive disengagement or under-stimulation—it was an active discomfort, a restless craving for something else.

We found that boredom was 4.2 times more likely to occur in the presence of another negative emotion than a positive one. And boredom wasn't just loosely correlated with negative emotions—it strongly co-occurred with them, often at strikingly high rates. A person experiencing loneliness was 496 percent more likely to also report feeling bored in the same moment. Anger increased the likelihood of boredom by 126 percent, sadness by 89 percent, and worry by 79 percent. These findings painted a very different picture from the traditional notion of boredom as a neutral or low-energy state. Instead, boredom appeared deeply intertwined with frustration, restlessness, and distress—far closer to high-arousal emotions like anger.

These findings challenged the dominant theories of boredom. If boredom were truly a passive state, why did it so often appear alongside feelings of serious psychological distress? If boredom was just about the lack of stimulation, why did people report feeling bored during some objectively stimulating activities, such as work meetings? And if boredom was about the absence of meaning or purpose, as some researchers have argued, why did people report it most during activities that were clearly meaningful, such as studying or working?

Back to Attention

Boredom often leads to mind-wandering. I confess this sometimes happens in the middle of a conversation with my wife. She'll suddenly interrupt herself and say, "You're not paying any attention to what I'm saying!" And, invariably, she's right. I've drifted off, even if I won't fess up to the fact.

Why would such a distracting emotion be useful? In evolutionary terms, boredom plays a critical role in helping us manage attention, one of our most precious mental resources. In a world filled with competing demands, we need some way to automatically shift focus from less valuable activities to more valuable ones. If early humans didn't feel the urge to redirect their attention when staring at the same patch of woods, they might have missed important opportunities—a rustle in the bush that signaled prey, or an approaching threat. Our ancestors who were better at reallocating attention had an adaptive advantage: they probably avoided more predators, found more food, and pursued more socially or intellectually engaging activities.

People can, with some effort, control or make conscious decisions about where to focus their attention. After my wife calls me out, I can deliberately choose to focus on what she's saying—at least for a few moments. But effortfully deciding where to aim our attention is mentally taxing. The problem is that choosing how to use attention consumes the very resource we're trying to manage.

Boredom solves this problem by kicking in automatically. When the brain senses that what we're doing isn't worth the attention we're giving it, boredom acts as a mental prod—pushing us toward something more rewarding. But what does boredom actually feel like? Psychologists describe it as a state of discomfort, but its defining feature is restlessness—both mental and physical. When people are bored, they fidget, shift in their chairs, check their phones, doodle.

Just as boredom signals when we should shift our focus, the polar opposite feeling—what is called *flow*—signals when our attention is exactly where it should be. When the brain perceives that we're spending our attention wisely, we enter a mental state of total absorption, in which our focus locks onto a task so completely that the rest of the world seems to fade away. In such a state, the idea of time recedes, effort becomes effortless, and shifting attention away from what we're doing feels almost painful.

For a paper with my colleagues Nick Chater and Zachary Wojtowicz, I borrowed a term from economics—*opportunity cost*—to describe how boredom and flow help us conserve attention. In economics, opportunity cost refers to the value of the best alternative—Option B—which we sacrifice when we choose Option A. If you spend an hour watching recipe videos on Instagram, the opportunity cost is whatever else you could have done with that time—reading a book, exercising, actually cooking one of the dishes you saw being prepared. In other words, boredom and flow function as "opportunity cost calculators" for attention, helping us continuously measure whether we are spending this finite resource wisely.

Understanding boredom as an attention-conserving mechanism helps us make sense of a mystery that I mentioned earlier: why some tasks that are extremely stimulating are also unbearably boring. Among the most boring activities reported in our time-use survey were work meetings. This might not surprise anyone in the corporate world, but think about it for a moment: Why are meetings so dull? After all, they are socially and informationally rich experiences—involving plenty of interaction, spontaneity, and opportunities to learn, perform, judge, and be judged. Why don't they hold our attention? Why, for many of us, do we squirm our way through the half hour, screaming inside our heads how desperately we want it to be over?

The problem lies in the subtle judgment the brain makes between how much value it *expects* to get from the information it's receiving, and how much it actually gets. In other words, boredom arises from disappointment. Meetings create an unconscious expectation of stimulation—after all, people are talking, ideas are being exchanged, important decisions are being made. But if the conversation drags, repeats itself, or lacks stakes, the brain compares the actual experience to its expected level of value—a kind of counterfactual judgment of the type discussed in Chapter 6—and finds it lacking. That mismatch generates the boredom signal.

The fact that boredom arises from disappointment—from situations in which we think something will or should be more interesting than it actually is—helps to explain something a whole lot more consequential than why work meetings are boring; it helps to explain why we are collectively becoming ever more bored despite ever-expanding sources of mental stimulation.

A growing body of research suggests that boredom has increased dramatically over the past two decades. One large-scale study of US teenagers found that boredom steadily rose between 2010 and 2017, based on surveys of high school students. Another study, analyzing boredom levels among Chinese college students from 2009 to 2020, found a similar trend—young people today report feeling bored more often than students did a decade ago.

The opportunity cost theory of boredom suggests that these rising boredom rates are occurring not *despite* increasing opportunities for engagement, but *because* of them. By bombarding us with opportunities for mental stimulation—social media, TikTok, email, porn, Reddit, and so on—the modern world has ratcheted up our expectations of how much we should be mentally stimulated at every point in time. The result is that we're often bored or distracted even when engaged in something—like caring for our children or speaking to our spouse—that we know, at least upon reflection, is worthy of our full attention. Activities that we used to enjoy, or at least tolerate—like cooking, cleaning, taxes, childcare—now seem crushingly boring, and we need to constantly multitask to keep ourselves sane.

Go to a playground these days, and notice what the parents are doing. Who knows, but whatever it is they are doing, they are doing it on their phones.

Why Are Dreams So Boring?

It's natural to think that the antidote to boredom is surprise. A dull commute home can be brightened by an unexpected story on the radio or even the sight of a new building under construction. But not all surprises are equally interesting. For many people, the strangest and most unpredictable experiences they have occur in their dreams—and yet listening to someone describe a dream is, almost without exception, excruciatingly boring.

My colleague Simon DeDeo, who has studied dream reports through the lens of information theory, offers a compelling explanation. The problem isn't that dreams are surprising—it's that they are *surprisingly* surprising. Dreams are full of bizarre twists: a car becomes a living room, a cat is covered in tattoos. But the surprises in dreams don't follow the narrative rules we're used to. In a well-told story, even if we don't know what will happen, we know *something* is coming. The structure and language signal that a twist is on the way, and they often provide clues about what that twist might be. In dreams, surprises arrive without warning or obvious purpose.

This is what makes listening to someone describe a dream such a tiring and tedious experience: we can't anticipate the turning points, and we have no sense that the story is heading anywhere. In a conventional story, the detective follows the suspect to their hideout, and we get to savor the tension, waiting for the unexpected to arrive. In a dream, the car simply turns into a living room for no reason at all. We're left scrambling to make sense of the new situation, but without the pleasure of having seen the turn coming. Worse still, we often lack the personal context the dreamer has—the associations or emotional undercurrents that give the dream meaning.

From the perspective of the opportunity cost model, dreams are a perfect storm of boredom: our attention is engaged in processing surreal, complex information, but that input fails to deliver on the kinds of cognitive or emotional payoffs we're wired to expect. So we quickly tune out.

Just How Bad Is Boredom?

As mentioned earlier, there's a perception that boredom isn't all that bad—and to some extent, I share this view. After all, in my long descent through the varieties of psychic misery, I've placed boredom only on the second rung. It is not, by my estimation, the worst form of suffering. And yet I think most people underestimate just how aversive boredom really is, and the great lengths we'll go to in order to spare ourselves from it.

In one well-known study by Timothy Wilson and colleagues, participants were asked to sit quietly with their thoughts for a set period of time. Many found the boredom to be so unbearable that they chose to administer mild electric shocks to themselves, simply because it was *something to do.*

Sadly, the link between boredom and self-destructive behavior is seen not only in laboratory settings. Research has found that individuals who are more prone to boredom are more at risk for substance abuse, compulsive gambling, reckless driving, and other forms of impulsive decision making. When people are unable to tolerate boredom, they often seek relief in ways that can ultimately harm them.

While people sometimes hurt themselves just to avoid feeling bored, what bores them depends a lot on the perceived value of what they're doing. Drawing on a series of experimental findings, Erin Westgate shows that people are often more bored by tasks that demand some effort but feel pointless (for example, scanning pages of digits to circle certain numbers) than by tasks that are objectively harder but somehow meaningful (like puzzles or brainteasers, which are, at least, a workout for the mind). This reinforces the idea that what bores us more than anything is the feeling that our attention is being wasted.

In *The Conquest of Happiness*, his 1930 guide to living a meaningful life, the philosopher Bertrand Russell devotes a substantial part of his essay to boredom, to which he attributes "half the sins of mankind": "Wars, pogroms, and persecutions have all been part of the flight from boredom; even quarrels with neighbors have been found better than nothing." Russell argues that people in his time were not necessarily more bored than they used to be, but rather *more afraid* of boredom. "We have come to know, or rather to believe, that boredom is not part of the natural lot of man, but can be avoided by a sufficiently vigorous pursuit of excitement."

He contrasted this with the grim monotony of the Middle Ages, when boredom wasn't an occasional inconvenience but an inescapable fact of life. Winters were long and dark, with nothing to do but tend the fire and wait for the thaw. In Russell's view, by the twentieth century, even modest access to technology and urban life had upended those expectations. A housemaid, he noted, now demanded "at least once a week as much excitement as would have lasted a Jane Austen heroine throughout a whole novel."

What struck me, reading Russell's argument nearly a century later, was not just how prescient he was—but how quaint his anxieties now seem. If he worried that 1930s consumer culture was raising our expectations for excitement, what would he make of an economy built around the promise of instant mental gratification? Today, we carry in our pockets a portal to endless stimulation. And yet, far from eliminating boredom, it seems to have made us more sensitive to it, less able to tolerate even a flicker.

This aligns with the argument I made earlier—that boredom is less about a lack of stimulation than it is about expectations being disappointed. Russell believed the solution to boredom was to cultivate the ability to sit with it, to accept it rather than frantically trying to escape it: "A certain power of enduring boredom is therefore essential to a happy life, and is one of the things that ought to be taught to the young."

But given the world we now live in, I'm not sure we are capable of that anymore. The fear of boredom has become ingrained. And so, instead of learning to tolerate boredom, we have built a world to protect ourselves from it, even as those efforts simply increase our susceptibility to the very misery we so assiduously try to avoid.

11

Anger

Alice could feel *rage* rising in her and it frightened her. She didn't want it to rise. She knew it would spoil things, and she was afraid of it, but there it was, rising and boiling in her.

—John Steinbeck, *The Wayward Bus*

Boiling Point

The facades people present to the world can be astonishingly deceptive. Our next-door neighbors once seemed like the perfect couple—until the day he moved out. And I would never have guessed that one of the calmest, most put-together friends I know would send me one of the most searing reflections on anger I've ever read.

As I mentioned in the introduction, after I began working on this book, I invited friends and colleagues to share any personal insights they had on negative emotions. I expected anecdotes, maybe a few vulnerable disclosures. I didn't expect this.

"I started writing this a million different ways," my friend began, "trying to find the right starting point—the right amount of background to explain the depth of the anger I felt. I didn't enjoy getting back into that mindset. But I'm just going to go for it, come what may."

She and her husband had been together for four years and married for one. After undergoing IVF, they had a single viable embryo, which was implanted shortly after their wedding. The pregnancy was grueling—emotionally and physically. She suffered from near-constant nausea, full-body hives ("like getting 100 mosquito bites"), and a deep depression brought on by the hormone treatments. What hurt even more was the creeping realization that her husband seemed less interested in caring for her than in preserving his own independence.

Three months after their son was born, they traveled to her parents' house for Mother's Day. After an endless night trying to sleep-train a hysterical baby—"I felt like a monster for not responding to him," she wrote, while her husband just rolled over and put a pillow over his head—she finally stepped away for a moment of peace. She took a long shower, and as she was drying herself off, she mindlessly picked up her phone.

The email was from a stranger, who apologized for reaching out on her work account but said he thought she needed to know: his girlfriend—a twenty-six-year-old whom both she and her husband had met through mutual friends—had been having an affair with her husband just before the baby was born. And, he added, it had recently started up again.

She showed the email to her husband. He confirmed it was true. What followed was "the longest and deepest bout of anger I've ever experienced":

> There were other emotions too, of course—sadness, shame, regret, envy, despair—but those didn't wake me up in the night and keep me from falling back asleep. That was uniquely anger.
>
> It felt like a huge battery in my gut, leaking acid that I swear I could taste. It felt physically harmful, like it could burn holes in my organs. It was easily triggered if I wasn't feeling it, easily exacerbated if I already was.
>
> I gave up on sleep training the baby immediately, but now I was kept awake all night by rage, and sleep deprivation heightened my sensitivity to all negative emotions, fueling a terrible feedback loop. Sleep medications always worked easily on me before, but now nothing kept me asleep. Even if a drug was successful in putting me to sleep, I would have nightmares that shot me awake—or more

accurately, shot at the battery pack in my stomach, exploding the acid out into my core.

I felt like I was being physically eaten from the inside. My body couldn't contain it. At particularly frustrating parts of arguments, I found myself punching the mattress, stomping on the ground, even hitting myself. It was a choice, but just barely—like whatever physical machinery moved Dr. Strangelove's arm that he had to consciously fight against.

Meanwhile, she was still living with the man who had betrayed her—sharing space, co-parenting, maintaining appearances. "Cosplaying my own life by day," she wrote, "and lying awake internally acid-washed by night." Talking to him only made it worse. He refused to take responsibility for her pain. "That would put me into the closest to a blind rage I have ever experienced," she wrote. "I never felt blinded, but I did physically feel anger burst through my whole body, aching to be unleashed."

"It Eats You Alive"

Psychologists and philosophers often describe anger as arising when we're blocked from attaining a goal by someone else's wrongful action. As the novelist Anthony Trollope expressed in his autobiography, "One does not become angry with a madman; but while a man has power in his hands over others, and when he misuses that power grossly and cruelly, who is there that will not be angry?"

Anger, in other words, usually presumes agency and blame. But not always. While normally reserved for people, anger can also be directed at inanimate objects. A 1988 article in the *Journal of the American Medical Association* documented fifteen injuries—three of them fatal—resulting from "vending machine rage," when people attacked machines that failed to deliver their drinks. In the fatal cases, the machines fell on them.

Anger is generally discouraged in society and usually feels bad in the moment. So why is it so common? The evolutionary answer is that anger served adaptive purposes. It helped our ancestors defend against threats, demand fairness, and deter future mistreatment. Physiologically, anger primes the body for confrontation—raising heart rate and blood pressure—and it broadcasts signals meant to discourage aggression. Early humans quickly learned that stepping on toes—literally or figuratively—came with consequences.

In the Misery Survey, I wanted to isolate the kind of anger that doesn't feel good—not righteous indignation, but what I called "corrosive anger," the kind that "eats at you."

The academic literature on anger reinforces the impression that this kind of corrosive anger afflicts nearly everyone, at least some of the time. In the Misery Survey, the most common targets for anger were ex-spouses, parents, bosses. Women were more likely to direct anger toward family members. Men reported anger mostly tied to work—supervisors, coworkers, or the abstract figure of "my company." Perhaps the most striking common feature among the responses was that the events that provoked this anger were often years or even decades old.

Why does anger have such staying power? Unlike other feelings such as pain or fear, anger stays with us because it is usually generated by thoughts—that someone cheated you or took advantage of you, say—and thoughts can be reproduced at will, or indeed, often against one's will (as discussed in the chapter on intrusive thoughts). Simply recalling the original offense can reignite the emotion, sometimes with its original intensity.

Adding to this staying power is a widespread misconception: that expressing anger helps us release it. The idea that one must "let it out" in order to move on is a legacy of Freudian psychoanalysis, which treated emotion as a kind of hydraulic force building up in the psyche. This gave rise to the popular notion of "catharsis"—that venting anger by yelling, punching pillows, or recounting grievances would be therapeutic.

But decades of research suggest the opposite is often true. In a series of experiments, psychologist Brad Bushman found that participants who hit a punching bag while thinking about someone who had angered them became more aggressive, not less—both in how angry they felt and how likely they were to retaliate afterward. Participants who distracted themselves, in contrast, calmed down. Bushman's conclusion was blunt: "Venting to reduce anger is like using gasoline to put out a fire."

Anger may also linger because people are reluctant to "let go" of it, in part because doing so feels like invalidating their suffering up to that point in time. And the longer you don't let it go, the stupider you will feel—for suffering unnecessarily—when you finally do. Anger can, in this way, become a form of self-imposed imprisonment, chaining the person ever more tightly to the pain of reliving their grievance.

One woman in her seventies, divorced twenty years ago, said she could still get angry thinking about something her ex did *thirty* years earlier. Another wrote that she spent "an inordinate amount of energy" mentally rehashing her ex-husband's betrayals. "Maybe trauma-anger never goes away," she said. "It just sits in the background forever, and the best one can do is reduce the reactions to triggers." Another respondent, a man laid off at age sixty after a lifetime of dedication to his job, described it this way: "The experience left a type of anger that has followed me almost to the current day. I know it's harming me. But it just hasn't left. Always having it there just keeps renewing the trauma."

Many respondents expressed a desire to get even—at least imaginatively. One man, bullied relentlessly in high school, still carries resentment toward the teacher who ignored his pleas forty-four years earlier. "I wanted to scream: 'How about I heckle you while you try to teach, and you ignore me? Let's see how well that works for you.'" It's as if he's spent four decades angrily rehearsing this comeback line.

Some of the most articulate reflections came from those who had tried to understand the roots of their own anger. One man observed: "Anger is never just anger. It's also sadness, disappointment, fear." Another said: "Being angry is like drinking poison and expecting someone else to die." That image—poison—is apt. Again and again, respondents described anger as inwardly destructive. It "eats you alive," said one. "It weighs on me," said another. "Not just the initial burst—but the way it lingers, gnaws at you from the inside."

Some described the feeling as a burden. "It's like carrying a weight that never lets you stand up straight," one woman wrote. Another woman, who grew up with an explosive, unpredictable father, said she learned early on that showing anger only made things worse. So she aimed her rage at "safe" targets: customer service reps, salesclerks. "I'm not really angry at them," she wrote. "But it leaks out into those low-consequence relationships."

Anger, like many other emotions in this book, is self-perpetuating. "It's a vicious cycle," one respondent said. "The anger feeds off itself, growing darker and more intense, until it becomes this heavy cloud that colors every thought and interaction." Another reflected: "What makes this kind of anger so corrosive is its ability to distort reality. When I'm angry, I lose touch with clarity. I can't see people or situations for what they truly are. Instead, I see them through a lens of hurt, betrayal, or frustration. Every comment, every perceived slight is another wound—even when it's not meant that way. It's suffocating, like I'm constantly bracing for a blow."

Social factors also typically act as an anger accelerant. Those who are psychologically astute know that it is risky to dismiss another person's anger; doing so is likely to make you the next target of the angry person's animus. Armed with this insight, a common pattern is to "indulge" an angry person by telling them that their anger is understandable and justified. Such tactics may benefit you, but rarely the person who is angry; most often they just end up fanning the flames.

The Value of Rage

The evolutionary function of anger seems obvious: it triggers aggression. It does so in part by desensitizing us to the likely consequences of that aggression. When someone is in what is sometimes aptly referred to as a "blind rage," they will attack a much more formidable foe. Anger can in some cases provide the motivating force to defeat an adversary; though anger-driven aggression tends, like drunken aggression, to be fairly myopic and mindless. A calm, deliberate opponent can often counter an angry person simply by letting them tire themselves out with ineffective attacks before delivering a lethal counterstrike. Revenge, as the famous saying goes, is a dish that's best served cold.

While anger undoubtedly prepares us to fight, the real evolutionary value of this emotion may be more as a deterrent. In his important book on the functional basis of emotion, *Passions Within Reason: The Strategic Role of the Emotions*, the economist Robert H. Frank contends that anger plays a strategic role in social life by driving us to retaliate without pausing to tally the immediate costs. As he puts it, "Someone who becomes enraged when dealt with unjustly . . . will seek revenge because he *wants* to, even when, in purely material terms, it does not pay." Such a response may seem irrational in the moment, especially against a stronger aggressor, yet often proves advantageous over repeated interactions.

Precisely because anger overrides short-term calculations, the threats we make when we feel we've been mistreated carry weight. Far from being purely disruptive, Frank writes, anger is "a vital force, enabling individuals to insist on fair treatment even at a cost to themselves." He argues that people have an incentive to form a reputation for becoming angry when mistreated, because this will make them less likely to be mistreated in the first place.

Thomas Schelling, likewise, in the book that probably won him the Nobel Prize—*The Strategy of Conflict*—explores how appearing irrational or unstable can be a source of bargaining power in situations of conflict, especially in the context of nuclear deterrence and international diplomacy. If one side believes the other might be "crazy enough" to press the nuclear button, for example, that belief alone might deter aggression. The threat doesn't need to be rational—only credible. As Schelling writes, "A careless or even self-destructive attitude toward injury . . . can be a genuine strategic advantage." Nixon's foreign policy during the Vietnam War, when he tried to convince adversaries that he was volatile enough to use nuclear weapons, was sometimes referred to as the "madman strategy."

In this book, I have generally steered clear of neuroscience, despite having done my share of work in the area. One of the reasons I quit working in the area was that its interpretation of fMRI brain scans—which have become the main workhorse of the field—seem to me, in many if not most cases, to be not much more reliable than reading tea leaves. However, I was intrigued by an observation that Iain McGilchrist makes in his synthesis of two decades of left-right brain research. He argues that, although the right hemisphere handles most emotional processing, there is one exception to this rule: anger. It shows robust left-frontal activation. If McGilchrist is right that anger is processed differently than most emotions, it may explain why otherwise unemotional people (men in particular, I suspect) have no apparent difficulty experiencing anger with all its corrosive effects on themselves, and destructive effects on others.

Wounded Pride

The psychologist Richard Lazarus argued that anger arises not from harm alone, but from a specific kind of harm: one that feels personal, unjustified, and demeaning. Generally speaking, according to Lazarus, we reserve anger for people who, we believe, *could* have easily treated us better, but didn't. Anger is therefore another example of an emotion that arises, at least in part, from counterfactual thinking. It also frequently involves another psychological mechanism we've already discussed: self-esteem.

In his 1991 book *Emotion and Adaptation*, Lazarus wrote, "the basic motive to preserve or enhance self-esteem against assault must . . . be activated for anger to occur." In other words, anger doesn't emerge unless self-esteem is at stake. If someone steps on your foot by accident, you may feel pain. But if they do it with intent, or in a way that implies you don't matter, the pain acquires moral weight—and anger ignites. As Lazarus explained, each emotion has a characteristic "action tendency"—a kind of built-in behavioral urge. Anger's action tendency is to *fight*. It prepares the body for confrontation and motivates us to retaliate.

That said, Lazarus's definition may be too narrow. We often experience anger or something very close to it in situations (like the aforementioned "vending machine rage") where there's no obvious assault on self-worth. When you stub your toe on a chair or spill a latte on your shirt because someone jostled you on the way to an important meeting, the feeling can certainly feel like anger, even if no one is truly to blame. Sometimes the affront is not to self-esteem but to reality itself: a kind of existential protest against the indignity of dumb, impersonal misfortune. Perhaps we should create another category for this type of existential anger—which can feel unfair even if no one is really to blame.

Because anger is rooted in the defense of self-worth, it is closely entangled with status. As the contemporary philosopher Martha Nussbaum writes, "Anger is not always, but very often, about status-injury. . . . We are prone to anger to the extent that we feel insecure or lacking control with respect to the aspect of our goals that has been assailed—and to the extent that we expect or desire control. Anger aims at restoring lost control and often achieves at least an illusion of it."

Her point about illusion is important. In motivating us to protect ourselves, anger holds out the false promise of retribution—of getting even. That's all I could think about after I received the errant email I described in the first chapter of this book, the one from a colleague accusing me of failing to credit their work adequately. I felt mischaracterized, wronged, even insulted. But once the heat passed, I recalled times when I had felt similarly overlooked—and moments when I might have done the same to others. My anger didn't vanish completely, but it no longer felt like it needed to be avenged.

The Ones We Hurt

It starts out small. A father is giving driving directions to his son, who's at the wheel.

"I told him to turn at the next exit," the father explained in his survey response, "and then, about five hundred meters later, as he's about to pass the exit, I told him to turn *now*. He argued that I should have said 'turn at *this* exit,' since the 'next' exit means the one after the upcoming one."

The semantic debate, he said, became ridiculously contentious. They went back and forth, looking up "information about terminology" and even asking ChatGPT "for its assessment," as the father became increasingly irritated.

"There are times when I just want him to stop talking, and I'll tell him to just shut up," he wrote. "And, for whatever reason, he's unable to and needs to keep pressing his points, and I'll tell him to shut up again, and more loudly, and I feel myself getting angrier and angrier, and I'll end up shouting at him."

What followed was not relief, but remorse.

"Then, afterwards, I feel miserable that I wasn't able to control myself during the episode. My only insight is that such episodes of anger seem primal and uncontrollable, and though I mentally 'know better' and try to remind myself that such things don't matter, they still lead to (a short-lived) misery."

One of the most painful patterns to emerge from the Misery Survey was how often people reported directing their anger at those closest to them. Not at bosses or strangers, but at children, spouses, parents, and friends—the people they love and who love them most. And how frequently this anger was followed not by satisfaction, but by guilt, shame, and isolation.

As one respondent wrote: "When I became a mother, I became an angrier person."

Deprived of sleep, unsupported by her partner, bombarded with advice from her mother, she described experiencing "flashes of anger that made me visualize shoving or somehow otherwise hurting my child," followed by a predictable meta-emotion: waves of guilt and remorse.

"It's shameful," she wrote. "The people who are the 'victims' of my anger are those closest to me, who love me and want me to be happy. Yet I can't seem to make myself stop lashing out at them. I see their sadness or fear or resentment or confusion . . . and it hurts my heart because I know it's because of me. I feel like a terrible person. And I didn't used to be like this."

Another female respondent, describing her partner's attempts to reach her emotionally, explained how her rage sometimes feels like a protective shield but actually is more like a prison: "I wonder if people can even see the real me through the mask of bitterness or frustration I wear. I've been in relationships where my anger pushed people away without me even realizing it. In that way, it becomes its own form of self-sabotage. The anger tells me I need to protect myself, that I need to guard against the hurt, but in reality, it just drives the very people I want close even further away."

These expressions of regret and emotional isolation echo themes explored earlier in this book: that we are often victims of ourselves, and that our defensive strategies—meant to guard the ego, or restore control—can end up hollowing out the very relationships we most want to preserve. As the Roman philosopher Seneca wrote in an ancient treatise on the topic, "Anger, if not restrained, is frequently more hurtful to us than the injury that provokes it."

But turning your back on that impulse—choosing not to lash out—can bring its own kind of misery, too. As the colleague whose story opened this chapter can attest, suppressing justified anger in the name of repair may leave you stewing in silence. She tried, earnestly, to rebuild trust with a husband who had betrayed her, but the anger persisted.

Lying awake one night, her husband snoring beside her—each exhale stoking her fury—she decided to get some help. With the aid of a therapist, she has managed to transform the volcanic anger into a slow burn.

"It's been rocky, and I don't know where I will land, but I experience anger less frequently and feel its grip less intensely. It's a new concept of forgiveness for me, one that has very little to do with the forgiven. I had always thought of forgiveness as pardoning, condoning, okaying the wrong that had been done. The new concept was that my husband had thrown the hot potato of his internal struggles at me, burning my hands, making my fingerprints unidentifiable—and forgiveness was to drop the potato."

I've shared this story with a bunch of my friends, and, to a person, their reaction is "I can't believe she doesn't leave the creep." My own reaction, which I expressed when she first described the situation by phone, is that she should forgive him. I make no claim that this position represents some higher level of ethics; quite likely the opposite.

12

Envy

> I envy people who don't have to constantly translate themselves just to be tolerated. Who don't have to over-explain, or mask, or recover from a five-minute conversation that left their nervous system wrecked. And then, I get angry at them for having what I want. And angrier at myself for wanting it at all. Most of the time, it just sits with me. Quiet and bitter. A reminder that I am not okay with being who I am, not all the way. And that is the part that hurts the most.
>
> —Twenty-five-year-old female respondent to the Misery Survey

The Pain of Measuring Up

Most definitions of envy treat it as a compound of two things: pain and desire. First, the pain—an uncomfortable jolt of comparison, aroused by someone else's qualities, achievements, or possessions. Then, the desire—a wish to have those things for oneself. The first part must always be present for envy to occur, but the second is optional. *Sometimes* we genuinely covet what others have. But envy isn't always paired with longing. We can feel envious even when we don't actually want what someone else has—or at least wouldn't trade what *we have* to get it. Take, for example, a female respondent to my Misery Survey who described an experience from her senior year of college:

> Many of my friends were getting engaged and were planning their weddings. I attended many of these weddings, and even though I was happy for my friends, I was envious. My plan was to go to graduate school and prepare for a career. While I focused on career rather than a relationship, it still made me anxious.

She knew she didn't want to be married at that moment, yet watching her friends enter that stage of life left her with a nagging sense of unease. A decade later, she did marry and—partly from watching the longer-term trajectories of her friends, which weren't generally as "enviable" as she had imagined—her envy vanished.

At its core, envy is deeply tied to self-esteem. In my earlier discussion of self-esteem, I defined it as our own dynamic assessment of our *relational value*—our standing in the eyes of others. Envy usually arises when we recognize in someone else a trait that throws our own perceived inadequacy into harsh relief. The feeling can be disturbing, often making us second-guess our choices or fantasize about alternate realities.

Take another respondent to the Misery Survey, whose feelings of envy seemed, at first glance, straightforward—she didn't have friends and envied those who did:

> In the last few years, I've become more aware that, although I have close and loving relationships with my spouse and my family, I don't really have close friends. I've noticed that the other moms of kids who go to school with my kids seem to be friends with each other: texting, meeting up for coffee, inviting each other and their kids to go on outings together. Although they are all friendly to me—saying hi when we see each other, chatting while we wait for the kids outside of school—they do not respond to my bids to actually be friends.

On the surface, this is a story of loneliness—of wanting to connect with the other moms as easily and naturally as they seem to connect with each other. But the more she describes her experience, the more the focus shifts—from them to her. Nowhere does she express much of a desire to actually be part of their social world. Her envy is less about the friendships themselves than what those friendships signify: that they are magnetic, socially desirable, fun—and she is not.

> The reason I feel misery because of this envy is that it makes me feel that something must be wrong with me. If I were more likable, better at small talk, more interesting . . . surely people would want to be my friend. The fact that they don't means that I am in some way deficient.

The fact that they're polite and welcoming only sharpens the sting. If they'd been cold or dismissive, she could have written them off. But their friendliness makes her exclusion feel personal.

Envy is often directed at qualities we feel inadequate about—intelligence, attractiveness, charisma. A male respondent who struggled with programming in graduate school described envying classmates who grasped difficult subjects with ease: "I had a sophomore tutor me in Java, and I could tell he was frustrated by my inability. In my work at [a big technology company], I envied colleagues who could go much deeper into concepts and ask more meaningful questions."

Yet sometimes, the source of envy is more idiosyncratic. One female respondent reported envying people who could tell stories: "People who, when you're in their company, draw you in and hold you with their ability to weave tales from personal experience. While I'm articulate and well-spoken, my cognition and creativity don't work that way—it frustrates me and makes me feel inadequate and uninteresting."

Self-esteem operates in the background of all these experiences. When we envy someone, we are not just noticing their success or abilities—we are measuring ourselves against them and, too often, finding ourselves wanting.

Envy Thy Neighbor

What is the opposite of envy? Smugness, pride, gratitude—none of these entirely capture the inverse of the bad feeling we experience when confronted with the (seemingly superior) qualities, possessions, or status of others. Envy, it seems, is yet another negative emotion without a perfect positive counterpart, at least in English. And the asymmetry is more than linguistic—we simply do not feel an equivalent surge of pleasure for the things we *have* as intensely as we feel envy for the things we *lack*.

As discussed earlier, most of our social comparisons are made *upward*. Though we *could* compare ourselves to anyone, our natural—and almost impossible to override—tendency is to look toward those who are better off.

Yet *not much* better off.

We may admire champion athletes, Nobel laureates, billionaire businessmen, and other paragons of achievement—but unless we are clipping at their heels, their success does not unsettle us. What provokes the sharpest feelings of inadequacy, and therefore envy, are the people *just* ahead—the ones whose success feels close enough that it *could have been ours*.

This is not a new observation. Writing in 1739, David Hume—the great Scottish philosopher and close friend of Adam Smith—described how envy arises not from great disparities, but from *proximity*:

> A common soldier bears no envy for his general compared to what he will feel for his sergeant or corporal; nor does an eminent writer meet with as much jealousy in common hackney scribblers, as in authors that more nearly approach him. A great disproportion cuts off the relation, and either keeps us from comparing ourselves with what is remote from us or diminishes the effect of the comparison.

Two centuries later, Bertrand Russell echoed this idea, observing that envy is a function of competition:

> We do not envy a good fortune which we conceive as quite hopelessly out of our reach. Beggars do not envy millionaires, though of course they will envy other beggars who are more successful.

Recall Leon Festinger's social comparison theory from the discussion about self-esteem. Festinger argued that our inclination to compare ourselves with another person—and thus to envy them—sharply decreases as the difference between their abilities or attributes and our own increases. In other words, the less someone resembles us, the less their successes feel like our own failures. This is one of the most profound truths about envy: though it *seems* to be based on a perceived difference (between what others have and what we lack), it is actually triggered by similarity (between them and us).

Inequality Breeds Envy

Humans have a deep-rooted preference for fairness—even if life persistently frustrates this ideal, confronting us again and again with situations that feel unjust or unequal. When we find ourselves confronted with inequality—particularly inequality among peers—our envy becomes supercharged with righteous indignation. We're no longer merely envying what someone else has; we feel a conviction that we're trying to make the world, or at least our little slice of it, a bit more just. This blend of envy and moral outrage is powerful enough to sour even an otherwise contented person's satisfaction with their own circumstances.

A particularly striking illustration comes from a study conducted by economists at the University of California, Berkeley. Researchers wanted to see how employees' feelings about their own salaries changed when they learned how much their colleagues earned. UC workers were given access to a new website listing the salaries of all university employees, allowing them—for the first time—to see exactly how their pay stacked up against others in similar roles.

The results were not subtle. Employees who discovered that their salary fell below the median of their peer group suddenly felt much worse about their jobs. Learning that their peers earned more bred resentment and dissatisfaction, and made them significantly more likely to look for another job elsewhere. Tellingly, those employees who found themselves above the median didn't suddenly feel significantly more satisfied or loyal.

Instead, their attitudes remained largely unchanged. The knowledge of being "ahead" hardly provided much of a lasting boost. These findings underscore an important psychological truth we've seen elsewhere in this book: we adapt to good news quickly, but bad news gnaws at us.

This same asymmetry plays out in more mundane, everyday forms of inequality—ones that don't require obtaining access to salary databases. Consider, for example, the uneasy social drama that unfolds every time passengers board an airplane. Those in economy class often glance resentfully at business- or first-class passengers, envying the extra legroom and free-flowing champagne. But I suspect those privileged travelers in the upper classes aren't entirely basking in superiority—at least during the boarding process. Instead, they probably feel a subtle sense of guilt or discomfort as the coach passengers shuffle past, aware of the inequity of the arrangement. After all, if envy is unpleasant, so, too, is being envied—at least if you're self-aware enough to notice it and sympathetic enough to feel bad for those doing the envying.

Misjudging Others, and Ourselves

Festinger's point is that social comparison kicks in precisely when we lack objective measures of our relative standing—so we rely on other people as benchmarks. But our perceptions of others, and even of ourselves, are notoriously *un*reliable. A striking example from the Misery Survey is a woman who remained haunted, more than four decades after the fact, by how much emotional energy she wasted envying a classmate in high school:

> I was skinny, nerdy, and not too rich. I wore thrift-store clothes and was shy and awkward around people I didn't know. There was this one girl, I'll call her Susan. She was pretty, popular, smart, a cheerleader, had the lead in the spring musical, and the best boyfriend. I was absolutely green with envy. She had, I believed, everything I wanted. I would lie in bed at night crying because I wasn't her. I even tried to dress like her, but it wasn't, of course, me. I was so unhappy as a teen, so longing to be pretty and popular.

It took decades, but eventually she came to understand just how distorted her comparison had been. "In hindsight," she explained, Susan was "anorexic, capricious, and probably full of the same self-doubts that I felt."

The story about Susan might suggest that there is a tendency to exaggerate the positive qualities and attainments of those we envy; and maybe that is true to some degree. But perhaps it is more accurate to say that we are most likely to envy those whose qualities and attainments we exaggerate. Envy makes us fixate on people's most visible markers of success, wealth, or status while overlooking the broader reality of their lives. We assume that excelling in one area—especially one we're insecure about—translates into an enviable life overall. But as psychologist Ed O'Brien and his colleagues have shown, this is a *focusing illusion*—a cognitive bias that leads us to overestimate how much someone's most conspicuous advantages shape their overall well-being.

O'Brien and his colleagues offer an intriguing answer to the question we raised earlier about the inverse of envy: they argue that the opposite of envy is pity. As they explain, "Envy and pity reflect complementary judgments: envy arises when another's life seems uniformly better than our own; pity arises when another's life seems uniformly worse." Note that pity may be the opposite of envy, but rather perversely (and fittingly for our purposes), it is yet another negative emotion.

When we envy someone, we zoom in on a single, obvious advantage—a bigger house, a higher salary, a more attractive spouse—while ignoring the fuller picture of their daily lives. To test how this distortion plays out in the real world, O'Brien and his colleagues recruited two groups of individuals: those with relatively high incomes (the "enviable") and those with relatively low incomes (the "pitiable"). They asked both groups to track how often they experienced everyday joys (small pleasures, moments of peace) and everyday annoyances (stressors, irritations). Meanwhile, a separate group of observers predicted how often these high- and low-income individuals encountered such ups and downs.

The findings echoed classic adaptation studies: the actual daily lives of high- and low-income individuals weren't nearly as different as observers imagined. Observers significantly overestimated how pleasurable the lives of enviable individuals were, neglecting the regular annoyances they faced.

Conversely, they exaggerated how relentlessly negative life was for pitiable people, ignoring the small joys they frequently experienced.

But envy doesn't just make us selectively misjudge individuals—magnifying certain traits we admire while ignoring the ones we wouldn't want. It also encourages us to mash together cherry-picked traits from different people. We end up comparing ourselves not to real people with strengths and weaknesses but to a monstrous composite-person who has one friend's professional success, another's financial security, and yet another's perfect family life. Rather than recognizing that none of these individuals is enviable across all aspects, we stitch together their best features into a single, unforgiving standard that we can never possibly meet.

Keep Your Good News to Yourself

When it comes to sharing personal updates, I've mentioned my tendency to share bad news. The corollary is that I tend to keep good news to myself. Sure, friends may seem—or, more to the point, *act*—genuinely pleased to hear about something going well in my life: getting a paper published, my child landing a job, or one of my granddaughters riding a bike not long after most kids are just learning to walk.

But it's highly unlikely the recipients of my exuberance are experiencing anything close to the pleasure that I'm deriving from such events. More likely, if the news is truly good, it elicits a faint twinge of envy—followed by the uncomfortable meta-emotion of guilt for feeling that way, and maybe even a flicker of resentment toward me for having caused it.

There are a few exceptions. Your parents might be one. Maybe, if you're very lucky, your romantic partner might be another—though I know a surprising number of couples who seem competitive with each other, and even some parents who seem to compete with their children. Almost everyone else will insist they're happy for you. But it's probably a good thing we don't walk around with hedonometers—hypothetical devices that measure and display moment-to-moment happiness—strapped to our foreheads. If we could monitor people's actual emotional reactions, some of the pleasure we take in their apparent vicarious joy might vanish on the spot.

I once coauthored a paper titled "You Call It 'Self-Exuberance'; I Call

It 'Bragging'" (with Joachim Vosgerau and Irene Scopelliti), documenting the asymmetry between the joy people assume their good news elicits and the lack of joy—and, in fact, often, actual misery—that listeners report experiencing. In a series of studies, we asked people to recall times when they enthusiastically shared good news about themselves and had them predict how listeners reacted. Meanwhile, we separately asked listeners to reflect on how they actually felt when someone "enthused" in their direction. Listeners reported being notably less happy and proud—and far more annoyed and irritated—than self-promoters predicted.

Why do people so often make this mistake? The answer lies in what psychologists call *projection bias*—the tendency to assume that other people's internal emotional experiences closely match our own. When we have exciting news, we project our happiness outward, confidently (and incorrectly) assuming everyone else feels the same; unfortunately, we are far less likely to perspective-take and recall how we felt when we were in the listener's (or should I say victim's) position. This creates a profound emotional misalignment; the speaker's sincere enthusiasm is received as unwelcome boasting.

Yet another source of discomfort might stem from the listener's own guilt: upon hearing someone else's good news, listeners often sense that they *should* feel genuinely happy for the person—but they don't. The envy or irritation they feel instead seems to imply something unpleasant about their character—that they dislike seeing their friends succeed or, worse, that they want them to fail. Part of the reason we resent bragging is because our negative reaction to good news makes us feel morally compromised.

People rarely admit to experiencing envy partly because they are ashamed of it. Envy was one of the least-reported-on negative emotions in the Misery Survey, which I suspect has more to do with the shame it arouses than its actual rareness. However, plenty did acknowledge experiencing it, and wrote about it. For example, one middle-aged woman from my survey, who had chosen not to have children when she was younger, confessed to envying her friends with grandchildren "about once a week." But envy alone wasn't the whole source of her suffering. She was tormented (8 on the 0-to-10 intensity scale) not just by the feeling itself—which she said "poisons" her brain—but by the fact that it arose so often: "I feel guilty for even having the thoughts."

Because people are ashamed of their envy, they typically hide it from others, so that, as Alain de Botton writes in *Status Anxiety*, "evidence of the inner drama is uncommon, limited usually to a preoccupied gaze, a brittle smile or an over-extended pause after news of another's achievement." But when pressed—or in the comfort of an anonymous survey—people can be unusually candid about envy's corrosive effects. One female respondent in her forties vividly described the complexity of emotions envy creates even within close friendships:

> I can divide my friends into two groups: those I only feel happy for when things go well for them, and another group whose successes make me envious, and whose failures bring me—not happiness, exactly, but a slight relief. I hate it. It makes me feel like such a bad person, and it really brings misery into my life. An example is when a friend does something cool or technically demanding in sports, and instead of being impressed, I feel like I'm not good enough. It's insane! It also shows that it's related to self-doubt . . . The strange thing is that I have many friends for whom I don't feel this way at all. I think it depends on two factors: (1) if the other person acts in a competitive way, and (2) if the activity involved is something central to my self-image.

Of course, the factors that determine whether a friendship feels easy and supportive or strained and competitive can change over time. That's what happened to me with my second-oldest friend, Getz. We had been introduced decades ago by a mutual ex-girlfriend, who was convinced that we'd hit it off. She was right. We became fast friends, and over the years took countless expeditions together: mountain climbing, kayaking, canoeing, sailing. Our separation started when my wife and I were trying, and failing, to have children, and Getz (or rather his wife) effortlessly popped out three of them in a row. I found the envy intolerable. So I just disappeared from his life—for about five years.

When we finally reconnected, after Donna and I had adopted our son, I sheepishly explained my absence. Getz, characteristically unfazed, told me he had barely noticed. He'd been so deep in the trenches of parenting that five years had gone by in a blur. I didn't fault him for not missing me, and he didn't fault me for being so envious. Thankfully, we were able to pick up right where we left off—climbing and hiking together, for nearly another three decades now.

If only every relationship derailed by envy could have such a happy ending.

13

Jealousy

O, beware, my lord, of jealousy!
It is the green-eyed monster which doth mock
The meat it feeds on.

—William Shakespeare, *Othello*

The Green-Eyed Monster

While jealousy and envy are often confused, they have distinct meanings: Envy, as we've seen, frequently involves wanting what someone else has. Jealousy is a different beast—it involves feeling threatened or fearful of losing what you already possess, especially another person's love or affection.

The famous passage above from *Othello*—perhaps the greatest work of literature on the subject—captures not just jealousy's intensity and self-destructiveness, but the way it mocks the person in its grip. It can lead you to spy on someone who has nothing to hide, to act cold or hostile toward perceived rivals, or to torture yourself by imagining betrayals that are probably never going to happen. You sense, deep down, that your suspicions are absurd—yet somehow you can't put them to rest.

Although I've seen *Othello* multiple times—it is my favorite of Shakespeare's plays—I find each time agonizing. Othello is driven mad, and Desdemona is ultimately killed, by a false belief: that she's unfaithful. Even though I don't think "straying" in marriage should be treated with the kind of moral absolutism it often receives, I still find Othello's jealousy more painful to watch precisely because it's unjustified. If Desdemona had truly been "cheating on him" (to use the unfortunate contemporary term), the tragedy would feel less tragic.

Why are we built this way, to torment ourselves over threats that don't exist? Why do we so often fear losing people who are not, in fact, going anywhere, or who might not have gone anywhere—if jealousy hadn't gotten the better of us? Jealousy does, after all, often become a self-fulfilling prophecy: we accuse, obsess, cling too tightly, and in doing so, we drive away the very person we so fear losing, sometimes into the arms of the person we are jealous toward.

The problem begins with the way jealousy distorts perception. A single hint—a delay in response, a changed tone, a short message where a long one is expected—is enough to trigger a feedback loop that turns suspicion into conviction. Psychologists call this tendency *confirmation bias*—the habit of interpreting the world in a way that supports what we already believe.

Confirmation bias results, in part, from the way we collect data. When tasked with assessing whether someone is an extrovert, you might ask, "What would you do to liven up a party?"—a question that assumes the very trait you're supposed to be testing. Another cause of confirmation bias has to do with the biased way we *interpret* ambiguous data. Jealous people do something similar. In one scene, Othello touches Desdemona's hand and finds it warm. That simple fact becomes, in his mind, evidence of something sinister:

> Hot, hot, and moist. This hand of yours requires
> A sequester from liberty, fasting and prayer,
> Much castigation, exercise devout;
> For here's a young and sweating devil here.

And Shakespeare, as if to generalize the madness, offers this:

> Trifles light as air
> Are to the jealous confirmations strong
> As proofs of holy writ.

The Origins of Jealousy

Jealousy is not confined to romantic relationships. One can feel jealous when a close friend grows close to someone else, or when a sibling seems to be favored, or when the new guy at work starts getting the compliments you used to receive from the boss. We can jealously guard almost anything we have—wealth, health, possessions, time, status—and we do sometimes use the word *jealousy* in those contexts. But the term is most commonly associated with romantic and sexual relationships. Which makes good sense, since that's probably where the emotion first evolved—and where it still wreaks the most havoc.

Jealousy, evolutionary psychologists posit, is an evolved mechanism—one that developed to protect reproductive interests. And like so many evolutionary stories, this one diverges by gender. For men, the key uncertainty is paternity: whether the child they're raising is genetically their own. A partner's *sexual infidelity*, in this view, represents a reproductive threat, something to guard against. For women, who have no such uncertainty, the evolutionary risk is different: being left to raise a child without support. For them, the greater fear is *emotional infidelity*—a sign that a partner may be pulling away, investing elsewhere, or preparing to abandon the family unit.

This theory leads to a striking and testable prediction: that men should be more upset by sexual betrayal, and women by emotional betrayal. And considerable research supports such a view. In an early study, the American sexologist Alfred Kinsey and his colleagues found that 51 percent of divorced men said their partner's sexual infidelity played a major role in the breakup, compared to just 27 percent of divorced women—even though the men were twice as likely to have committed adultery. Later studies have tended to reproduce the finding.

For example, the psychologist David M. Buss and colleagues presented participants with hypothetical scenarios about sexual versus emotional infidelity and observed the same pattern as seen in the Kinsey survey: men reacted more strongly to sexual infidelities; women to emotional ones. Robert Pietrzak and coauthors took it a step further and measured physiological responses (e.g., heart rate and sweating) to infidelity scenarios, and again men showed stronger reactions to sexual infidelity and women to emotional infidelity.

Other differences by gender seem to reflect similar evolutionary pressures—though not all of these align neatly with the theory. Men, for example, are more likely than women to feel threatened by a rival's wealth or status. Women are more likely to be distressed by a rival's youth or physical attractiveness.

While evolutionary psychology may tell us something about the *kind* of jealousy men and women feel, it doesn't fully explain why some people are just more jealous than others. That question was at the heart of a large study of Finnish twins designed to tease apart nature and nurture in romantic jealousy. The researchers studied over a thousand twin pairs, including identical (monozygotic) twins, who share 100 percent of their genes but often end up in very different romantic situations. The logic was simple: If jealousy is mostly biological, then identical twins should have similar jealousy levels regardless of their experiences. If it's shaped more by the twists and turns of life, then their individual relationships—who they dated, how secure they felt—should matter more.

They found, first, that men and women did not differ much in overall jealousy. Women scored higher, but gender was by no means the best predictor of jealousy. About 29 percent of the variation in jealousy was attributable to genetic factors (inferred by comparing how similar jealousy scores were among identical versus fraternal twins). But the remaining 71 percent came down to non-shared environmental influences—presumably, at least in part, the personal, relationship-specific experiences unique to each twin.

What were those experiences? The study highlighted several, including whether they distrusted their current partner, whether they'd been "cheated on" in the past, and whether they felt they were dating "up" (meaning they believed their partner was more desirable than themselves). All these factors strongly predicted jealousy.

As important as relationship dynamics and someone's own romantic history are in determining feelings of jealousy, sometimes the seeds are planted as far back as childhood. One female respondent to the Misery Survey described her jealousy as so consuming it bordered on paranoia. "I am highly jealous and something as simple as a text, phone call, or email can set me off." Although, to her knowledge, she had never been cheated on, she couldn't shake the belief that an act of infidelity could happen at any moment. "I simply do not trust that this could not happen to me." This respondent traced her own jealousy not to personal betrayal but to the betrayals she had witnessed as a child: "I believe it occurs due to my mom and dad divorcing when I was five, and his new wife, my stepmom, used to be my mom's best friend. Growing up, most betrayals came from people who were either family members or good friends."

Only after twenty years of marriage did the feeling begin to loosen its grip, thanks in part to the sense of (seemingly problematic) control she had established in her relationship. Her spouse worked from home. The respondent had "full access to everything," so there was "no way they could cheat."

What Makes Jealousy Worse

Uncertainty is a potent catalyst for misery, as we've learned. In the case of hope, uncertainty keeps us from adapting to bad news. In the case of impatience, not knowing whether something will happen drains the pleasure from anticipating good things and makes waiting for bad ones feel like "suffering twice." Jealousy, too, feeds on uncertainty.

To understand how, consider the hypochondriac. In a sense, the hypochondriac is jealously guarding their health—vigilant for symptoms, alert to every twitch and twinge. They imagine elaborate illnesses where none (or only minor ones) exist. They are ceaselessly suspicious of their own bodies. And yet, when they actually fall ill, I've noticed, something strange sometimes happens: they handle it with surprising equanimity. The uncertainty is gone. The imagined has become real. They are no longer preparing for disaster—they are living it, and sometimes discovering it to be not as bad as they'd imagined.

The real hell of jealousy comes in not knowing whether and to what extent our fears are justified. One Misery Survey respondent, a man in his sixties, described a night out with his wife and one of her old friends named "Chap"—a charismatic, alpha-male figure who had been close with the man's wife during her first marriage. There was nothing overtly inappropriate about their interaction—just a tone, a glance, a certain warmth that struck him the wrong way. And that was all it took to send his mind spinning into a web of scenarios he couldn't untangle: "DID she ogle this guy? DID anything happen between them? WAS her first husband clueless and cuckolded? . . . Or it was all completely normal, nothing happening. Or Sue just thought Chap was hot and enjoyed the scenery. I dunno."

Naughty or Nice

People's emotional reactions to jealousy vary so widely that it's tempting to propose two subspecies: a hot kind (rage, possessiveness, door-slamming), and a cold kind (quiet devastation, scrolling through old messages at 2 a.m.). Each version distorts the way we think and remember. The hot kind, which makes us angry, brings to mind earlier betrayals. The cold kind, earlier abandonments. Thinking about these past events reactivates old emotions associated with them and makes the possibility that they'll recur seem more plausible, and so the feeling deepens—another downward spiral.

That's how jealousy affects us internally, and its outward expression on our behavior follows a similar logic. Psychologists who study romantic relationships have noted that jealousy tends to elicit one of two patterns of behavior: punishment or reward. In the literature, these are called *cost-inflicting* and *benefit-provisioning* mate-retention strategies. The benefit-provisioning approach is the carrot: give gifts, shower compliments, lavish your partner with attention. The cost-inflicting approach is the stick: monitoring your partner's whereabouts, monopolizing their time, inducing guilt, or undermining their self-confidence. At its most extreme, this can include emotional abuse, and even violence.

Though psychologists have long assumed that jealousy evolved to trigger these kinds of behaviors, surprisingly little experimental research has tested whether it actually does. To fill that gap, Steven Arnocky and colleagues brought over two hundred college students in committed relationships into a lab. Half were asked to imagine their partner in a neutral, everyday situation. The other half were instructed to imagine a scenario in which their romantic partner was flirting with an attractive stranger. Jealousy ratings in this second group shot up.

More telling was what that jealousy seemed to motivate. Participants who felt jealous were more likely to say they'd engage in cost-inflicting behaviors—monitoring, guilt-tripping, low-grade emotional coercion—than in benefit-provisioning ones like giving compliments or affection. The researchers noted that these defensive reactions may once have helped early humans preserve pair-bonds. But they also acknowledged that in modern relationships, these behaviors are often actively harmful. The stick is more likely to break the bond than preserve it.

Still, jealousy does have one possible upside. It can jolt a person out of complacency. When you're suddenly afraid of losing someone, it becomes harder to take them for granted. As Alain de Botton writes, "There is no doubt that a person's charms are less frequently a cause of love than a remark such as: 'No, this evening I shan't be free.'"

Research by psychologist Jeremy Dugosh suggests that, in some relationships, a bit of jealousy may actually be a good thing. Dugosh studied 134 undergraduates at the University of Texas at Arlington, all of whom were in committed heterosexual relationships. He rated them based on standard psychological measures for romantic love, jealousy, and overall relationship satisfaction. The results were revealing: among participants who reported strong love for their partner, higher levels of jealousy were actually associated with greater satisfaction. In small doses—and in strong relationships—jealousy may reinforce a bond.

But that "sweet spot" is very small indeed. Across the full sample—including the less satisfied couples—Dugosh found that people who reported more jealousy also tended to report less love. Which suggests that outside of that narrow band—where love is high and jealousy is mild—the emotion begins to chip away at the very foundation it's trying to protect.

David Hume understood this very well. He conceived of jealousy as a "subordinate passion" that could sometimes support a romantic relationship—but once it rises past a certain point it "swallows up the affection it before nourished and increased. Too much jealousy extinguishes love."

Because jealousy is often a self-defeating emotion—one that leads us to do things that damage, and sometimes destroy, the very relationships we want to protect—it often gives way to regret . . . another misery, which we'll get to shortly. For now, I'll leave you with this—one of the more devastating responses I received from the Misery Survey, submitted by a man reflecting on an experience of jealousy from more than fifty years ago.

In its quiet way, it strikes me as just as tragic as the fates of Othello and Desdemona:

> When I was a freshman in college I met my first real "true love." She was a sophomore who actually picked me up at a party. For about two months we were inseparable, making love at every occasion, going places together, even going through the shock of thinking she was pregnant that turned out to be a false alarm. The intensity was both thrilling and unnerving. I traveled with her back to her hometown just before Thanksgiving to meet her high school friends. We went to a party. There I felt she was ignoring me, flirting with her old flame, and I became enraged with jealousy, even leaving the party and hitchhiking back three hours to school. After Thanksgiving she broke up with me and I was heartsick. She decided it was best to change schools and over Christmas transferred across the country to Arizona. In early January she fell off a horse, rupturing her spleen and suffering massive injuries. Her family chartered a plane and was flying her home. She died en route. Her sister told me during the flight she kept calling my name. I have never been jealous again.

14

Rejection

My ex-husband and I met in 1987 and married in 1988. He told me he loved me every day during the three decades that we were together: when leaving for work in the morning, when we spoke on the phone during the day, before going to sleep. Then, the day before my fifty-sixth birthday, he said we should get a divorce. Obviously, I was dumbfounded and stupidly said, "But, but—you said you loved me!" To which he answered: "LOVE YOU?! I don't even LIKE you!" And thus, he broke me. My self-esteem, my sense of security in our home and in our marriage, my trust in humanity . . . all took a hit. At the time, I felt that he would have been kinder if he had just put a bullet through my head, because I was effectively dead inside.

—Sixty-two-year-old female respondent to the Misery Survey whose husband broke up with her seven years ago, who rates the misery of that rejection as a 10 ("horrendously bad") on the 0-to-10 badness scale

Sliced in Half

In Plato's *Symposium*, the character of Aristophanes relates a myth about how people once had a "double nature." Instead of one face, they had two.

Instead of four limbs, they had eight. Possessed of tremendous strength and agility, they could walk upright but also bend themselves into circles and roll around at high speed. Such fearsome creatures posed a threat to the gods on Mount Olympus. Should they be annihilated? Zeus chewed on the question for a long time before a eureka moment came to him.

"Methinks I have a plan which will humble their pride and improve their manners," he said. "Men shall continue to exist, but I will cut them in two and then they will be diminished in strength and increased in numbers; this will have the advantage of making them more profitable to us."

Zeus sliced the ur-people into two halves, and dispatched Apollo to clean up the mess. Apollo yanked skin, sculpted breasts, forged mouths. When he was finished, each person looked at their newly detached other half—and panicked. They flung their arms around each other, entwined, longing to be one again, until "they were on the point of dying from hunger and self-neglect."

Out of pity, Zeus made a few tweaks to save the species from extinction, but he left in place that aching desire to become whole. It's this pursuit of the lost half that Plato called love. With this myth, he introduced the idea of "soulmates"—the notion that each of us is searching for the one who will complete us. But at the same time, he offered a visceral explanation for why it hurts so much to break up.

When we describe the misery of rejection, we often reach for metaphors that evoke physical pain: heartbreak, open wounds, tearing of flesh. The British writer Diana Athill, in her memoir *Instead of a Letter*, offers one of the most vivid accounts I've come across. She was ghosted by her longtime love and fiancé, who left without even sending a note to explain why. The event haunted her for the rest of her life. Of all psychological pains, Athill believed that rejection is "nearest to the physical—to that of a finger crushed in a door, or a tooth under a drill."

The (sort of) funny thing about the fact that people use the language of physical pain to describe the misery of a bad breakup is that—as already touched upon in the first half of this book—we are almost completely unable to remember what *physical pain* feels like. The British clinical psychologist Stephen Morley distinguished three possible variants of memory for physical pain: (1) actually reexperiencing the sensory feelings of the pain; (2)

recalling the sensory, intensity, and emotional qualities of that pain *without* reexperiencing it; and (3) merely remembering the circumstances in which the pain occurred.

He conducted a study in which subjects were first asked to think about a painful event from their past and then answer questions designed to gauge how they remembered it. Fifty-nine percent were able to recall at least some aspect of the pain sensation (Morley's second variant), while 41 percent reported *no recall* of the pain sensation at all. In other words, they knew they had been hurt but forgot what it felt like. Not a single subject in the study reported actually reexperiencing their pain—Morley's first variant of pain memory.

It's ironic, then, that when we suffer from rejection and find ourselves at a loss for how to describe it, we reach for the *language* of physical pain—essentially, we're trying to convey the awfulness of one indescribable thing by analogizing it to another indescribable thing. Of course, the big difference between these two sensations is that, in the case of physical pain, we can't remember what it felt like, but in the case of rejection we can't seem to forget.

A little-known feature of pain is that it has at least two basic components. One is purely sensory, the feedback from nerve cells. A second is emotional, with fear being the most predominant emotion ("How bad is it?" "When will it stop?"). The dual nature of pain has important implications for coping with it. A common misconception is that the best way to deal with pain is to try to distract yourself from it, but a much better strategy, in part because it is much more easily implemented, is to do the opposite: to *focus* on the pain (I've found that this strategy also works for itching). The reason is that focusing on the objective features of the pain naturally distracts one from the emotional dimension, effectively cutting the pain in half. I raise this because who knows: Perhaps the same is true for psychic miseries such as the pain of rejection?

•••

What little research there is on romantic breakups shows that it is among the "worst events" that people experience. Over 40 percent of people struggle with depression in the aftermath of a rejection, and 12 percent classified these episodes as "moderate to severe." Women are more likely than men to report severe depression and hopelessness following breakups, but men are three to four times more likely to commit suicide. Heart attacks and strokes occur disproportionately following rejections, and rejected individuals often show symptoms that are typically associated with drug withdrawal, including anxiety, depression, crying, loss of appetite, and irritability.

After analyzing the survey responses about rejection, I believe that part of the reason why this particular misery is so devastating is because of how it undermines our self-esteem. If we had a relatively positive self-image before a breakup, it is often difficult to maintain it afterward. A sixty-year-old male from my survey captured this feeling when describing a breakup that happened thirty years earlier, which he rated a 9 out of 10 in severity: "When she moved on it was very hard for me to separate the fact that we probably weren't right for each other long-term from the idea that there was something wrong with me."

The connection to ego may help explain why rejections are so painful, even for people who had already been contemplating ending their relationship—but then their partner beat them to the punch. A thirty-five-year-old female writing about a rejection fourteen years earlier reported on the relationship in remarkably unflattering terms: "We were actually incompatible in a lot of ways and aside from his charisma and ambition, there were a lot of things I didn't like about him. I didn't respect a lot of his habits that weren't very healthy. And most strangely, I wasn't even physically attracted to him!" But none of this prevented her from being devastated when he dumped her: "It felt out of the blue . . . I was hung up for so long."

Discussing not a romantic breakup, but a relationship with his therapist that he himself was contemplating ending, Andrew Solomon, in his classic book on depression (which I draw upon heavily in the chapter on that topic), relates his reaction to news from his psychotherapist that she was retiring: "I had been feeling disconnected from our work together and had been considering terminating it; nonetheless, when *she* broke that news, I burst into uncontrollable sobs and cried for an hour. I don't usually cry much; I hadn't cried like that since my mother's death. I felt utterly, devastatingly lonely and entirely betrayed" (emphasis added).

While rejection can torpedo our self-esteem, it also can shatter the related sense of confidence we have that we know what's going on in the hearts and minds of our significant others. A fifty-two-year-old female recounting a rejection twenty-nine years earlier that she rated a 7 in badness wrote that "I came to the realization that I didn't—and possibly hadn't—ever meant as much to him as he meant to me. I'm still haunted by the 'Fool me once; shame on you. Fool me twice; shame on me,' and how I was willing to take him back after he'd previously cheated on me. As angry as I was at him, I was even angrier at myself for allowing myself to get hurt/used like this."

Results from the survey also supported the idea that *unexpected* rejection is especially painful. A sixty-two-year-old male whose wife rejected him four years earlier to "explore her sexuality" reported that the rejection was still an ongoing source of pain: "The marriage wasn't strong, but I was caught completely off-guard." An eighty-two-year-old man reported on a rejection that he rated a 10 on the badness scale, and that, twenty-one years later, he said, continues to be a source of pain:

> My second wife, a businesswoman, came home from work one day and said she bought a house. I said I will put mine up for sale. She said you are not coming with me. We subsequently divorced. I cried every day for 9 months. Then, she called me and said she had cancer and would I take care of her. I did.

Tossed Aside

As was the case with jealousy, rejection is perhaps most closely associated with romantic relationships—but of course, it isn't limited to them. We can and do experience rejection in all sorts of contexts: being ghosted by a once-close friend, having an idea shot down in a meeting, extending a hand for a high five that never comes. In the wrap-up comments I give at the end of my PhD course, I tell future academics that life in the ivory tower has some huge perks—long vacations, freedom to study what interests you—but it requires a thick skin. Your papers will get serially rejected, your most beloved ideas will be publicly disemboweled, and your students will sometimes be openly bored and inattentive, if they don't fall asleep on you.

Any kind of rejection hurts. But we might not appreciate just how deeply, how reflexively, or how irrationally rejection affects us if not for the foundational work of the Purdue social psychologist Kip Williams. Williams didn't begin by studying big, obvious rejections like getting dumped by your romantic partner. He started with something tiny.

One day, he was at the lake with his dog, stretched out on a blanket, when a stray Frisbee landed nearby. He threw it back to one of the two guys who'd been playing and got ready to sit back down—when the Frisbee came flying back. Just like that, he was in the game, happily tossing the Frisbee back and forth. Then, after a few minutes, something strange happened: "They just stopped throwing it to me. They just started throwing it to each other. At first, you know, I'm thinking they're toying around with me a little bit, and I'm maybe smiling. And then I realized it's just never going to get to me again."

When that realization hit, Williams felt two things in quick succession: an emotion (the sting of rejection), and a meta-emotion (embarrassment over just how much it stung).

"I felt terrible," he said.

And: "I couldn't believe how amazingly awful I felt for such a silly thing."

He slunk back toward his blanket and his dog, and then it hit him: this setup—or something like it—was the perfect way to study social exclusion in the lab.

He began with a simple in-person game. Three participants (two of whom were actually confederates) tossed a ball around in a triangle. After a few rounds, the confederates stopped including the real subject in their game of catch, quietly leaving the third person out.

The emotional effects were immediate—hurt, confusion, lowered self-esteem. Williams later developed a computer-based version called Cyberball to re-create the experience virtually and saw a similarly sharp drop in mood and self-esteem. In a follow-up study, Williams tested whether it mattered if the other players were computer programs instead of actual humans. It didn't. Even those participants who were explicitly told they were playing against artificial agents still experienced the pain of rejection. Cyberball revealed that rejection isn't a social judgment we reason our way through. It's a reflex—like flinching when someone's about to strike us.

Later studies added physiological and neurological evidence. During the game, the rejected participants showed heightened stress responses, including spikes in blood pressure. And in an fMRI study that tracked brain activity while people were playing Cyberball, researchers found that rejection activated the dorsal anterior cingulate cortex—a brain region also involved in processing physical pain. This may help explain why, as I noted earlier, we tend to describe rejection by employing physical metaphors like heartbreak or gut-punch. Inside the brain, physical and social pain are nearly indistinguishable.

There are very good evolutionary reasons why rejection stings as much as it does. For much of human history, being left out of the group could get you killed. So rejection is a strong signal pushing us to do whatever we can to get back into the fold. Ideally, it pushes us to repair a relationship, adjust our behavior, make new connections. In such cases, the pain of rejection may be miserable but it's also purposeful—and usually temporary, even if we are forced to relive it from time to time thanks to our less-than-charitable memory.

But for certain people the feeling of rejection—or more to the point, the *fear* of it—never leaves them. Due to a mix of temperament and early experience, such people are called *rejection-sensitive* by psychologists. These individuals live in constant fear of being cast out. So constant, in fact, that they often preemptively reject others just to avoid the pain of being rejected themselves.

Rejection sensitivity distorts how we read other people. In one study by Sandra Murray and colleagues, when rejection-sensitive people encountered ambiguous behavior from their partner—delayed responses, vague feedback, emotional distance—they were more likely to interpret this behavior as a hostile act: *Why is she ignoring me?* Meanwhile, people who were not rejection-sensitive had a more neutral interpretation: *She's just distracted.* Taken to an extreme, rejection sensitivity can sometimes turn into *rejection sensitive dysphoria*, in which people obsessively scour their social interactions, turning gentle criticism or even neutral questions from others into catastrophic episodes of rejection. The cycle is yet another example of a self-reinforcing feedback effect, leading to behaviors—reclusiveness, outbursts, intrusions of privacy—that often bring about the very kind of rejection the sufferer so fears.

Even those who wouldn't meet clinical criteria for dysphoria can let the fear of rejection warp their judgment. Another clever study by Sandra Murray and colleagues showed that people who have low self-esteem—a hallmark of rejection sensitivity—respond to disapproval from their partner very differently than those with healthy self-esteem. In one experiment, participants were led to believe that their partner harbored unspoken complaints about them. The high self-esteem group absorbed the blow and maintained their positive view of the relationship. But low self-esteem participants reacted defensively: they rated their partner more negatively, and reported feeling less close to them. In another study, people were led to believe their partner was privately listing everything they disliked about them—when in fact they were just jotting down the contents of their dorm room or apartment. Once again, the low self-esteem participants responded by pulling away. The upshot is grim: those most in need of connection are the ones most likely to sabotage it, rejecting others out of fear that they will be rejected themselves.

Picking Up the Pieces

Being rejected destroys the confidence we have—both in ourselves and the person to whom we're supposed to be closest. That may help to explain why, immediately after a breakup, we often feel paralyzed, unsure about what to do, convinced our partner was irreplaceable, and uncertain whether we'll ever be happy again. For the sixty-two-year-old woman I quoted at the beginning of the chapter, "the fears and uncertainties" that went through her head all coalesced into one question:

> What the hell am I supposed to do now? Figuring that out is taking me some time. Today, I cope by separating that feeling of despair and betrayal from the rest of my other feelings. I have no desire to ever marry again, but love comes in all shapes and sizes, and joy can

> be had from other, non-romantic, sources: from my dog (until he died), from reuniting the family from which my ex had isolated me, and from doing things I have always wanted to do, but to which he objected, etc. I survive by creating pockets of joy where I can, and/or simply enduring when I can't.

After a bad breakup, it's common to feel like you'll never recover, and the scariest thing about rejection—unlike many other forms of misery—is that sometimes these predictions are correct. A sixty-eight-year-old white woman—whose partner, a Black man, left her after he was rejected by her family because of his race—reported her rejection as a 10 out of 10 on the badness scale. When asked how long it took to get over it, she responded: "I'm not sure how to answer this . . . it lasted years. I still cry over it. It was thirty-four years ago . . . I was broken and still am."

Some of the rejections reported as most persistently painful were from people who remained in daily contact with the person who had rejected them, sometimes years after the rejection. A fifty-seven-year-old woman who remains married to her perennially unfaithful husband rated her ongoing feelings of rejection as a 10 in badness. The pain she feels over this rejection, she reported, has robbed life of its pleasure: "Things that I used to enjoy, I no longer enjoy because I look at them differently." A sixty-nine-year-old male reported on a rejection from eighteen years earlier that he still finds painful: "My wife said she no longer wanted to make love. I was aged fifty, she forty-nine. We are still together and it is still quite painful as we have not had sex in eighteen years."

The one benefit of remaining in a relationship with a person who rejects you is that you are unlikely to romanticize someone you still are in contact with. This is not the case for other kinds of heartbreaks, which are very susceptible to memory biases. Over time, our memories of past experiences tend to get more positive, a phenomenon known as "rosy retrospection." Although this bias might seem to be happiness-promoting, when it comes to rejection, the opposite is the case. Rosy retrospection often makes the pain of being apart worse because one remembers the relationship as having been even better than it was.

A sixty-four-year-old male, for example, who reported a rejection two years prior as a 9 on the badness scale, and who said that it took him a year to get over it, seems to have been aware of the memory bias, and tried to consciously counteract it: "The difficulty was remembering and yearning for the times when I felt we had a normal relationship." After much introspection, he began to realize that his memory was filtering out the bad times. "Now, I wonder if we really had a normal relationship at all . . . [it] makes me think even the good times were an illusion."

The good news is that while the pain of rejection *can* last a lifetime, usually it doesn't. A majority of survey respondents claimed to have fully recovered from their worst rejection. Therapy, religion, and friends helped many people cope with a bad breakup. Others needed a new relationship to get over the old one. But in the largest number of cases, time itself was the most effective medicine. Hedonic adaptation, which, as we learned in Chapter 7, takes the sting out of our losses over time, can be so effective that one doesn't even recognize when it has occurred—a bit like a nagging pain that bothers you for a long time only to disappear without you even noticing.

One seventy-three-year-old nonbinary respondent experienced a breakup at age forty that took them a full decade to get over. Sometime later, they reported, "I found out she would be coming to work where I was employed. At first I had some of the old feelings, then realized that she was no longer important to me."

How Do You Fix a Broken Heart?

After being rejected, a person is faced with a key decision: whether to devalue your past relationship or maintain a positive perspective despite your broken heart and whatever new (and often upsetting) information you learned about your ex in the course of the breakup. Each strategy has a different downside. Denigrating the relationship—deciding, for instance, that the rejecter was evil, dishonest, unworthy of your respect or time—devalues your own history, in effect consigning the whole relationship to the trash bin. Maintaining a positive outlook on the relationship, in contrast, preserves memories and history, but renders the demise of the relationship more painful.

A seventy-seven-year-old female respondent decided to take the high road: "I had a twenty-five-year relationship with someone who was married. It suited me well since I do not like being married and the relationship was rich in connection, mutual support, and yes, love. As we both aged, continuing was untenable. I was bereft for a while when it ended but now feel grateful; the many years we had together was a gift." Representing the opposite strategy, a seventy-year-old male reported on a relationship twenty years prior with an "attractive professional woman that was much younger." Though extremely happy with her at the time, he decided after she ended the relationship that he had made a mistake, given their differing romantic expectations and gap in ages.

Thank God, the man thought, *I dodged a bullet.*

What causes a jilted lover to adopt one coping strategy or the other? Undoubtedly, one determinant is the actual quality of the relationship—it is easier to denigrate a bad relationship than a good one. Another is the length of time one spent together. The damage to one's history and memories is much less severe for a relationship that lasted a month than one that lasted a decade. In *Instead of a Letter*, Diana Athill articulates the trade-off between preserving history and mitigating immediate trauma, and explains that she came out in favor of the former due to the quality and duration of her relationship to her beloved fiancé, Paul, a particularly noble stance considering how poorly he treated her at the end:

> If I had known him less well the whole thing might have been over comparatively quickly: I might have written him off as a monster, dropped all hope, and have been cured. Two things prevented this. One was the reaction common to almost everyone in such a situation: the terrible knowledge that if you accept the unworthiness of the object of your love, then your love itself is discredited and all the good in its past becomes poisoned retroactively. The other was the plain fact that Paul was not a monster. I had known him for so many of the longest years in a life-time, I had grown up with him, I had loved him, after the first spell of childish infatuation, with the sort of love which brings knowledge rather than illusion: I was unable to make a grotesque of him.

Another decision that those who are rejected face, at least if anger is mixed in with sorrow, is where to direct that anger. If you catch your significant other *in flagrante* with another person—and a very large fraction of rejections are connected in one way or another to infidelity—you face the decision of whom to blame: your partner or their love object. Even when this decision is seemingly made on the spur of the moment, my guess is that it incorporates an element of rationality. If the cuckolded partner still harbors a hope of remaining together, then the natural target is the lover, who can be blamed for "corrupting" the loved one. But if the victim of infidelity really wants out of the relationship, they will blame their partner.

A sixty-one-year-old female from my survey, for example, whose boyfriend met a new woman on a bike trip, reported thoughts of revenge. "I daydreamed about killing myself, so he would really feel bad about what he had done, and also about going to confront her / hurt her (I'm not a violent or suicidal person and would never have done so)." Tellingly, she did not contemplate hurting or killing *him*.

Reluctant as I am to dispense advice in a book so skeptical of self-help, I'll make one suggestion: if reconciliation is possible after a rejection—and if the person has other redeeming qualities—it may be worth trying to forgive them. I was struck by how many respondents ended up back with the person who had cheated on them or broken things off. In some cases, that choice clearly led to more pain. But in many others, it turned out to be the right call.

A fifty-one-year-old female reported on a rejection thirty years earlier that she rated an 8 in badness: "I fell in love with this man who had a girlfriend in another town. He cheated on her with me for several weeks, then he went back to her. I was devastated even though I knew he was going to do that. I spent months trying to talk myself into disliking him so I wouldn't feel bad about it."

The story, however, has a happy ending: "We met again years later, became friends, dated, and we've been married for twenty years. I still felt a little bit of the hurt from before, but he declared that that was in the past. I've always had a hard time holding a grudge against people I love, so I agreed to go out with him again. I let my guard down and let him in."

15

Guilt

The first house we owned had been built in 1830. The basement had a whitewashed stacked stone wall that made it a bit porous. There were beautiful salamanders that sometimes showed up and I loved that they did. They were harmless and kept bugs at bay. One day, when I was doing laundry, I caught motion on the floor out of the corner of my eye and STOMPED what I thought was a bug. It was a baby salamander. To this day, when I think of it, it is like a jab in my gut. I got a tattoo of a little salamander as an apology and act of contrition.

—Sixty-six-year-old female respondent to the Misery Survey

Guilt Versus Shame

I agonized over whether to write separate chapters about guilt and shame, which—like jealousy and envy—are closely related, at least in the public's mind. Shame and guilt are both, along with their weaker cousin embarrassment, what psychologists call *self-conscious* emotions: they involve evaluations of the self. But guilt and shame are not quite the same. Guilt is usually about what we do, want to do, or fail to do—essentially, *behavior* that harms others or violates a moral code (*I did something bad*). Shame is less about behavior and more about identity, *being*: the feeling that in some way we are fundamentally deficient (*I am bad, or at least other people think so*).

This is why when we offer an apology that's accepted or when we are forgiven, our feeling of guilt can be mitigated—at least somewhat, sometimes—but such things do little to assuage feelings of shame. Someone else's forgiveness does not undo the fact that one misbehaved, or the implications of that fact for one's self-evaluation. Guilt, according to psychologists, is more likely to lead to "reparative action"—even if in the vast majority of cases it does not—whereas shame is more likely to lead to withdrawal, hiding, and sometimes aggression.

These and other differences between guilt and shame are hinted at by the metaphors used to describe the two forms of misery. Guilt is often (including multiple times in the Misery Survey) described as a weight—one respondent observed that "the misery may be psychic, but in many ways it feels like a physical weight that refuses to disperse." Other common guilt metaphors involve stain or contamination—"A *blot* on one's conscience" or "unclean" or "dirty hands." Shame, in contrast with guilt, is more about one's public reputation (although, as I discuss in a moment, it can be a purely private affair), and its metaphors reflect that, involving exposure ("caught with your pants down") or hiding ("wanting to disappear" or "crawl into a hole").

Guilt is, in some ways, a subset of shame. Guilt almost always comes wrapped in shame, but shame often arises without guilt—when we have not harmed anyone, and indeed may have "made their day" by giving them something to laugh about. Tripping over a microphone cord during a wedding toast, or emerging from a bathroom with a long tail of toilet paper stuck to one's shoe: such moments are mortifying to the person experiencing them, but amusing to everyone else. Because guilt tends to involve specific wrongdoing, while shame can be provoked by something as simple as standing exposed before others, it seems fitting to begin with guilt—the narrower, more circumscribed emotion—before turning to shame, the broader and more engulfing one.

Though I have plenty of things to feel guilty about (my sister and I recently compared our top offenses, and the lists were impressive—or should I say, depressing), one incident stands out. It can still cause a stab of pain when recalled now, more than sixty years later—a testament to guilt's staying power.

I don't remember exactly how old I was, only that I was young enough that no adult would have thought I was ready to play with fire—which, of course, is exactly what I did. One afternoon, my friend Matthew and I built a small fire in the woods behind my house. We were, I suppose, mature enough to extinguish it before anything terrible happened.

That night, during dinner (eaten on the same kitchen island where we anxiously awaited my sister's prom invitation), the phone rang. My father answered it while the rest of us tried to guess who was calling and why. After a short conversation, he hung up and turned to me.

"That was Mrs. Naiman," he said. "She says she saw you playing with fire in the woods; you know you're not permitted to do that. Were you?"

I responded that I had definitely *not* been playing with fire.

"Okay," he replied. "I guess she was wrong. I'll always believe what you tell me."

My mother was known as the psychologically astute one in the family, but if my father wanted to inflict maximum punishment—or most effectively deter future lies—he couldn't have done much better. One of the predominant functions of guilt is to deter misbehavior. And I can report that I rarely lied after the incident—or at least, rarely lied *to my father*. To this day, I carry the burden of guilt of having lied to someone who believed me so completely.

Unforgivable

As I noted earlier, guilt can sometimes be alleviated by forgiveness—by an apology that is accepted. But in many situations, forgiveness is no longer possible. Perhaps the clearest example is when the person we wronged has died, which may help explain why so many enduring feelings of guilt are tied to those who are no longer alive.

One female respondent to my Misery Survey, for example, described neglecting to visit a beloved uncle who was dying of endocarditis during the early days of Covid. Her father (the uncle's brother) urged her to go, she reported, but her husband talked her out of it. Her self-report is especially poignant because she has made many attempts to assuage her guilt—none of them successful. Her uncle died in the hospital about a month later, and several years on, she writes: "It makes me cry even today. Mainly sadness but also a lot of guilt to not have shown him how much I loved him by being there."

The guilt is even worse if we feel in some way responsible for what happened.

"I discovered my mom, dead, on the top of a set of stairs in her home," wrote one male respondent. "It looked like she was trying to get to a phone—too far for her to reach. At her advanced age, I should have been more proactive about getting her a wearable emergency call device. She might still be alive." Two years after the incident he reports that "I will always have that memory of finding her that way."

A third respondent, estranged from her half-brother and feeling helpless to make amends, already anticipates the permanence of guilt after his death: "I am sure this guilt will haunt me even more after my half-brother dies."

It is sometimes said that you should live each day as if it were your last. But perhaps it should be broadened to say we should treat everyone we love as if it were their last day, too. As one woman wrote: "The week before my mom unexpectedly passed away, I got into a huge fight with her over the phone—over wedding invitations, because she hadn't reviewed the proof I'd sent. She wasn't feeling well. I've felt tremendous guilt over our last conversation being a fight over something that now seems absolutely trivial."

Even if the people we've wronged are still alive, some sources of guilt are so far back in time—and deeply entrenched in our personal histories—that they feel impossible to atone for. One elderly man reported still being haunted by his behavior at a fraternity party when he was in college: "I may well have overstepped the bounds of consent. The woman was very much a 'straight arrow'—she expected better behavior from me, and I failed. I have had a guilty conscience to this day (for a scant sixty years or so)."

A great deal of guilt also stems from things done in childhood, viewed later through the harsher judgment of an adult. Having been bullied is a common and powerful source of anger (see Chapter 11); having been the bully oneself is a common and enduring source of guilt.

One sixty-two-year-old woman, for example, reports still being tortured by an act she committed when she was about seven years old—an incident she rated a 10 on the badness scale:

> A couple of my friends and I played a nasty trick on a small three-year-old girl who lived next door to me. I think we did it more than once. We'd convince her to pull down her underwear and then bang on her door and tell her mother that Anna pulled her pants down. This memory has always been a guilt-ridden one for me. I meditate a lot now, and when this memory comes up I offer the memory of Anna my deep apologies, usually with tears.

Another respondent, a man in his sixties, described a similar experience: "When I was eleven or twelve, I was miserable in school and was frequently mocked and bullied. One day while walking home I came upon several boys mocking another boy who was basically in the same boat I was in. Much to my shame, I joined in." Reflecting more broadly on the experience, he noted the finality of some forms of guilt—the feeling, much like guilt toward the dead, that it's impossible to truly make amends:

> I think I experience it acutely because there is literally nothing I can do to make it better. I have made rash or foolish decisions in the past that have affected my life negatively, but I find it easy just to accept them and move on. I feel like I don't have any way to move on from this. Even if I remembered the name of the boy (I don't), I can't undo the harm I participated in.

The Curse of Knowledge

One reason guilt can feel so overwhelming is that it rarely seems confined to our private conscience. Even if no one else knows what we've done—or if those we've wronged have died or moved on—some part of us continues to believe our transgressions are somehow *known*. Earlier in the book, I introduced Adam Smith's idea of the "impartial spectator"—an internal judge who always holds us to account. Some experience that presence as a quiet inner voice; others feel watched by something larger and more mysterious—God, karma, the moral order.

This exaggerated sense of being observed, even in solitude, can be partly explained by a psychological phenomenon I studied with my colleagues Colin Camerer and Martin Weber: *the curse of knowledge*. The curse of knowledge refers to the difficulty people have in setting aside what they know when trying to understand what others do—or don't—know. In one early experiment, we found that participants who knew the correct answer in a simple guessing game systematically overestimated how likely others—who lacked that information—were to correctly guess it. Even when explicitly instructed to take the other person's perspective, they couldn't fully do it. As Edgar Allan Poe's "The Tell-Tale Heart" dramatizes—a story in which a man, certain that the police can hear the beating heart of his dead victim beneath the floorboards, confesses to his crime—people often overestimate how obvious their moral failings are to others, a distortion that magnifies guilt. As Shakespeare put it, "They whose guilt within their bosom lies, imagine every eye beholds their blame."

This same bias can, somewhat paradoxically, keep us from apologizing for our misdeeds. It's easy to see why people hesitate to admit fault when others are watching: public apologies risk reputational damage. But most moral failures are private, involving just ourselves and the person we've wronged. In such situations, when we already know we're at fault, why resist fessing up? The answer, according to research I did with Shereen Chaudhry, is that people imagine an *outside observer*. An apology rarely tells the aggrieved party anything they don't already know. But to this invisible moral scorekeeper, it does something more consequential: it fixes responsibility.

The perversity is that the very act we avoid for fear of sealing our blame—apologizing—is the one most likely to ease our conscience, not to mention fix broken relationships.

The Punishments Do Not Fit the Crime

Reading through the Misery Survey responses about guilt, I was struck by how often even serious-sounding confessions seemed forgivable—at least to me. Many, if not most, of the events that inspired lifelong guilt struck me as surprisingly minor, though perhaps that says more about my own moral standards than about guilt itself. Again and again, I noticed a mismatch between the perceived severity of the wrongdoing and the intensity and persistence of the guilt it caused.

One woman recalled a first-grade memory that still troubles her thirty-five years later. On a field trip to a museum, students were given little metal pins to wear. She left hers on her desk while going to the bathroom, and when she returned, it was gone. A friend told her that a boy who "liked" her—a boy she didn't like back, and who wasn't especially popular—had taken it. He denied it, but she told the teacher, who forced him to give her his own pin. Later, she found her original pin on the floor beneath her desk.

As an adult, she still feels guilty for not returning the boy's pin or apologizing. "I just really didn't know how to handle it," she writes, "or how to handle his unwanted attention." Looking back, she suspects he may have come from a troubled home—"He was often asleep in class"—and grieves her inability, even then, to respond with more compassion.

Another respondent described a moment that still pains her decades later. As a teenager, her older brother—less outgoing than she was—showed up unexpectedly at a small gathering of her friends. She was "so surprised to see him" that she blurted out, "What are you doing here?"—in a tone that, she now realizes, "made him feel like he didn't belong." What haunts her is not just her casual cruelty, but the contrast to *his* behavior: he "always made me feel welcome and introduced me to his friends." Thinking back on this moment, she writes, "I still feel the sadness in my heart."

Perhaps the most extreme illustration of how trivial acts can produce enduring guilt comes from a woman who, more than a decade ago as a teenager, found a baby mouse near a dumpster at summer camp. Thinking it was "precious," she picked it up to examine it more closely. The mouse wriggled free, fell from her hands, and died from the fall:

> I felt like the worst type of monster (I still do) . . . I took this beautiful, tiny life, selfishly meddled with it, and it died. I didn't sleep that night, thinking about the suffering I inflicted . . . wondering if one day it would come back to me somehow.

As her guilt persisted, it was joined by another burden, the loneliness of feeling guilty about something most people would dismiss:

> Was there something wrong with me, that I'd made myself miserable over a mouse? . . . There was no good scenario that would come out of telling someone. Either they'd confirm my worst fear—that I *was* a monster—or they'd laugh it off.

Guilt often arrives like this—not as a pure emotion, but as a *meta*-emotion. We may feel guilty for feeling relief when a friend fails, or deflated when they succeed; guilty for not grieving enough after a loved one dies, or for not crying at their funeral. Absurdly, we can even feel guilty—after we've done something wrong—for *not* feeling guilty.

One woman, a working mother struggling to balance parenting and a demanding job, came to see that the things she felt guilty about—missing deadlines, not playing enough with her kids—weren't, in the grand scheme, so terrible. But that insight didn't free her from guilt; it only layered another guilt on top:

> I feel guilty (!) that I feel guilt at all. If anyone else was to describe these feelings to me, I would tell them they shouldn't let it bother them.

16

Shame

> Being forgiven creates a peculiar shame. I felt hot, and not just from the blanket. I felt held close, stifled, as if it was not air I had to move and talk through in this world but something thick as cotton. This shame was physical, but went far beyond sexual shame, my former shame of nakedness; now it was as if not the naked body but all the organs inside it—stomach, heart, lungs, liver—were laid bare and helpless. The nearest thing to this that I had ever known before was the feeling I got when I was tickled beyond endurance—horrible, voluptuous feeling of exposure, of impotence, self-betrayal.
>
> —Alice Munro, *Lives of Girls and Women*[*]

Exposed

If self-esteem reflects the moment-to-moment fluctuations in how we think the world sees us, reputation is the slow accumulation of those moments

---

* Alice Munro was, herself, shamed posthumously, if that is possible, by the revelation that she had stood by her husband though she was aware that he had sexually molested her daughter.

over time—a kind of reservoir of social worth. And, as is true of so many of the other emotional phenomena in this book, there's an asymmetry between how reputations are made and unmade. A good reputation typically takes a long time to develop (though in some special cases a particularly brave or wise act can bolster it tremendously), but it takes very little to blow a hole in one's reservoir and to lose it in one fell swoop.

The likelihood of such a fall is amplified because reputations are multidimensional. A good reputation entails being a good (or at least not horrendously bad) parent, coworker, manager, friend, spouse, driver, neighbor, and so on. Having a good reputation is typically what psychologists refer to as a *conjunctive* process; all the relevant dimensions need to be at least above some threshold. A bad reputation is, by the same token, *disjunctive*; all it takes is one bad dimension to bring down the house of cards or, to revisit the earlier metaphor, to crack open the reservoir.

In my own field, three people with stellar reputations who were at the pinnacle of their careers were abruptly brought down—two by accusations of data fraud, and one by accusations of sexual impropriety and abuse of power. Leaving aside the details of each case, I can't even imagine how horrible it must feel to lose one's standing (not to mention livelihood) in a single stroke. As Adam Smith observed, "Compared with the contempt of mankind, all other external evils are easily supported." Perhaps Smith and other wise men of the Enlightenment understood something important about shame that we have since forgotten. Benjamin Rush, a physician and founding father of the United States, once asserted that the shameful punishments common in his time—stocks, the pillory, the whipping post—might in some respects be harsher than the gallows: "Ignominy is universally acknowledged to be a worse punishment than death."

People experience shame when their social standing or reputation is tarnished—or when they believe it *might* be. While public disgraces are clearly shameful incidents, shame can also be entirely private. What matters is not the actual judgment of others, but the *imagined* judgment—the anticipation of how others would see us if they knew the truth. This helps explain the phenomenon of imposter syndrome, in which people who are admired or perceived positively by others secretly believe they are undeserving of that regard.

The experience of imposter syndrome is often framed today in terms of workplace anxiety, but at its core, it's a form of internalized shame: the fear of being found out, unmasked, exposed as a fraud—unworthy of the position you've been granted. Consider John Quincy Adams, who upon his election to the American Academy of Arts and Sciences responded with characteristic ambivalence:

> Honours like these produce in my mind humiliation as well as pride. In this particular instance, I am mortified at being raised to the head of a learned Society, with qualifications so inadequate to the Station.

Perhaps Adams was simply being modest, but the sense of mortification or physical discomfort caused by shame is very real. When I asked one of the disgraced academics why he wasn't attending an event he logically should have been part of, he told me that walking into the room—appearing before his colleagues, knowing what they'd be thinking about him—would have been so stressful that he would have vomited. People, quite simply, are not built to withstand such an onslaught of shame.

As Jon Ronson points out in his insightful book *So You've Been Publicly Shamed*, public shaming is one of the worst psychic miseries a person can endure. He documents what he calls "a great renaissance of public shaming" ushered in by the internet:

> After a lull of almost 180 years (public punishments were phased out in 1837 in the United Kingdom and in 1839 in the United States), it was back in a big way. When we deployed shame, we were utilizing an immensely powerful tool. It was coercive, borderless, and increasing in speed and influence. Hierarchies were being leveled out. The silenced were getting a voice. It was like the democratization of justice.

But that early glee, he observes, was tragically shortsighted:

> It didn't seem to be crossing any of our minds to wonder whether the person we had just shamed was okay or in ruins. I suppose

> that when shamings are delivered like remotely administered drone strikes nobody needs to think about how ferocious our collective power might be.

Like drone strikes, the shaming comes "out of the blue" for many of the targets, and the effects, as he documents in many interviews with those who have been shamed, are devastating. Reputations destroyed. Widespread ostracism. Long-term psychological harm. In some cases, the shame has been so intense that individuals have become unable to leave their homes.

Nothing to Apologize For

Shame and guilt often travel together. As noted in the previous chapter, guilt arises when we believe we've done something wrong—when we've hurt someone, broken a rule, violated a moral code. In those cases, shame usually comes along for the ride. But shame doesn't require wrongdoing. Consider this painful story from a female respondent to the Misery Survey:

> When I was about twelve years old I had my first period while in school and it stained my uniform and also my seat. The worst part was that we had to do an exercise where we moved to different seats. I didn't know I was staining the seats and then someone saw a stain on their seat and then on other seats. It came out that it was me and the whole class and maybe part of the school found out.

Obviously, the respondent knows she did nothing wrong. Yet her shame, which she rated a 9 on the badness scale, was intense and, given that it happened twenty-five years earlier, seemingly unforgettable. This is the experience of shame via *exposure*.

Yet in other cases we experience shame when we've done nothing wrong—*but others believe that we have.* That was the kind of shame felt by a friend of mine who, when I mentioned I was writing a book about negative emotions, immediately named humiliation as his dominant misery. At my request, he sent me the following story:

> The train station at Cambridge is a little outside of town. You can walk, or take a bus, but many people take taxis. When the train arrives from London, there's usually a large crowd. People line up, and the taxis pull up in order. Knowing that there would be a big line, I got out of the station quickly and got into a cab. The driver told me that I had jumped the queue; I told him that I hadn't, but he told me to get out of the cab (and of course I did). He was firm, and impolite, but didn't shout or anything—it was like being disciplined. By the time this conversation had unfolded, a big line had formed. Everyone could see me getting out of the cab, and the driver then pulling a few feet further forward to take the person at the front of the line. I walked into town. I felt completely humiliated, and have never forgotten it—one of those flashbulb memories where I can see the interior of the cab, the beige seats, the back of the driver's head, the line beginning to form through the windshield, and my leaning over to open the door again.

Many of the most devastating stories of public shaming described in Jon Ronson's *So You've Been Publicly Shamed* reflect a similar dynamic—though on a far greater scale. The person at the center of the storm is often innocent—or, at the very least, not guilty of what they've been accused of. But the crowd acts as prosecutor, judge, and jury, often on the basis of partial or misinterpreted evidence. Which, alas, doesn't exactly distinguish it from many real-world trials.

In her classic 1946 study *The Chrysanthemum and the Sword*, anthropologist Ruth Benedict famously distinguished between "guilt cultures" and "shame cultures." In guilt cultures (like the modern West), morality is typically internalized: people feel bad when they violate their conscience, even if no one knows. In shame cultures (as Benedict characterized Japan), morality is externally regulated: what matters is not the internal reckoning but the eyes of others. A misdeed is shameful if, and because, it damages your standing in the group.

Shame, like guilt, evolved because it benefited either individuals or the groups they were embedded in. Just as fear protects us from external threats, and pain helps us avoid injury, shame serves a social regulatory function. It creates an internal punishment system for violating group norms, helping to deter behaviors that might threaten cohesion—and sparing us, in many cases, from the risk of ostracism. Emotion researchers have noted that the physical manifestations of shame—lowered gaze, slumped posture—may serve as appeasement signals. These signals communicate submission and remorse, reducing the likelihood of retaliation and facilitating reconciliation. A closely related theory suggests that shame evolved to preserve attachment bonds. Because abandonment was particularly dangerous for our ancestors—especially for human infants—shame may have functioned as an adaptive response to threats of rejection, motivating us to restore social harmony. These evolutionary accounts help explain why shame feels so excruciating: it was designed to protect us from one of the greatest threats to our survival—being cast out.

Human Stains

Unlike guilt, which is usually tied to a specific act, shame often attaches to who we are—our identity. That's why it can linger long after the triggering event has passed. It becomes a kind of stain: a mark on the self. That word—*stain*—came up again and again in the Misery Survey. Respondents described feeling "permanently marked," "tainted," "unclean," "contaminated"—not only by what happened to them, but by how others saw them afterward.

One man described being discharged from the Navy for a "personality disorder"—a bureaucratic euphemism, he said, for not being able to handle the stress. Afterward, he found himself constantly lying or evading when asked about his military service: "It's like an insidious fight-or-flight response. If the subject comes up, my mind instantly moves into a keyed-up state. Do I answer, deflect, lie?"

A woman recounted a different kind of shame, born not from failure but from rejection—by her own child: "Our son sent me a harsh message saying that he didn't want to be in touch with us. Perhaps it was I who was specifically the target. Though I have sincerely done nothing to deserve the harsh words, it has left me with a crushing feeling of shame. I feel that everyone on the road knows that my son rejects me, and I feel like hiding out of sight."

The most harrowing account came from a woman, now in her fifties, who was raped by some male classmates at age fourteen and then disbelieved by her best friend, who insisted the boys "would never do that kind of thing":

> The boys told a different story at school. I was already geeky and unpopular and from that moment on I was labeled a slut. Every day since that moment was consumed by shame. Despite that I was a virgin before that night, I thought about what I should have known and should have done differently. I was left with a lot of fear and self-doubt. I knew that people could not be trusted . . . Even though I don't actively think about it every day and I consider my life to be happy, the experience is always in the background of my mind. I'm very jumpy. Any type of reference to sexual assault on TV hits me in my gut. I'll probably have nightmares tonight after filling out this survey.

The stain metaphor works for another reason: defending someone with a stained reputation can leave a mark on the defender, too. Once a person has been publicly condemned, the condemners acquire a stake in upholding their verdict—otherwise they risk being seen as false accusers. The consequence is that anyone going to the defense of the fallen individual is themselves at risk. And who wants to put themselves on the line in a (typically futile) attempt at public rehabilitation?

In the case of the disgraced academic who admitted to me he couldn't attend an event in his field for fear of vomiting, I had private information that might have partially exonerated him—information that the judging masses were, I knew, largely or entirely unaware of. But I chose not to speak out in his defense and continue to believe that was the only sensible decision. It is a decision I'm not proud of—damn it, that I'm ashamed of.

17

Anxiety

Anxiety is a special kind of misery—it's not just fear or worry; it's the feeling of being trapped in an invisible vise, squeezed by scenarios that haven't happened yet but feel as real as if they had. It's living in a state of hyperawareness, where every decision feels like a game of chess with unseen consequences, and every possible move has the potential to bring regret. One of the most agonizing aspects of anxiety is how it distorts time. It drags the future into the present, making uncertainty feel unbearable. It replays the past like a broken record, amplifying mistakes until they seem unforgivable. It's exhausting because even when nothing is happening, everything is happening in my mind.

—Fifty-seven-year-old female respondent to the Misery Survey

Trigger Warning

One late night, on a flight from London to Toulouse—where I was scheduled to teach a single day of a weeklong PhD course in behavioral economics—I decided to glance through the faculty lineup to make sure I wouldn't be repeating anyone else's material. I was hoping for a little peace of mind. Instead, I was seized by a sickening realization. A research collaborator had already given a talk at the course, and her presentation almost certainly overlapped with mine.

In a panic—I was already jittery and sleep-deprived from earlier travel—I stayed up all night reworking my lecture from scratch. I decided to present an overview of emotions (a topic most economics students know nothing about). I focused especially on fear and anxiety, topics I happened to know well, thanks in part to a sabbatical year at the Center for Advanced Study in the Behavioral Sciences, where I rubbed shoulders with three leading scholars in the field: Susan Mineka, Mark Bouton, and David Barlow. Barlow, who occupied the office next to mine, had quite literally written the book on anxiety—*Anxiety and Its Disorders*. In my hastily revised Toulouse lecture, I spent a fair amount of time on fear and anxiety, including an extended discussion of panic attacks, much of it drawn from Barlow's work.

Several months later, back in Pittsburgh, I was on the phone with a CMU graduate student who had attended the course in Toulouse. It was 11 p.m.—I used to stay up, and work, late—and at some point in our otherwise normal conversation, the student interrupted: "Sorry, but I have to put the phone down." I asked him what was up, and he explained that, while we had been talking, he started having a panic attack.

"Do you need me to come over?"

I wasn't really on such personal terms with the student, had no idea where he lived, nor experience dealing with panic attacks, so I was a bit dismayed when he said yes. I jumped in my car, made what turned out to be a short drive to his apartment building, and did my best to calm him down until he said he felt well enough for me to leave.

During the course of our conversation, I asked him when he had first begun to experience panic attacks, and was shocked by his answer: "Right after I learned about them from your lecture in Toulouse!"

Anxiety, it turns out, can be learned. It can be absorbed and transmitted—not just from one person to another but collectively. The British psychiatrist Simon Wessely has catalogued dozens of episodes of what used to be called mass hysteria, going back centuries. In one early case from 1787, a group of Lancashire mill workers became ill after believing they had been poisoned by contaminated cotton. One worker collapsed, then another. Soon, dozens followed. The fear of contamination, initially sparked by a single fainting episode, rippled outward through the group, producing real physical symptoms—dizziness, nausea, hyperventilation, unconsciousness—in people who were perfectly healthy. What was being transmitted wasn't poison. It was anxiety.

More recently, as described in the podcast *Hysterical* (which mainly focuses on a case of mass hysteria among female high school students in upstate New York), a similar kind of collective anxiety gripped law enforcement officials. Beginning in the mid-2010s, reports began circulating that police officers were collapsing or nearly dying after briefly touching or being near fentanyl during drug busts. Media outlets and law enforcement agencies amplified these accounts, claiming that even incidental skin contact or inhaling trace amounts could be fatal. However, toxicologists and medical experts quickly debunked these claims, explaining that fentanyl cannot be absorbed through the skin in dangerous quantities and that the reported symptoms were consistent with panic responses, not opioid overdose. Despite the scientific evidence, the myth persisted for years, shaping police training, policy, and public fear about the drug.

Anxiety Versus Fear

I don't suffer much from anxiety—as my mother would say, *Gott sei Dank* (thank God)—but, thanks to the Misery Survey, I've had a more intimate glimpse into it than I ever could have gleaned from theory or secondhand observation. The outpouring of stories was overwhelming—there were so many eloquent, heart-wrenching accounts that a huge number ended up on the cutting-room floor. After depression, anxiety was rated by respondents to the survey as both the most common and most intense form of misery from the twelve emotions I asked about—and by quite a considerable margin.

Before delving too deeply into what anxiety is and how it operates—especially in its more extreme forms, like panic disorder or OCD—we have to get clear on what it's not. It is not the same thing as fear. Though they are closely related, there is a virtual consensus among researchers that fear and anxiety are distinct. As Joseph LeDoux, a neuroscientist at NYU and expert on fear circuits in the brain, points out, fear is a response to *present danger*, while anxiety is a state of heightened vigilance in preparation for *future danger*. It's roughly the difference between camping in woods where there might be bears (anxiety) and finding one outside your tent (fear).

The single scariest moment of my life was losing my son—then three years old—in an airport. We had been walking down a hall, with him trailing behind. When I looked back, he was gone. The panic was instantaneous. I ran through the airport yelling his name, asking guards—none of whom spoke English—if they had seen a lost child. I had visions of him being kidnapped, sold into sex slavery. Finally, a kind woman approached me and told me a child had been found behind a ticket counter. Finding him there, happily chatting with a uniformed airline worker, was, along with discovering Peter alive after our canoeing mishap, one of the best moments of my life.

I'm sure I never let him lag behind me in an airport again. But while *I* may have learned a lesson, our ancestors didn't have the luxury of this kind of trial and error to develop their fear responses. Nature couldn't afford to wait for us to get kidnapped or eaten. Instead, it built in mechanisms that favored survival on the first try. This is why the fear response is triggered so quickly; it is designed to steer us away from danger before we even understand what it is.

All animals are programmed by instinct to fear certain things, even if they haven't experienced them. Rats raised in laboratory cages with no prior exposure to predators display signs of fear when presented with the scent of cat fur. Humans, similarly, are primed to fear spiders and snakes, looming forms, and open spaces below us—even without prior exposure.

Some fears follow predictable developmental patterns. Separation anxiety, for example, is common in infants, starting between eight and twelve months of age, and has been linked to adult attachment styles and relationship dynamics. A vestige of separation anxiety probably helps explain why romantic rejection can be so excruciating (see Chapter 14); the mechanisms that keep us bonded to caregivers in infancy don't simply vanish in adulthood. Stranger anxiety (or what parents sometimes term "stranger danger") likewise emerges universally across cultures in infants between four and nine months, peaking around 12.5 months, even when the child has never had a bad experience with a stranger.

While some fears are preprogrammed by instinct, others can be easily learned by example. Sue Mineka's experiments revealed that rhesus monkeys raised in captivity showed no initial fear of snakes. But after viewing a movie of an adult monkey reacting fearfully, they developed strong and lasting snake fears of their own. Notably, this vicarious learning only occurred with *evolutionarily relevant* threats. Captive monkeys who observed concocted films of adult monkeys reacting fearfully to flowers or rabbits did not develop similar fears. A key consequence of this preparedness is that many ancient threats—predators, snakes, spiders—can still trigger intense fear responses, even though they're far less dangerous now. Conversely, modern threats that didn't exist when we evolved—guns, UV radiation, microplastics in the water supply—don't frighten us as much as perhaps they should.

Jonathan Haidt, in his influential book *The Anxious Generation*, argues that the dramatic rise in anxiety and depression among adolescents—especially girls—reflects this mismatch. Modern parents often protect their children from risks that aren't truly dangerous (like roughhousing or unsupervised play), while failing to shield them from those that are—namely, the internet. Many parents won't let their children walk alone for fear of predators, but permit unlimited access to social media platforms that expose them to actual predators, hardcore pornography, and an unwinnable contest for social validation.

Another intriguing—and unsettling—feature of fear is how stubborn it is. Mark Bouton, the third fear-and-anxiety researcher I spent time with during my sabbatical year, has shown that certain fears don't go away easily. Even after we "unlearn" them—typically through repeated exposure to the feared thing without any bad outcome (a process known as extinction)—they can come back. In studies with rats in his lab, Bouton has documented the phenomenon of *spontaneous recovery*, where a fear that seemed to be gone suddenly returns out of the blue, and *reinstatement*, where a fear gets reactivated after we're exposed to something associated with the original event—like a ringtone or siren that was playing during a traumatic moment.

Other fascinating work by Joseph LeDoux suggests that even those fears we seem to have conquered or grown out of are still buried inside us, suppressed by higher-level brain processes. In one experiment, LeDoux conditioned a rat to associate a flashing light with an electric shock, triggering a fear response. He then extinguished the fear by flashing the light without the shock, until the rat stopped reacting. But when LeDoux disabled the rat's *infralimbic cortex*—the brain region responsible for suppressing fear—the animal immediately relapsed, reacting fearfully again to the light. The fear hadn't disappeared. It had been overwritten—but it was still there.

This research shows just how deeply embedded these fear responses are: they can be activated even when we're not consciously aware of our fears, or when we believe we've long since "gotten over" whatever frightened us. In all those cases, however, the fear response is still tied to an *immediate threat*, whether that's a snake, a stranger, or a missing child. Anxiety is what happens when those same fear circuits start firing in the absence of clear and present danger, a kind of suffering that emerges not from what *is*, but from what *if.*

The Panic Button

What struck me most while working on this chapter—and talking with friends and colleagues about their experiences—wasn't just how many people live with anxiety, or how intense it can be, but how often it overwhelms us by spilling from the mind into the body, spiraling into full-blown panic attacks and other acute forms of suffering.

One friend—a risk-taking, thrill-seeking, borderline-reckless extreme athlete—confessed that her anxiety takes a very different shape than you'd expect. Despite routinely putting her life in real physical danger, what unravels her is not any of those concrete risks, but the mere *idea* of death. "My anxiety has always been about dying or suffering related to dying," she wrote in an email. "I think I first realized that I was mortal at age eight. My parents had to say 'see you tomorrow' every night, I went crazy otherwise as I thought it was an indication that I would die during the night."

Her first panic attacks came in high school—one likely triggered by "too much coffee and cigarettes"—with a racing heart, disorientation, and distorted vision. Later, the attacks started arriving unprovoked. On a flight to London, she hallucinated smoke in the cabin. Now, they happen mostly at night, just as she's falling asleep. "They are all related to death. I can't accept that I will die at some point. The thought is too frightening. I handle the attacks by telling myself that I'm having a panic attack, and that it is okay to be afraid, but that I should not think about it because there is absolutely nothing I can do about it."

Panic attacks have the nasty habit of being both extremely common and extremely horrible. The academic literature emphasizes that the *first* panic attack is especially damaging, because it often creates a traumatic memory that can be retriggered—sometimes by nothing more than the *fear* of having another panic attack. As one female survey respondent put it: "While I was fortunate to understand what I was experiencing, it took me many years to overcome the ongoing anxiety that I experienced in worrying constantly about whether I was going to have another panic attack. I avoided situations and places where I felt trapped, and became incredibly frustrated that I needed to avoid the simplest experiences that other people took for granted."

This pattern is so well-documented that researchers strongly recommend early intervention after a first attack, to reduce the risk of *fear conditioning*—a process in which the brain learns to associate otherwise neutral situations (a car ride, a crowded room, even falling asleep) with the trauma of a previous panic episode. The result of such conditioning is a kind of learned vulnerability: panic becomes something you fear not just *in* the moment, but *before* the moment, in anticipation of its possible return.

Another respondent, a male in his thirties, described a panic episode that unfolded over weeks, and which he initially misread as a medical crisis:

> It began with gradually increasing chest pains I couldn't shake in December, and evolved into severe sleeping disturbances, nausea and stomach pains, pins/needles sensations and numbness around my body, muscle pain points, etc. . . . I drove myself to the ER to be admitted. . . . My doctor finally suggested my issues might be rooted in anxiety. I began taking an SNRI—and within a week or two nearly all of my symptoms vanished completely. I never would have imagined the physical symptoms anxiety could manifest.

In addition to panic attacks, anxiety researchers have linked the condition to a wide range of other diagnoses—including autism, ADHD, and OCD—all of which were mentioned by survey respondents. One woman described a classic loop of obsessive thoughts that assailed her while she was trying to have fun at a party the previous evening:

> I immediately worried that I may not have locked the back door. . . . If the door is unlocked, then an intruder could enter and if they do not close the door behind them, then my dog could get loose. I also worried that I forgot to turn off the space heater and that it will start a fire, destroying personal possessions and putting my dog's life in danger. . . . These intrusive thoughts required focus from my brain and distracted me from fully engaging with family and friends.

Anxiety Feeds on Itself

Anxiety, like most miseries in this book, is self-reinforcing. Psychologists often describe it as a kind of mental alarm system that can be triggered all too easily. These false alarms—what researchers call *type I errors*—can be psychologically costly. Once the system mistakenly flags danger, the resulting anxiety puts us on edge, sharpening our vigilance and making us even more likely to over-detect threats. In trying to protect us, anxiety can wind up doing us much more harm than good.

This dynamic was painfully clear in a story from one survey respondent—a computational researcher who once prided himself on his productivity. When he developed a repetitive strain injury that left his hands partially immobilized, he couldn't type and had trouble feeding himself. But it wasn't just the physical limitations that undid him. It was the spiral of anxiety that followed—worries about losing his job, that his wife would leave him, that an undiagnosed neuromuscular disease would paralyze him:

> Pretty soon my nervous system was so on edge that the skin on my neck became hypersensitive. I could no longer wear shirts with tags

> on them . . . I couldn't endure noisy settings. Even supermarkets with too much clutter became too much to bear.

Another reinforcing element is rumination, especially at night. As previously noted, our psychological defenses are lower in the middle of the night. Objectively terrible events weigh heavily, but even trivial concerns can loom absurdly large. One respondent in her forties described her nightly torment with a kind of frustrated clarity:

> It usually manifests in waking up around 1 or 2 a.m., and being unable to relax back into sleep. All my thoughts have an urgency that pushes me to stay awake and give them my attention. . . . It would almost be better if I had something significant to worry about, but it's as though, however easy my life is, the top 20 percent of issues or challenges make me anxious—even if it's remembering a book I want to buy. . . . It drives me insane.

That same tendency to spiral—from a single concern to a flood of unanswerable questions—showed up in another account. A male respondent in his forties who, seven years earlier, had been tasked with deciding whom to lay off at his company described the emotional fallout not just from the act itself, but from the endless mental echo:

> Anxiety-based misery is one where you easily spiral into the what-ifs. What will happen to those people who I have to let go? How will they react? How long will it take them to find a new position? How will they survive? Will they still be friends with me? How will I survive without them here? etc. An endless loop of questions that get worse and worse the more you think about it. It puts you in a constant state of alert and is incredibly draining both physically and emotionally.

The cruel irony of anxiety is that it often prevents the very behaviors that might relieve it. Other evolutionary "sticks"—like pain or hunger—drive us to act: to escape, to eat, to correct the problem. Anxiety, by contrast, tends to immobilize us with worries. The most effective treatment for many phobias and anxiety disorders is *exposure therapy*—the gradual, repeated confrontation of the feared stimulus. But fear, being aversive by design, pushes us to flee rather than face what frightens us. This creates a motivational paradox: getting better requires doing the one thing anxiety urges us to avoid.

Bertrand Russell saw this clearly. He observed that people often use the wrong technique for handling fear—trying to distract themselves instead of confronting it. "Now every kind of fear grows worse by not being looked at. The effort of turning away one's thoughts is a tribute to the horribleness of the specter from which one is averting one's gaze; the proper course with every kind of fear is to think about it rationally and calmly, but with great concentration, until it has been completely familiar."

It's a noble idea—to look fear in the eye, calmly and rationally—but for many people with anxiety it feels impossible. That's the trouble with this particular kind of misery: the more we avoid it, the more powerful it becomes.

What Makes Us Anxious

Sometimes anxiety doesn't just interrupt a life—it derails it. One respondent in his sixties described a moment during his freshman year of college that began, as so many anxiety stories do, without warning or obvious cause. In the middle of a large lecture, he passed out. He woke up confused, drenched in sweat, with dozens of classmates staring at him. He didn't even know what the lecture had been about; later he learned it was a discussion of medical issues related to sexuality. The attack had come out of nowhere.

But it was what happened afterward that altered the course of his life. Word spread quickly. That night, he overheard students in the dorm laughing about the guy who fainted in class when the professor mentioned sex. They didn't know it was him—not yet. Within twenty-four hours, someone did. When they mentioned it, his face flushed with heat. "I just turned and slunk into my dorm room. I didn't come out for two days." He couldn't bring himself to ever return to class. Before long, he dropped out of school entirely.

Most episodes of anxiety, while less dramatic, have similar themes: isolation, self-recrimination, and retreat. In the Misery Survey, people described a wide range of things that made them anxious—some predictable, others less so. Health problems were the most common source, usually their own but sometimes a spouse's, parent's, or child's. Other triggers included children's difficulties, financial insecurity, public speaking (a perennial classic), fraught relationships, and politics. While financial, political, and health anxieties tended to ebb and flow based on real-world conditions, social anxiety emerged in the survey as one of the most pervasive and enduring types. For many, it wasn't just about shyness or awkwardness. It was about being physically unable to enter a room, say a word, or make eye contact—and then feeling ashamed for that inability.

One woman, married to the manager of an engineering office, described sitting frozen in the car outside her husband's office Christmas party. Despite having dressed up and made it all the way to the restaurant, she felt unable to open the door and go inside.

"I physically couldn't get out," she wrote. "Now as soon as I hear about a situation where I'll be anxious, I don't agree to attend from the jump."

One man in his fifties described a recent experience of being seized by anxiety at a dinner party. The initial trigger—feeling inadequate and socially awkward—was soon displaced by more pressing worries: the feeling that he was trapped at the table, the idea that others would notice that he had begun to sweat profusely. "My self-consciousness from the sweating exacerbated the cycle," he wrote. "I sweated completely through my shirt." He eventually escaped to the bathroom to try to calm down, then returned and tried to salvage the evening.

Others described their anxiety as being so severe they never even make it out the door. "I knew getting out would help me in many ways," one woman wrote, "but every time I'd think of speaking to anyone I would pull up the bedclothes and just shake."

Social anxiety is rarely eased by social contact—exposure that should, in theory, be therapeutic can backfire when others respond to visible fear with discomfort or rejection. As several respondents noted, people tend to look away, change the subject, or quietly recoil when confronted with shaking hands or a drenched shirt. "When it does become observable, it often creates this sense that I should be avoided," one female respondent wrote. "You feel like a freak, and their facial expressions confirm my self-diagnosis of being a wimp who will never amount to much because of the anxiety."

In many cases, this dynamic leads to a second layer of suffering—shame about the anxiety itself. One female respondent in her thirties, who had long struggled with a phobia of driving, described how therapy initially helped, but her fear soon returned. What she came to realize was that she wasn't just afraid of driving. She was afraid of *becoming anxious while driving.*

"The anticipation of anxiety is what fueled my phobia," she wrote. "Instead of just experiencing the anxiety and letting it unfold, I was layering suffering on top, making it many times worse than the 'clean' anxiety itself . . . I feel like misery and anxiety create a vicious cycle, each of them deepening the other."

Anxiety, like all the emotions in this book, is subject to empathy gaps: when you're not feeling anxious, it's surprisingly hard to imagine what it would be like if you were. Unlike emotions that arise from clear lines of thought—anger, guilt, even envy—anxiety often feels irrational and inaccessible once it's passed. This makes it hard to explain and easy to dismiss. It also distances anxious people from those around them.

Several respondents compared anxiety to chronic pain—not just in intensity, but in *invisibility.* "Both are mostly invisible to others," one male in his fifties wrote. "Both have a big impact on my happiness, quality of life, and interactions with others. Both are easily dismissed by some because there's no objective diagnostic test."

It's curious, in a way, how little death featured in the survey. Given its claim as the alpha—and certainly the omega—of all anxieties, I expected it to loom larger. Aside from my colleague, the risk-loving daredevil whose panic attacks were rooted in the terror of her own demise, there was only one other notable instance of death anxiety.

It came from a thirty-five-year-old father who had lived with "existential dread" since childhood. His anxiety was constant, lurking in the background even during his happiest moments. When he felt content, a voice would whisper: *How many more times do you think you'll get to feel this way before the end?*

"Nothing helps alleviate it," he admitted. "But at least I try my best to cherish every moment with my kids and other loved ones. I feel like I don't take them for granted since I have this little clock ticking away and alerting me constantly of how short my time is." It almost sounds like a silver lining—the idea that watching out for what might go wrong helps us savor what's going right. But the trouble with anxiety is that it rarely leaves us calm enough to enjoy it.

18

Regret

> I regret not telling anyone I was sexually abused as a child until many years after the fact. I regret not replying to an email from a friend who ended up killing herself two weeks later. I knew she was struggling and I feel like I could have helped her. I regret losing my close relationship with my father when I was a reclusive teenager, and never recovering it. I regret so many things, and the thoughts of them, the big regrets and the little ones and everything in between, come into my mind constantly and lead me to feel all kinds of negative ways: angry, depressed, sad, guilty, hopeless. I feel like regret is particularly painful because there just isn't anything you can do to change what's already happened.
>
> —Twenty-nine-year-old female respondent to the Misery Survey

Commissions and Omissions

Even though the Misery Survey was entirely anonymous, it still felt like an act of remarkable bravery when people shared certain stories—not just because they were painful, but because they required putting into words things no one says out loud, and many people wouldn't even admit to themselves. One woman, a successful professional, told a story about motherhood gone terribly wrong. She had never wanted biological children. Since her teenage years, her vision of parenthood was guided by altruism: she planned to adopt a "special needs child" who otherwise might not have had a chance. Eventually, she and her husband found a child who was medically fragile, emotionally stunted, and developmentally delayed. They spent hundreds of thousands of dollars on therapies, hired specialists and caregivers, and eventually she gave up her career to care for him full time. Her dedication paid off. He began to speak, to grow, to flourish.

But the years that followed were marked not by gratitude or connection, but by increasing alienation. The boy became, in her words, "spoiled, privileged, and utterly ungrateful." She described feeling not just exhausted, but defeated—unable to see the values she tried to instill reflected in the young man he was becoming:

> I simply cannot wait for him to finish high school and move out. This sounds absolutely horrible, given that he would certainly have died if we had not adopted him, but I regret adopting my son. I just don't think he will grow up to be a "good person" or a positive contributor to society, despite my having poured my heart and soul (not to mention savings) into trying to raise him "right." The regret—and the guilt for feeling the regret—are overwhelming.

One of the most important distinctions that researchers draw between different types of regrets is between *regrets of commission*, which revolve around actions we took that we wish we had not, and *regrets of omission*, which arise from actions we could have taken, but did not.

In a toxic mixture of both variants, one respondent described how he had once dreamed of a life in the theater. He had enough talent—or so his professors insisted—and imagined himself not just performing, but writing, directing, even teaching. But life took a different turn. He married "the wrong woman," and got on the "hamster wheel" of a more lucrative, if much less exciting, career—all regrets of commission. But his crowning regret in life would be better described as a regret of omission: "One of the last words one of my disappointed theater professors said to me was, 'You could have been one of the greats.'" Although this was ostensibly intended praise, he mused, "I wonder if that comment wasn't actually, in a way, a curse."

For years, researchers have debated which type of regret—*omissions* or *commissions*—makes us more miserable, and why. That debate came to a head in the late 1990s when the psychologists Daniel Kahneman and Thomas Gilovich engaged in what they called an "adversarial collaboration," an attempt by people who have fundamental disagreements about an academic issue to agree on a study that would definitively determine which side had it right.

In this case, Gilovich believed regrets caused by inactions loomed larger and haunted us for longer; Kahneman took the reverse position, that it was our actions that produced the greatest regrets. They agreed on a study together, ran it, but—as has been true for all examples of adversarial collaborations that I've witnessed—in the end couldn't agree on the interpretation of the results. However, they did publish a joint paper that attempted to reconcile—or at least articulate—their differences.

Gilovich and his colleague Victoria Medvec argued that, though regrets of commission could be extremely painful, that pain usually dissipates thanks to the magic of hedonic adaptation (see Chapter 7). So when we look back on our lives, it isn't the mistakes we made and have already punished ourselves for that still sting, but the roads not taken. Kahneman mostly agreed with this formulation, but he said that most regrets of omission were not painful in the same acute manner as regrets of commission—but more *wistful* and "not terribly troublesome." Many respondents to the Misery Survey, and at least one close friend, would not agree.

One of my good friends confessed in an email that he was tortured not by one missed opportunity but by a torrent of them—erotic regrets that ambushed him without warning, always attached to a prospective romantic partner who was ready and willing but whom he didn't pursue.

There was "X," who presented herself "in full 1960s lingerie as I was plastering my parents' dining room ceiling. I kept plastering." And another "X," who invited him to a clearly romantic dinner party at her house. "We sat on the couch for an interminable period with me unable to make an obvious and easy move—twenty minutes into this standoff (with myself), she said she felt like I was her brother . . . and got up to do the dishes."

And one more in which he and his girlfriend at the time were in the shower when a beautiful mutual friend stepped in to join them. It was, by all appearances, an open invitation. And yet he froze. Said nothing. Did nothing. What tortures him isn't just what didn't happen—it's how close it came to happening, and how effortlessly he can still imagine a version of events where it did happen.

Now, much older and celibate for over a decade, he finds himself constantly assailed by regrets of omission—thoughts of what could have been:

> I respond by acknowledging their presence (ouch), then actively put the thought down, trying to think about something else—a hot water heater that needs fixing, an upcoming doctor's appointment. It has occurred to me that I could greet these memories, welcome them in and play them out instead of shushing them away. Lots and lots of room for fantasy . . . But alas, no—I chase my memories of the multitude of X's away from my consciousness as quickly as I'm able to. The pangs of regret and self-disgust are too much.

In 2011, Bronnie Ware, a palliative care nurse who spent her career giving hospice care to terminal patients, published a memoir with the compelling title *The Top Five Regrets of the Dying.* Adding more anecdotal evidence to support Gilovich's position, four out of the five regrets Ware listed were regrets of *omission*, including the biggest regret: "I wish I'd had the courage to live a life true to myself, not the life others expected of me." The only regret of commission to make her Top Five was "I wish I hadn't worked so hard," a regret that, she wrote, came from "every male patient that I nursed."

As with a lot of academic debates, the best answer to the question of which kind of regret hurts us more—actions or inactions—is probably: *It depends.* The woman who adopted her son out of altruism only to rue her fate—a regret of commission—doesn't seem to have adapted to her regret at all; my now-celibate friend isn't "wistfully" nostalgic about the women he failed to pursue—a clear set of regrets of omission. In both cases, these people are, to varying degrees, actively *tortured* by their ongoing regrets.

It's also worth noting that the line between regrets of omission (what we didn't do) and commission (what we did) is often blurrier than it seems. If you regret not taking the road less traveled, are you mourning the path you missed (omission) or lamenting the one you took (commission)? The distinction is often more about how regret is framed in the mind.

While it's hard to make any sweeping generalizations about which type of regret is worse, I do think regrets of omission tend to stay with us longer. Earlier, in the chapter on meta-emotions, I mentioned a study I recently conducted with colleagues in which I asked people whether they've taken too many, too few, or the right number of risks over the course of their lives. Recall that, while half of the respondents said they were satisfied with their level of risk-taking, most of the remaining respondents said they took *too few* risks. This suggests, again, that it was their inactions—the job not taken, the love never confessed—that they regretted more in retrospect.

In his bestselling memoir *Born a Crime*, the comedian Trevor Noah made the bold claim that he never regretted anything he's ever done in his life or any choice that he's made. "But," he added, "I'm consumed with regret for the things I didn't do, the choices I didn't make, the things I didn't say. We spend so much time being afraid of failure, afraid of rejection. But regret is the thing we should fear most. Failure is an answer. Rejection is an answer. Regret is an eternal question you will never have the answer to."

Remorse: The Importance of *Why*

Whether regret stems from something we did or something we failed to do, the emotional engine driving it is the same: *the comparison between what is and what could have been*. Regret, like a number of other painful emotions, is powered by counterfactual thinking—the mind's ability to imagine an alternate version of events. "It's the not-knowing that creates the misery—*What would my life and future be if I'd made that one different choice?*" said one thirty-three-year-old respondent to the Misery Survey. "I once told someone it's like you're suffering from futures lost."

Like many emotional processes, counterfactual thinking has a negative bias. We don't tend to imagine how things could have been worse—we imagine how they could have been better. And those upward comparisons are especially vivid and emotionally charged. Regret is the most familiar form this suffering takes. But it doesn't stand alone. Researchers distinguish between three closely related emotions that arise from counterfactual thought: *disappointment*, *regret*, and *remorse*.

Disappointment is no picnic but it's the mildest misery of the trio: it occurs when you compare what could have happened to what actually happened. You're disappointed when you buy a scratch-off lottery ticket and win nothing. You're disappointed when you show up at the airport and your long-awaited flight to Hawaii has been canceled.

Regret cuts deeper. It involves a sense of agency—the feeling that *you* made a choice, and that a better outcome was within reach. You regret booking the Delta flight that's now delayed when you see that the United flight you almost chose is departing on time.

Still, regret and disappointment are just pinpricks compared to the third: *remorse*. Remorse adds one key element to regret—not just that a different decision would have led to a better outcome, but that you *should have known better*. When people talk about the things they most regret in life, they are usually talking about remorse (although oddly, there isn't a verb corresponding to the noun).

I'm still haunted by a story I read years ago in *The New York Times*, about a father who took his eight-year-old son rafting on the Green River in Utah. After a safe day on the water, the father suggested one more run through the rapids—an extra, spontaneous thrill to cap the day. It ended in tragedy. The remorse—the knowledge that this final, unnecessary outing deviated from the plan and cost him his child—is something the father must wake up to every morning. I find it almost unendurable even to think about.

This detail—the fact that the outing was *extra*—is significant. Many of the decisions we regret most are often the ones that deviate from our routines. Daniel Kahneman and Amos Tversky demonstrated this in a classic 1982 study, in which participants were presented with two nearly identical scenarios:

> Mr. Adams was involved in an accident when driving home after work on his regular route. Mr. White was involved in a similar

accident when driving on a route that he only takes when he wants a change of scenery.

Then they were asked: Who would feel worse? Eighty-two percent of respondents said Mr. White—the man who strayed from his usual path. The implication is clear: when something bad happens during a deviation, we not only suffer the outcome—we torment ourselves for the choice to deviate at all.

The fact that remorse is so much worse than regret—at least as decision researchers define it—points to a more general insight about psychic misery: usually, *why* something happens is much more important than *what* happened.

This explains why getting cheated or scammed is so unbelievably painful. Not only does it tell you that the world is a dangerous place populated by unscrupulous people who want to exploit you; it also vividly conveys that you're a chump. I've been scammed twice in my life (that I know of): once for fifty dollars in China, and once for fifty euros in Sicily. Even though the first time was twenty-five years ago, and the second a few years ago, and even though I have a terrible memory, I can still recall both extended episodes in gruesome detail.

My index of how bad something is corresponds to how long it takes before I can recount it in a lighthearted way. Almost killing Peter in the canoe took two years; but I still find it painful to relate the stories of getting scammed. Losing vastly larger amounts on the stock market is, by contrast, a nonevent; in fact, in a weird instantiation of meta-emotions, I sometimes feel good when I lose a lot of money just because I don't feel *that* bad.

Reading through the myriad accounts of regret from my Misery Survey, one thing that struck me was how many respondents agonized over *why* they made the decisions they ended up regretting. Quite a few cited bad parenting or bad advice. Some blamed their youth or naivete. But many blamed themselves for errors they saw as unforced. How fair are these ex post facto judgments?

One reason we judge ourselves so harshly is *hindsight bias*—a phenomenon identified by my former colleague Baruch Fischhoff. As captured in the cliché that "hindsight is 20/20," Fischhoff's experiments showed that people who know the outcome of an event are far more likely to see it as having been predictable—and to believe they *would* have predicted it—than people who don't know how it ends. This illusion affects everything from medical diagnoses to political outcomes, and it applies to professionals as much as laypeople. Hindsight bias accentuates self-blame, and hence regret, because it greatly increases the feeling that we should have known better.

I tend to think that many nagging regrets about what could have been are based on faulty memory or poor self-knowledge. As I discussed in the chapter on empathy gaps, we're basically incapable of reentering the emotional frame of mind we were in at the time when we made our fateful decision. We forget how afraid we were or how tired or lonely or excited. We assume that because we feel differently now, we must have been capable of making a different choice then. But that's often an illusion.

This point hit home for me when I happened to see my old high school crush a decade or so after we graduated. I had always thought of her as "the one who got away." She was a bit older—blonde, popular, out of my league—and I spent a lot of time regretting the fact that I'd never worked up the courage to speak to her. Years later, when I learned she was enrolled in one of my mother's social work classes, I imagined a second chance. I waited outside the classroom for a moment to talk to her. But when she finally stepped into the hallway, all the emotions that had paralyzed me in high school came rushing back. I remembered exactly *why* I had never spoken to her—basically, her awesomeness left me breathless and flustered—and I let her walk right past me without saying a word. I realized then that what I had been regretting wasn't a missed opportunity. It was a fantasy.

Hell Is Other People (Who Chose Wisely)

Remorse is even worse when not only does it seem obvious—fairly or not—that you should have made a different decision, but there's also someone in your immediate orbit who *did* make the right one. Your neighbor, for instance, who bought into the stock market the day after Trump was elected in 2016—while you, in a moment of panic, sold everything just before its meteoric rise. People not only suffer more when they see that someone has made the correct choice where they've erred—they fear it happening, and that fear can lead to worse decisions.

I've done research on a phenomenon called *takeover aversion*, in which people continue to invest in a project of dubious value simply because they are afraid that if they drop it someone else might pick it up—and take it all the way to the bank. This happens in academia all the time. I've often chased research ideas out of a fear that if I don't pursue them, somebody else will, and I'll rue the decision to have given up.

Economics teaches that we should invest based on expected value—looking only forward, not back. If a project isn't working, it shouldn't matter how elegant the idea was or how much effort you've already put in. The rational move is to cut your losses. But research has shown that in such situations people often care more about minimizing their regret than actually minimizing their losses. If you give people the option of taking a risky gamble that may pay off, they will usually opt to play it safe—provided they have no way of knowing what would have happened if they had rolled the dice. But if given the chance to see a "what if" scenario, they will be much more daring. The possible regret of having "missed out" on a jackpot is enough to keep them in the game.

Takeover aversion is based on this exact kind of fear, but the negative feelings are even more intense because the comparison is not between your decision and a hypothetical alternative choice that you could have made—but between your decision and someone else's.

Seeing someone else succeed after you gave up allows you to imagine the counterfactual very easily: *If only I had stuck it out, I would now be receiving the rewards that they are enjoying.* It also makes you question your judgment; you can more easily blame yourself for quitting when you know that someone else had good reason to believe the same investment was worth pursuing.

Regret Blackmail

My friend and colleague Marcel Zeelenberg from the University of Tilburg in the Netherlands is one of the world's experts on the psychology of regret.

One day he received an advertisement in the mail exhorting him to try his luck in the Dutch Postcode Lottery. The text read: "If the summer jackpot (of 10.2 million euros) falls in your postcode, will you be standing empty-handed congratulating your neighbors?"

The Dutch Postcode Lottery is peculiar. Unlike the more conventional Dutch National Lottery, in which people buy tickets and a winner is drawn at random, in the Postcode Lottery your ticket number is your postcode. This means that if your postcode wins but you didn't decide to play that week, all your neighbors become millionaires, and you are left with nothing but the knowledge of what could have been.

"It's emotional blackmail," Zeelenberg said.

And, as is often true of blackmail, it works. Though the Postcode Lottery is much less generous with its jackpots than the National Lottery, paying back winners only around 30 percent of what it takes in (compared to 60 percent for the National Lottery), it is still the second-largest lottery game in the Netherlands and generates hundreds of millions of euros per year for charity, as well as a nice revenue stream for its for-profit organizers.

Zeelenberg studied the psychology of the players of the National Lottery and the Postcode Lottery and discovered that the latter group was much less happy with their experience—they were begrudgingly motivated by the fear of regret instead of aspirationally motivated by a fantasy of wealth.

The Dutch Postcode Lottery and other so-called regret lotteries have inspired many behavioral scientists looking for a powerful way to nudge people toward more healthful behaviors. I've used regret lotteries in some of my own research interventions, and found, for example, that they were effective at getting workers at a company to complete health risk assessments (HRAs). They were also effective in motivating people to lose weight, although, when the incentives were removed at the end of the study, not only did participants stop losing weight; they gained back the weight they had lost when the incentives were in place.

Regret Without End

Regret lotteries, like in the example above, are one narrow way to harness regret for good. But the utility that most people draw from regret is educational—the pain of having made a costly mistake can be a "teachable moment," perhaps even a life-changing one. Such regrets often anchor transformation stories: the bankruptcy that taught a future mogul more than business school ever could, the jail sentence that sent an ex-con down a straighter path.

But not all regrets come with an inspirational second act. Some are simply final. They don't make us wiser or better—they just live on as pain or guilt. One seventy-five-year-old woman described a regret that had followed her since the 1980s AIDS epidemic. A very close friend of hers was dying, and she stopped seeing him—not because the friendship didn't matter, but because another, even closer friend was also dying of AIDS.

"I didn't have the emotional maturity to deal with both of them," she wrote, "so I cut off contact with the former. It caused so much pain to the friend I dropped."

Commiserating with friends who understood her predicament—and excused her actions—hasn't helped. "I will go to my deathbed regretting what I did."

Another man recalled sitting at his mother's bedside through her final hours.

"We took good care of her," he wrote, "but when her organs were shutting down, she asked me to hold her. Tears were running down my face, and I took a minute or two to wipe them in the bathroom. By the time I returned, she was into her final sleep. I regret that I didn't grant her that last wish."

One woman recalled the anguish of watching her mother die when her mother did not know that she was in fact dying. In 1977, her mother had been in and out of the hospital with cancer. A doctor told the woman and her father that she had six weeks to live—but to not tell the patient. Her father insisted they keep quiet and follow the doctor's orders. She disagreed, but in the end she said nothing.

"My mom died six weeks later. I know for a fact that she did not know she was close to dying. Not telling her . . . has haunted me ever since." The only benefit of such regrets about how we treated someone else is that they can shape what we insist on for others, or ourselves. Now, she makes one thing clear at the outset of any new medical relationship: "If you ever withhold information about my health, we are done."

•••

Geoff Dyer's unclassifiable memoir *Out of Sheer Rage* is a great case study in the varieties of counterfactual misery. He agonizes about whether to work on a novel or a book about D. H. Lawrence, and ends up doing neither; about whether to move or stay in his apartment; whether to go to the theater or to hear music. "Being with you," his girlfriend complains, "is like licking sugar through a glass . . . You're never quite there."

Acknowledging the charge, he observes that his thoughts are always trapped by alternate realities: "When I'm working I'm wishing I was doing nothing and when I'm doing nothing I'm wondering if I should be working." Summarizing an earlier period of his life, he relates that "at school a teacher warned that if I spent all my time playing football and not studying then I would regret it in later life. As it happens I regret wasting so much time studying when I could have been playing football, but he almost had a point. What he should have said was that whatever you do you will regret it."

19

Loneliness

> Lizzie felt herself alone in a crowd. Who does not know that terrible feeling, and the all but necessity that exists for the sufferer to pretend that he is not suffering—which again is aggravated by the conviction that the pretence is utterly vain?
>
> —Anthony Trollope, *The Eustace Diamonds*

Showing Up

In January 2025, as his second term as US Surgeon General drew to a close, Dr. Vivek Murthy published a thirty-two-page document titled *My Parting Prescription for America*. The disease he was trying to cure was not physical, but social:

> In different ways, people tell me they feel something is missing in their lives. . . . The idea of approaching someone you don't know to strike up a conversation, calling a friend to say hello, or opening up about your struggles feels increasingly uncomfortable. Social media has turbocharged a culture of constant comparison that too often undermines our self-worth and makes us feel dissatisfied with our lives. The decline of civic institutions has made knowing where to

> go for community harder. And underneath these trends, the pendulum of self-reliance has swung so far to one end that needing others is seen as a sign of weakness, leading to a vicious cycle of stress, isolation, and more stress.
>
> The messages that surround us in advertisements, articles, and our online feeds often urge us to fill the emptiness by optimizing ourselves—with more dollars, more likes, more achievement, more stuff—or by drowning ourselves in distraction and substances that can numb the pain.

The cure for this crisis, Dr. Murthy said, was deceptively simple. "We can start by reaching out to people we care about each day," he wrote, "and prioritizing time for regular connection even if it is brief." He suggested people commit to performing "one act of kindness each day"—"dropping off food to a friend who is overwhelmed, checking on a work colleague . . . welcoming a new neighbor." These, he argued, were "small, but . . . powerful acts of community that can build trust, create belonging, and renew our faith in each other."

While his "prescription" focused on mending America's frayed social fabric in general terms, Murthy has elsewhere applied the same logic to loneliness in particular. In his *US Surgeon General's Advisory on the Healing Effects of Social Connection and Community*, he encouraged Americans to build "connection rituals"—habits like sharing meals without devices or scheduling weekly calls with loved ones—to combat the sense of disconnection that is a hallmark of modern life.

That the nation's top doctor would devote so much of his tenure to loneliness reflects a growing recognition of just how pervasive—and costly—the problem has become. Recent surveys suggest that more than one in five US adults now report feeling lonely on a regular basis. Among young adults aged eighteen to thirty-four, the figure rises to 43 percent. Because perceived social isolation is strongly linked to depression, anxiety, substance misuse, and suicide, the loneliness epidemic is also fueling what economists Anne Case and Angus Deaton have termed "deaths of despair." Between

1999 and 2021, annual deaths from suicide, drug overdose, and alcohol-related illness more than doubled, reaching 176,386 lives lost per year and becoming the fifth leading cause of death in the US. While loneliness is hardly the sole cause, the CDC notes that lonely adults are up to three times more likely to experience frequent mental distress, and more than twice as likely to report depression and substance use—all key risk factors.

Murthy deserves credit for using his position to elevate loneliness and social disconnection to matters of national medical concern. But there's reason to doubt whether his proposed antidote—the "connection rituals" that encourage us to "show up" for one another—has any real hope of saving us from this particular poison. What if the problem with loneliness isn't that we don't "show up," but that when we do, we still feel invisible?

I've asked myself that question more than once. I'm not someone who lacks for social interaction. I teach, I go to meetings, I spend time with friends and family. And yet I've gone through periods where I've felt very lonely. Sometimes it's a vague sense of disconnection, a background feeling that lingers for weeks. Other times, it's an acute emptiness that arrives all at once. I hardly think I'm alone in being surrounded by caring friends and family and nevertheless susceptible to loneliness. But I wondered what exactly drives this feeling of disconnection in people like me who, objectively, are not isolated.

When I looked into the research for answers, I was surprised by what I found. For all the public calls for acts of kindness and social connection, there's little evidence that loneliness is caused by a lack of social contact—or even by a mismatch between how much interaction someone wants and how much they actually get (the fallback position of those who believe it is about social connections when confronted by the lack of supportive evidence). In fact, I believe, loneliness has less to do with our social circumstances than with what we think those circumstances *say about us*.

This interpretation helps explain why so many behavioral interventions designed to fight loneliness fail to deliver. A rigorous 2011 meta-analysis of loneliness-reduction programs grouped existing efforts into four broad categories: those that (1) helped people build social skills, (2) increased their sense of support, (3) gave them more chances to interact, or (4) changed the way they thought about themselves and others. Of these, only the last one—changing people's beliefs about themselves—worked consistently.

Many well-funded efforts fell into the third category: interventions that increased social contact. These often looked promising on paper. Some paired lonely adults with others through buddy programs. Others organized group-based social activities such as community walks, singing groups, or aerobics classes—anything to get them "out there." I'm sure that many if not most of these interventions had positive effects; I applaud them. But in study after study, the effect on *loneliness* was weak, inconsistent, or even nonexistent.

The same meta-analysis also evaluated efforts to teach people how to interact more effectively—how to read social cues, ask follow-up questions, or modulate their tone. These had little to no effect on improving loneliness. Likewise for interventions focused on shoring up people's support systems—therapy groups, advice networks, peer mentoring. These were often experienced as helpful or uplifting, but they didn't reliably move the needle on loneliness.

The problem, I believe, is that these programs misunderstood what loneliness is. Even—and perhaps especially—when a lonely person is surrounded by others, they can still feel unwanted. Even when they're equipped with the right "social skills," they may still expect rejection. As the late John T. Cacioppo—a foundational figure in loneliness research and a coauthor of the meta-analysis—put it: what's needed is "changing how people who feel lonely perceive, think about, and act toward other people."

And in practice, that often means changing how lonely people think about themselves—a prescription that is exceedingly difficult to fill.

What Loneliness Is—And Isn't

The event happened more than thirty-five years ago, but he still remembered it with cinematic clarity: the day the yearbooks were passed around at school. Everyone else clustered into little groups, flipping through the pages to spot themselves and their friends—portraits, candid shots, team photos—and laughing at the bad pictures. He sat alone at his desk. He flipped to the index to find his name. There was one page number, for "one lonely portrait photo":

> Then, the books started changing hands because you had to get your friends to sign your yearbook. This made things worse because not only was I alone in the middle of these groups of happy people, but . . . now, there was pressure for me to find someone to sign my book. What if no one wanted me to sign theirs? No one did.

He got up from his desk and moved around the room anyway, pretending to do what everyone else was doing, "hoping no one noticed the perfect unsigned book" in his hands. He wasn't so much desperate to be included as terrified of being exposed as the boy with no friends. It was not the last time he would have to conceal his loneliness:

> The thing is, though, once you've become really good at hiding it, it's hard to stop hiding it—and fix the problem. You just feel hollow and sad and afraid that someone will see how hollow and sad you are. Not all the time, weirdly not when you're alone. Just times like this when everyone else seems to get it, or something happens, and it'd be really nice to have someone to call.

In his classic book *Loneliness*, the sociologist Robert Weiss describes this state as "gnawing . . . a chronic distress without redeeming features." As persuasive as his description is elsewhere in the book, his line "without redeeming features" struck me as odd. To the sufferer, loneliness may feel that way—pure pain with no purpose. But evolutionary psychologists would argue otherwise. Like the pain of a burn that warns us away from fire, the pain of loneliness played a crucial adaptive role. It deterred us from cutting ourselves off from others, from abandoning the bonds that, in our evolutionary past, were essential for survival.

Indeed, antecedents of what humans experience as the pain of loneliness may have evolved far back in our evolutionary past—well before our species had even emerged. In our closest primate relatives—apes and chimpanzees—being isolated from the group is associated with elevated rates of mortality. But even studies examining the impact of social isolation on species as distant as fruit flies have uncovered diverse impacts on health, neural functioning, and life expectancy.

In humans, social isolation leads to physiological and psychological impacts similar to those observed in other species, including heightened vigilance for threats (similar to anxiety), stress responses such as the release of cortisol, and weakened immune function. Studies have shown that loneliness is associated with increased risk of heart disease, depression, and cognitive decline, and a shorter lifespan on average. And, though the causal connection is difficult to establish, one meta-analysis of studies examining this link found that deficiencies in social relationships were associated with a 32 percent increase in incidence of stroke, and were comparable in their impact on life expectancy with smoking fifteen cigarettes a day.

Perhaps most famously, the Harvard Study of Adult Development, which began in 1938 monitoring the lives of 724 men, revealed powerful links between loneliness and life expectancy. One of its most notable findings is that the quality of relationships, not wealth or fame, was the best predictor of long-term health and happiness. As Robert Waldinger, the study's director, noted: "Loneliness kills. It's as powerful as smoking or alcoholism."

Some of the studies, like the Harvard one, assessed loneliness through self-reports. Others relied on more objective indicators—like the number of close relationships someone had. But those aren't the same thing. Objective social isolation—not having friends or close contacts—is very different from subjective loneliness, or what's sometimes called *perceived social isolation*.

Plenty of people with close relationships can still feel lonely—as I can attest. Some of the loneliest people in the world are parents of small children, who may have constant companionship and deep love, but whose kids monopolize their time while offering little in the way of actual sociability. In her novel *Flight Behavior*, Barbara Kingsolver writes of her protagonist: "Being a stay-at-home mom was the loneliest kind of lonely, in which she was always and never by herself."

Objective social circumstances certainly matter—hence the strong correlations between objective and subjective isolation. Married people, on average, are less lonely (though relationship quality plays a big role), while those who are divorced or widowed tend to be lonelier. People who live alone, or who have infrequent or low-quality contact with friends and family, also typically report more loneliness.

But considerable research suggests that simply having a lot of social connections is not in itself enough to protect against loneliness. Consider this response from a thirty-six-year-old female:

> I am an extreme extrovert—I have a handful of best friends, a lot of close friends, and an endless supply of acquaintances. But I still have these moments, like the other night when I came home from an event and felt unwanted, where I feel like no one can relate to me, or I don't want to bother my sister yet AGAIN with my sad feelings. So I sit alone in my room and cry and feel incredibly alone.

While some people are overtaken by loneliness in acute moments like this, others describe it as a constant companion—a chronic, existential state that never quite goes away. As one sixty-year-old male respondent put it: "I have a general sense of loneliness I feel all the time. Even when I am at a gathering with friends and family . . . I feel like I have not found my place in the universe." A twenty-seven-year-old respondent echoed that sense of disconnection, describing his current life as one of "little to no meaningful contact with anyone." Although he has two close friends, distance and circumstance have eroded those ties. Online friendships have fizzled out. Most days, he wrote, are spent alone, studying or scrolling on social media: "No one to hug, to talk to about feelings and problems . . . I feel like I've lost connection even to the people I love the most, and I truly do not know how to reconnect."

The Role of Comparisons

If a lack of social contact isn't the key to loneliness, then what is? Some researchers have responded to the weak relationship between social contact and loneliness by suggesting that it's not the number of friends or interactions that matters, but how those relationships measure up against a person's "internal yardstick." That is, we feel lonely to the extent that our social life falls short of what we'd like it to be.

Personally, I find this account unsatisfying. For one thing, it's not clear what a person's yardstick actually is—or how stable or meaningful that self-reported ideal might be. If someone is already feeling lonely, of course they're likely to say they wish they had more or better connections. But this doesn't explain *why* they feel that way in the first place.

There's another possibility, which I find more plausible: that what drives loneliness is *upward social comparison*, the same thing that drives envy and feelings of low self-esteem. It's not that our own sense of social connection fails to meet some internal standard, but we look around and see others as being more connected, more wanted, and more surrounded—and that makes us feel inadequate by comparison. In my experience, and in responses to the Misery Survey, I've gained the impression that what triggers loneliness isn't so much the *absence* of people but the presence of (seemingly more connected) others that remind you of your own isolation.

Much of our discomfort about going out "solo" also makes sense through this lens of implicit comparison. Many people find it awkward to be the only single person at a dinner party, or to sit alone in a restaurant or movie theater—not necessarily because they mind the solitude, but because they look lonely in contrast to others who are paired or grouped. Recall the story of the lonely schoolboy, trying to blend into a crowd of laughing peers, terrified that someone might see him clutching a pristine yearbook that no one wanted to sign. For him, loneliness was worst "not when you're alone" but when someone else might "see how hollow and sad you are." In such moments when we are forced to compare ourselves to others, our own social inadequacies are reflected back at us. And the picture is not pretty.

If we don't feel lonely by comparison to others, we sometimes feel it in comparison to our past selves. A striking number of (often older) respondents to the Misery Survey described their loneliness as something made painful by contrast to earlier periods of connection, intimacy, or community. For example, a seventy-seven-year-old male respondent wrote:

> After divorce, I spent many years living alone and for the most part was perfectly happy. Living solo does have advantages. At some point

> I felt I might be ready for a long-term relationship, but was still not feeling lonely and was not actively looking for anyone. Then, purely by chance I met someone, not local, and we began a relationship. That is when I started to feel lonely when we were not together.

Another female respondent in her thirties described a period of deep connection during the pandemic, when she moved in with two friends. They shared everything, ate together, took memorable road trips, and supported each other through lockdown. She grew to adore, and rely on, that intimacy. When restrictions eased, the bonds dissolved. Her friends became more individualistic, and they grew irritated with her efforts to re-create their old rhythm. She tried to find new social outlets, "but really, I just wanted my friends back, and the closeness we had during the pandemic."

Back to Self-Esteem

If loneliness has less to do with the quality or quantity of our social connections and more to do with what those connections say about *us*—whether we feel lovable, likable, or wanted—then it starts to sound suspiciously like another concept we've already met: self-esteem.

Mark Leary's "sociometer" theory holds that self-esteem is not a stable measure of inner strength or self-love, but an evolved tracker of our "relative social value." Even mild rejection stings, not because we're thin-skinned, but because the sociometer is tuned to detect subtle threats to our social standing—and prompt corrective action.

It strikes me that Leary's idea of self-esteem is, in a sense, the inverse of my idea of loneliness. The former is often assumed to be about us, when it's really about other people. The latter is often assumed to be about other people (or their absence), when in fact it's deeply about us. The measures often overlap. Feeling rejected lowers self-esteem; it also intensifies loneliness.

There's data to support this link. In one study, lonely students were far more likely to attribute their social struggles to stable character flaws—being boring, awkward, or weird—rather than to anything they could change. Other studies found that loneliness correlated strongly with self-criticism, low self-esteem, and uncertainty of self-concept.

But of course, loneliness and self-esteem are not one and the same. To have low self-esteem is to doubt your own worth. To be lonely, regardless of what causes it, is to long for social connections that would affirm it.

Yet here we encounter the darkest part of loneliness: while it makes us long to connect with others, it also robs us of our ability to do so. As Cacioppo once put it: "Real relief from loneliness requires the cooperation of at least one other person, and yet the more chronic our loneliness becomes, the less equipped we may be to entice such cooperation."

Why Loneliness Is Self-Reinforcing

Like so many of the miseries explored in this book, loneliness is self-reinforcing. It alters perception, deepens pessimism, and changes the way people relate to others—often in ways that isolate them further. Lonely individuals tend to form more negative impressions of others, judge them more harshly, and recall social encounters in a more negative light—biases that often sharpen over time. Loneliness dulls the pleasure we get from social contact, when it does happen. At the same time, it sharpens vigilance for social threats, so ambiguous cues are read as rejection. As people turn inward to protect themselves, the mind begins to create substitutes for human connection. Lonely people are more likely to anthropomorphize animals or see faces in clouds; to name and talk to their gadgets; to form one-sided "parasocial" bonds with TV characters and, increasingly, with AI chatbots.

All these tendencies have social consequences that of course amplify a person's loneliness. Negative expectations generate off-putting behavior—"bad vibes"—which in turn confirms those expectations. Lonely people may push away the very individuals who could help them reconnect.

One forty-five-year-old male Misery Survey respondent captured this spiral with painful clarity. Referring to loneliness, he wrote:

> It's debilitating. It erodes trust in others and it compounds on itself. Like you try to address it by going out in public and then you feel worse because now you're surrounded by people; they're not lonely and even though you're around people you're not able to connect

> in any meaningful way with any of them, so you think, "Oh well I guess there's just something wrong with me." And eventually you end up in this self-reinforcing spiral of being socially awkward because you're lonely and being lonely because you can't seem to connect with anyone.

Even at the physiological level, loneliness appears to shut down the very systems that foster connection. In ordinary, healthy interactions, people automatically and unconsciously mimic each other's facial expressions—especially smiles. This mimicry is a social reflex, one that helps us build rapport.

But in a study by Andrew Arnold and Piotr Winkielman, participants were shown joyful faces while their own facial muscle activity was measured. Those who scored high in loneliness were significantly less likely to mimic the smiles. Among those who felt disconnected, the reflex to smile back had been muted, which of course only exacerbates the loneliness spiral.

One Misery Survey respondent seemed to intuit the way smiles could counteract chronic loneliness. She described a period of intense isolation after moving to a new state. Her husband was busy, her colleagues absent, her social life almost nonexistent. "People were polite," she wrote, "but I felt invisible." And so, in private, she developed a small ritual. After using the bathroom, she would stop at the mirror, smile at herself, and hold the expression for a moment. "It helped," she said. "Oddly."

This subtle disruption of our facial expressions is just one way that loneliness tricks us into making ourselves even lonelier. It tells us to withdraw when we should reach out, to protect ourselves in ways that only deepen our isolation. Perhaps most insidiously, it casts doubt on the very relationships we do have, which in some cases are loving and supportive. One female respondent described how, during stressful or unbalanced periods of her life, loneliness hijacked her mind:

> I have lived alone for most of my adult life. Alone does not equate to loneliness and indeed there have been times when I've felt the most alone in a room filled with people. But I experience loneliness most

> acutely when my life is out of balance for some sustained period of time, for example when work is especially stressful or I'm sick. That's when I feel the lack of someone at home to be there with a hot meal and a kind word or an ear to listen or a hug. That's when I tend to start chastising myself for not being in a relationship, so the loneliness gets compounded by spiraling self-esteem issues. When I give into that spiral, I disconnect from my networks of support which further erodes my mental well-being.

It's poignant but also a little dispiriting to see how little such self-knowledge does to help people suffering from loneliness. Among the most difficult survey responses to read was the story of a forty-year-old woman grieving a series of undisclosed "traumas," who knew that her loneliness was driving other people away, but she felt unable to stop it:

> I have never felt more lonely than I do now. . . . I try to go out, I invite friends to dinner, I love to socialize. However, since my traumas, I think I must ooze negativity or neediness, I'm too much and not enough all at once, and no one wants anything to do with me. I feel completely and utterly alone, and I don't know how to heal in isolation or connect with people while still in tremendous pain. . . . The lack of emotional intelligence often leads them to interpret someone very much struggling and traumatized as "obsessed," "just wanting attention," "not trying to get over it"—which only adds to the pain.

One of the central themes of this book is that we can understand exactly how the machinery of suffering works—and still be no better for it. Sometimes, in fact, insight only sharpens the pain: we see how self-defeating our emotions are, and yet we're powerless to interrupt the cycle. That's often the case with loneliness. But it may be even more true of depression, a fitting end to our descent into the depths of misery.

20

Depression

I think calling it sadness is misleading. It is a state of mind that most closely resembles sadness but that is not quite it. There is a hopelessness to it, there is a seemingly endless quantity of it, and I have always felt a strange seething anger associated with it. I say that it is not sadness, because people who are not aware will try to treat it like sadness, by trying to cheer you up or distracting you. But it is like an all-consuming beast with a vehemence to it that destroys anyone and anything trying to tame it. You will say things to loved ones trying to help that you immediately regret and that only pushes you deeper into the pit. Over time, you see them keeping their distance from you, which is what you simultaneously want and don't want.

—Thirty-nine-year-old male from the Misery Survey, who rated his depression a 10 out of 10

The Bottom of the Barrel

This book is not an exhaustive catalog of psychic misery. If I'd tried to write one, I never would have reached the end. There are simply too many varieties of suffering to count, let alone classify: anomie, grief, homesickness, awkwardness, sexual frustration, fear in all its many manifestations—of aging, of dying, of missing out. And then there are the bad feelings we don't have words for. John Koenig, in his sui generis book *The Dictionary of Obscure Sorrows*, coins names for negative states many of us have felt but never quite articulated: *lachesism*, a sudden desire for disaster—the wish for something terrible to happen, just to break the monotony of our lives; or *Altschmerz*, the weariness of facing the same old problems you've been struggling with for years. Paging through his book led me to conclude that there may be nearly as many ways to suffer as there are sufferers.

In this book, I've taken the opposite approach—focusing not on rare breeds but on garden-variety miseries, the kind suffering so many of us share. And I've saved two of the worst for last.

Sadness is the obvious one: the common emotional response to loss, disappointment, or pain. Everyone knows what it feels like to be sad. Psychologists define it as a "low-arousal state," marked by diminished energy, reduced interest in the world, and a tendency to withdraw. Biologically, it's linked to shifts in heart rate and drops in dopamine and serotonin. These changes help explain why sadness feels not just emotional, but physical—heaviness in the limbs, tightness in the chest, a fog behind the eyes, making it feel easier to cry (an act that may itself function as an emotional release valve, signaling distress to others and, ideally, helping the body reset). Unlike fear or anger, which galvanize us for action, sadness slows us down. It's a response that, usually, is *proportionate* to whatever loss or disappointment caused it.

Depression is an entirely different beast. It may resemble sadness from the outside, but it is its own, more elusive creature—less reactive, more engulfing, hard to explain, and harder to endure. Some people pass through life without ever truly encountering it. Others live with it constantly, or suddenly find themselves pulled under by it without warning or reason. Sadness might make you cry at the end of a movie. Depression makes the idea of watching one feel pointless. The difference can be tricky to convey—but those who know, know. And they are not few.

People have always suffered from depression, even if they called it something else: melancholia, neurasthenia, soul-sickness. But the modern term—*depression*—has never quite captured its full weight. William Styron, in his incomparable memoir *Darkness Visible*, objected to the name from the moment he realized he had been "laid low by the disease." He called it "a true wimp of a word for such a major illness."

Styron traced the shift to Adolf Meyer, the Swiss-born psychiatrist and Johns Hopkins professor who helped usher the term into psychiatric use. Meyer, he suggested, may have had "a tin ear for the finer rhythms of English" when he labeled the disease with the same word we use to describe "an economic decline or a rut in the ground." Despite its insufficiency, the term stuck—and for more than a century, the word has, as Styron put it, "slithered innocuously through the language like a slug, leaving little trace of its intrinsic malevolence and preventing, by its very insipidity, a general awareness of the horrible intensity of the disease when out of control."

Does Depression Serve a Function?

The evolutionary origins of many of the psychic miseries discussed in this book may be murky, but those of depression are especially hard to parse. Why would a brain, evolved for survival, generate a state so profoundly debilitating? Why would natural selection preserve a condition that drains motivation, blunts pleasure, disrupts cognition, in some cases erodes the will to live, and in other, more extreme cases, actually leads to self-destruction?

One popular theory is that depression, like other negative emotions, exists to signal that something needs to change. But this framing quickly runs into trouble. If depression is a signal, why is it so often incomprehensible, even to the person experiencing it? If it's meant to catalyze action, why does it so often leave its sufferers immobilized?

A variety of other evolutionary accounts have been proposed, but none strike me as particularly convincing. The *social competition hypothesis* suggests that depression evolved to manage social hierarchies: after a defeat or loss of status, persistent low mood lowers the drive to keep competing, thereby reducing risk. Some evidence from animal research seems to support this theory. British psychiatrist John Price observed that chickens who lost a fight would withdraw and act submissively, reducing the risk of further attacks. Price saw similar behavior in Vervet monkeys, where social defeat triggered striking behavioral and even physiological changes. As Randolph Nesse writes in *Good Reasons for Bad Feelings*: "The alpha male, who gets essentially all the matings, has bright blue testicles. Until, that is, he loses a fight with another male. Then he huddles into a ball, rocks, withdraws, and acts depressed as his testicles turn a dusky gray."

As colorful as this example is, it seems unlikely that evolution would employ such a blunt emotional instrument as depression to maintain social order, when we already have many other specialized aversive signals, like shame and loneliness, to keep us socially in line.

The *analytical rumination hypothesis* posits that depression helps individuals focus cognitive resources on solving complex problems—especially social ones. And while it's true that depression often gives rise to rumination, seldom in my experience—or in the accounts I've collected—does that rumination prove useful. It's not careful analysis; it's repetitive, self-sabotaging thought.

The *attachment* or *signaling hypotheses* propose that depressive behaviors—crying, withdrawal—exist to elicit care from others. But as with chronic loneliness, depression often seems to do the exact opposite: it drives away those people best positioned to help us.

The *energy conservation hypothesis* strikes me as slightly more plausible. In this view, depression is a kind of biological power-down—a way to conserve energy during times of inescapable stress, illness, or scarcity. The only problem with this theory is that no one emerges from a severe depressive episode feeling rested, replenished, or ready to act. It doesn't seem to conserve energy so much as drain it slowly and completely.

The *mismatch hypothesis* may be the most compelling of the evolutionary accounts. It suggests that the emotional wiring behind depression may *once* have been adaptive—helping our ancestors withdraw from danger or recalibrate after failure. But in the modern world, that same circuitry is exposed to stressors it wasn't designed to handle. As one paper put it: "Modern populations are increasingly overfed, malnourished, sedentary, sunlight-deficient, sleep-deprived, and socially-isolated. These changes in lifestyle each contribute to poor physical health and affect the incidence and treatment of depression." It's hard to tally the damage done by these mismatches, but they likely account for a great deal of modern suffering. As Edward St. Aubyn once put it, "People died of feelings all the time, once they had gone through the formality of materializing them into bullets and bottles and tumours."

Like so many evolutionary questions, the issue of whether depression is a feature or a bug of human nature may be ultimately unanswerable. My own view is that depression is "epiphenomenal": it serves no function of its own, but arises as a byproduct of other systems in distress. In that sense, depression is a fitting finale to this Hieronymus Bosch underworld of psychic torments—not just because it is so supremely awful, but because nearly all the other miseries, when they persist and accumulate, can give rise to it.

The Ultimate Empathy Gap

I remember going to an exhibit of the work of the Serbian conceptual and performance artist Marina Abramović, who, in a number of her shows, performed acts of self-mutilation. I got the strong sense from her work that she had powerfully depressive tendencies, and I wondered if the acts of self-harm were an attempt to produce an external manifestation of internal pain—something her audiences could finally *see.*

Andrew Solomon, in his superb memoir of depression, *The Noonday Demon*, writes that "the wish for a more visible illness was, I would later learn, a commonplace among depressives, who often engage in forms of self-mutilation to bring the physical state in line with the mental." One seventy-six-year-old respondent to the Misery Survey echoed this same yearning for visibility in gentler form: "I'd like to see black armbands to signify mourning come back," she said. "We walk around with no outer sign that we're in deep grief." Another respondent, a twenty-six-year-old woman, said that when she was in the grip of a major depression, she even found herself "jealous of coworkers who faced personal tragedies, because then at least they were 'allowed' to mourn or 'justifiably' took time for themselves." Her pain, by contrast, was invisible.

As Styron previously noted, depression presents a problem of language—a failure of communication between inner and outer worlds. Sufferers often turn to analogy in an attempt to bridge the gap. When respondents described their own episodes, what emerged was a rich catalog of metaphor.

Some Misery Survey respondents likened depression to a cunning adversary: "It knows your deepest secrets and your weaknesses and will exaggerate and distort things you thought you knew." Others imagined it as a shadow that stalks: "It follows you and whispers constantly at you." Many reached for metaphors involving weight: "You know the lead apron you wear at the dentist's office for X-rays? It was like that lead apron was draped over my feelings. I felt very numb." Others turned to geography: one was "stuck in a pit underground," another marooned on a "beige desert where nothing could touch me—not sadness, not joy, not curiosity." A third was "lost in the vast ocean, adrift without a direction or a paddle."

These metaphors, vivid as they are, essentially convey to non-sufferers only that depression is very, very bad. What they don't convey is what it actually *feels* like. And there's the rub.

Styron argued that this failure to describe depression is built into the illness itself. His own depressive episode struck in the late 1980s, as he approached the end of a long and distinguished literary career. In *Darkness Visible*, he described how it began almost imperceptibly: a growing sense of dislocation, insomnia, aversion to music and food he once enjoyed. A prestigious award ceremony in Paris—the kind of event that once thrilled him—instead felt like a death knell.

What he was experiencing, which drove him to obsessively consider suicide, was a "sensation close to, but indescribably different from, actual pain":

> This leads me to touch again on the elusive nature of such distress. That the word "indescribable" should present itself is not fortuitous, since it has to be emphasized that if the pain were readily describable most of the countless sufferers from this ancient affliction would have been able to confidently depict for their friends and loved ones (even their physicians) some of the actual dimensions of their torment, and perhaps elicit a comprehension that has been generally lacking; such incomprehension has usually been due not to a failure of sympathy but to the basic inability of healthy people to imagine a form of torment so alien to everyday experience. For myself, the pain is most closely connected to drowning or suffocation—but even these images are off the mark.

This incommunicability—this inability to make others *feel* what one is feeling—isn't unique to depression, but it may be the misery for which the phenomenon is most extreme. As we know from the earlier discussion about empathy gaps, it's practically impossible to share or understand a feeling if you're not currently experiencing it. When we are calm, it's hard to imagine the desperation of rage or grief; when we're no longer in pain, it's hard to remember why it felt unendurable. But of all the miseries explored in this book, depression may be the one most profoundly subject to this gap. It doesn't just separate sufferers from others—it divides them from their own past and future selves.

And the consequences of that gap are not just emotional but existential. Because depression feels permanent, sufferers often come to believe that it *is* permanent. They confuse a temporary state with a final truth. They make judgments—about their lives, their worth, their prospects—that feel rational, but are not. In some cases, as we will see, those misjudgments become life-threatening. The empathy gap doesn't just isolate people in their pain. It blinds them to the possibility that the pain might end. But empathy gaps also work in the opposite direction. Once we are no longer depressed, it's remarkably difficult to remember what it *felt* like, beyond the abstract knowledge that you were depressed, and thus to imagine—and prepare for—its recurrence.

This poses a serious barrier to treatment, especially for people with bipolar disorder, in which depressive episodes alternate with periods of elevated or manic mood. During depressive phases, patients are often diligent with medication. But in manic states, they lose touch with the memory of their former misery and stop taking their prescriptions. As psychiatrist John Mann puts it, "When a person is depressed, they have a problem imagining ever getting better. When they're well, they can't imagine getting sick again." Research by Jan Scott and Marie Pope found that roughly 50 percent of individuals with bipolar disorder discontinue medications like lithium—a pattern consistent with a cold-to-hot empathy gap.

Despite the power of empathy gaps, those who have emerged out of deep depressions can nevertheless appreciate how warped their worldview had become when depressed, as shown by this forty-year-old female respondent's experience:

> [Depression] negatively impacts my perception of everything, even that which is entirely unrelated. Colors in the world seem dull, the innocuous intentions of uninvolved others seem sinister, and I approached each day as something to get through. It became the exclusive topic of conversation with people closest to me, and work tasks seemed banal, pointless. Nothing about my relationships or work life had in fact changed, but it seemed that way. I would have been horrified if I'd made some kind of serious decision through this altered lens.

Depressed people are not entirely themselves. And yet, in such a state, they remain perfectly capable of making irrevocable decisions about their lives.

The Self-Destruct Button

One of the most corrosive aspects of depression is its effect on self-worth. It doesn't just make people feel sad—it convinces them they are irredeemably broken, unloved, and better off dead. Many of the people who responded to the Misery Survey described not just despair, but the conviction that they were fundamentally defective.

"My emotions can cause frequent bouts of feeling like everyone hates me," said one respondent. "When not in that state I can logically view and assess what happens. When in that state my head is hijacked and I am unable to tell myself it's not true or not nearly as bad as I believe it to be." Others described a persistent feeling of worthlessness: "It felt like the universe was screaming at me, '*You are not worth anything!*'" Another wrote: "I believed I was so defective I should not have been born."

One woman recounted how a painful episode of postpartum depression spiraled into suicidal thinking. She had just weaned her one-year-old and was grieving the sudden emotional shift, compounded by the rejection of a close friend—her triathlon coach. When that friendship ended abruptly, it felt to her not like the loss of one person, but like confirmation that the entire world was against her. "The peak of this sadness turned into contemplation of suicide while driving home one day—I thought of how I could crash my car into a median or oncoming 18-wheeler . . ."

Others described a long pattern of suicidal thoughts linked to loneliness, rejection, hormonal shifts, and the grinding weight of daily life. One woman in her early thirties, with undiagnosed depression during grad school in Pittsburgh, recalled the darkness that descended during winters, compounded by job-search anxiety and the loneliness she felt as a foreign student in a new city. Years later, after giving birth, she was diagnosed with premenstrual dysphoric disorder (PMDD):

> I became more depressed toward the end of the day. I would lie in bed and cry, and have terrible thoughts. I thought about what would happen to my family if I were gone and felt like they would be better off without me. This image played over and over in my head.

This is a common depressive fantasy—that the people we love would somehow be better off without us. A nineteen-year-old woman shared similar thoughts in a particularly upsetting response, describing a period of depression when she was just fourteen years old:

> I used to think that even though I had people in my life who loved me they would have other people near them if I was to die—that I could be replaced, and that the replacement was better. I struggled with self-harm to the point that I no longer felt pain; it was just an addiction to see the scars and cuts accumulate until I had no more space for them. Those scars are still with me and are my biggest insecurity. What made me stop cutting myself was when my younger sister asked me what happened to my arms.

In *The Noonday Demon*, Solomon writes about how frequently depressives believe their loved ones would be relieved if they were no longer around. He quotes the psychologist Kay Redfield Jamison, who nearly took her own life during a severe depressive episode: "I knew my life to be a shambles and I believed—incontestably—that my family, friends, and patients would be better off without me."

Not all suicidality is a response to feelings of worthlessness, however. Sometimes it's simply a desperate desire to escape psychic pain. One man, whose sister died by suicide decades earlier, wrote:

> I descended into a full-scale, devastating clinical depression. The pain I felt was more intense than any physical pain I had ever previously experienced . . . I wished I were dead, and even tried once, mercifully unsuccessfully, to take my own life. If you haven't been in this state, you cannot truly appreciate the pain.

Some suicide attempts are driven by calculated despair, or rage, or a sense of being trapped. As we discussed in the chapter on empathy gaps, one of the most striking findings from research on suicide survivors is how few of them ever attempt it again. Recall the study of individuals who were prevented from jumping off the Golden Gate Bridge: 94 percent were still alive or had died of natural causes decades later. That kind of data points to a crucial insight: the beliefs that lead someone to attempt suicide—the certainty that things will never get better, that they are unlovable, irredeemable, or that their pain is permanent—often dissolve with time.

This is not a self-help book, but if it finds readers, I anticipate that a high fraction may be individuals suffering from psychic misery. If you are, and are contemplating suicide, please reconsider, if only for the sake of others. My own observation, based on experiences in my extended family, is that committing suicide is like dropping a neutron bomb in the center of one's family—you are by no means killing only yourself.

From Bad to Worse

Thankfully, even serious cases of clinical depression only very rarely end in suicide. But it is troubling to see just how widespread thoughts of suicide are. In large US surveys of the general population, about one in ten adults report ever having seriously considered suicide, and roughly one in twenty report ever having attempted it. When depression does lead to suicidal thinking or action, it's often because the illness is self-reinforcing—building on itself, deepening over time, and becoming harder to escape the longer it lasts.

One common trajectory goes something like this: A major loss or disaster triggers abject misery; severe depression follows. Things may improve—circumstances shift, time passes—but the trauma doesn't vanish. When depression returns, it feels less justified, more internalized. It's no longer just a response to external tragedy; it starts to seem like something wrong with *you*.

Consider one female respondent whose depression was initially catalyzed by the unexpected death of her father, an opioid addict who had recently gotten clean. At just twenty-three, she found herself planning the funeral, holding her mother together, supporting her sister through addiction, and commuting hours by bus from her shared basement apartment to a dead-end job. The grief was enormous—but in some ways, the aftermath has been more bewildering:

> It has been over eight years since then, and sometimes my depression creeps back in, despite my sister being clean, my mom being okay, and me being married, a homeowner, with a steady job. On paper, life is immensely better. But the sadness persists . . . [T]hinking about starting a family of my own has caused a lot of pre-natal sadness. Will I hurt this potential child the way I was hurt? Do I deserve to be a mom? Do I deserve to even be?

This is a textbook case of what psychologists call the *kindling hypothesis*—the idea that once someone has experienced a major depressive episode, their threshold for future episodes lowers. As Solomon writes, "The more episodes you have, the more likely you are to have more episodes, and in general the episodes, over a lifetime, get worse and closer together." Over time, the original cause becomes less relevant. By the fourth or fifth episode, depression often seems to come out of nowhere.

One man described the long tail of his grief after his parent died of a brain aneurysm at a young age. Though therapy helped at first, his depression has become unpredictable and untethered from any specific trigger:

> A movie where the mother dies was tolerable, but sunlight dancing on a floating dandelion tuft could reduce me to a fetal position. Grief is mercurial, respecting neither timeline nor temper. Twenty-five years later, the only thing better is I can hold off a collapse long enough to get back home.

The same pattern recurs across lifetimes. One man, now in his sixties, described episodic depression that has haunted him since adolescence—sometimes triggered by fresh wounds, sometimes by the ghost of long-ago traumas:

> I don't know what triggers it. But when I think I know, it's often a situation where my self-esteem is attacked—by someone else's words, or just by memory. I was institutionalized at fourteen for suicidal thoughts. Sometimes I still think I would have been better off if I had gone through with it then—so I could have avoided sixty years of intermittent pain.

Depression is also self-reinforcing in ways that echo the pattern of almost every other form of psychic misery we've discussed so far. Some of these feedback loops affect how we think, others how we behave.

Take *mood-congruent memory*: when people feel low, they're more likely to recall memories that match their mood—blunders, failures, regrets, moments of guilt or shame. These recollections, in turn, deepen the depression, which only further amplifies the selective retrieval of negative material. A related process, *mood-congruent judgment*, means that we also interpret ambiguous events in a mood-biased way—assuming the worst, reading rejection from silence, seeing cruelty when it may have just been carelessness.

And, as in the case of loneliness, feedback effects don't just stay inside the head. They also shape how people behave—and how the world responds.

Depressed people can be withdrawn, passive, and irritable. And while most are painfully aware of how exhausting they can be, that doesn't make them easier to be around. The result is another vicious cycle: depression warps behavior in ways that elicit rejection, deepening the depression.

The psychologist James Coyne has analyzed exactly how this process works. Depressed individuals tend to evoke discomfort in others: their suffering is hard to witness and even harder to fix. Friends and partners may feel guilty or burdened, but they can't express their frustration without seeming cruel. So they offer scripted reassurances or polite support—gestures aimed more at soothing or managing than truly connecting. But these responses are often half-hearted or out of sync with what the depressed person needs. Over time, the mismatch becomes palpable. Sensing insincerity or detachment, the depressed person may escalate their distress, hoping to draw out genuine care or at least prevent abandonment. This only increases the discomfort of those around them, who retreat further.

This bleak interpersonal spiral was captured with extraordinary precision by Javier Marías in his novel *The Infatuations*. "When one suffers a misfortune," he writes,

> the effects on the victim far outlast the patience of those prepared to listen and accompany her; unconditional support never lasts very long once it has become tinged with monotony. And so, sooner or later, the grieving person is left alone when she has still not finished grieving or when she's no longer allowed to talk about what remains her only world, because other people find that world of grief unbearable, repellent. She understands that for them sadness has a social expiry date, that no one is capable of contemplating another's sorrow, that such a spectacle is tolerable only for a brief period, for as long as the shock and pain last and there is still some role for those who are there watching, who then feel necessary, salutary, useful. But on discovering that nothing changes and that the affected person neither progresses nor emerges from her grief, they feel humiliated or superfluous, they find it almost offensive and stand aside: "Aren't I enough for you? Why can't you climb out of that pit with me by your

side? Why are you still grieving when time has passed and I've been here all the while to console and distract you? If you can't climb out, then sink or disappear." And the grieving person does just that, she retreats, removes herself, hides.

Why We Spiral

By now, it should be clear that all kinds of misery feed on themselves. When we feel bad we often do things (or think thoughts) that only make us feel worse.

In high-stakes performances, we try our best—but the very effort to succeed makes us acutely aware of the possibility of failure. That awareness triggers physical symptoms: dry mouth, tunnel vision, a quavering voice. These symptoms in turn disrupt our performance, which deepens our fear, which worsens our symptoms, which sabotages us further. A bad mood cues up a mental highlight reel of regrets, blunders, and humiliations, deepening and darkening the mood. Jealousy makes us paranoid and accusatory—and in trying to cling tighter to a partner, we often push them away. Shame isolates us from others by convincing us to hide the very parts of ourselves most in need of acceptance. And once we do, we assume others don't share them—which only intensifies our shame. Loneliness distorts our perceptions of others' intentions, making us withdrawn, suspicious, or needy—precisely the behaviors most likely to alienate others and confirm our worst fears.

Why would evolution design emotions to behave this way? What adaptive purpose could there possibly be in a system that amplifies distress and pushes us further from the very things we seem to need? Earlier in this book, I promised to explain why feedback loops exist. The answer to that question begins with the man who gave the word *feedback* its modern meaning.

•••

Many of the miseries discussed in this book are intensified by *feedback effects*: self-reinforcing patterns in which people respond to a bad feeling in ways that only deepen or prolong it.

Source of Misery	Feedback Effects
Low self-esteem	Low self-esteem → selective recall of ego-wounding experiences → reinforces negative current self-view → other people respond in ways that further confirm that self-view
Choking under pressure	High-stakes situation → physiological stress reactions (dry mouth, tunnel vision, shakiness) → worsened performance → heightened awareness of pressure → further performance decline
Anger	Anger → heightened perception of unfairness or injustice in others' actions → more anger and reduced ability to de-escalate
Jealousy	Jealousy → increased clinginess or controlling behavior → partner pulls away → fear of abandonment is confirmed
Rejection (sensitivity)	Perceived rejection (even if ambiguous) → heightened rejection sensitivity → preemptive withdrawal or rejection of others → increased likelihood of actual rejection
Shame	Feeling ashamed → hiding traits or experiences we fear others will judge → assuming these traits are rare → intensified sense of isolation
Loneliness	Feeling lonely → behaving in ways that seem less warm or appealing → others avoid or disengage → deeper loneliness and isolation
Depression	Depressed mood → negative memory recall and interpretation → withdrawal from others → others avoid or disengage → further depressed mood

Norbert Wiener was one of the most visionary scientists of the twentieth century. A math prodigy and the son of a domineering Harvard professor, he entered Tufts at age eleven, earned his PhD from Harvard at age eighteen, and spent most of his career at MIT, where he became the archetypal absentminded professor: muttering to himself, trailing cigar ash through the halls, interrupting meetings to deliver insights that ranged from brilliant to baffling.

During World War II, Wiener was recruited by the National Defense Research Committee to work on a pressing engineering problem: how to direct antiaircraft fire to intercept fast-moving enemy planes. The problem was one of prediction. By the time a shell reached the coordinates of a moving aircraft, the aircraft would already be gone. So the gun needed to anticipate where the plane *would* be, and adjust accordingly in real time. That required a new kind of system, one that could monitor its own errors and use them to improve its performance—a loop that would feed back on itself, again and again.

Wiener quickly saw that this principle had broad, even universal applications, and that the same self-correcting logic existed throughout natural systems. Feedback, he argued, was a foundational property of life—present in the nervous system, in homeostasis, in adaptation. He laid out this sweeping vision in his 1948 book *Cybernetics: Or Control and Communication in the Animal and the Machine*. The book not only gave us the modern definition of *feedback*, but also the now-omnipresent prefix *cyber-*, which has since attached itself to everything—from crime to war to sex.

Wiener distinguished between two types of feedback: negative and positive. In everyday language, positive feedback means praise, and negative feedback means criticism. But in cybernetics, the meanings flip—somewhat.

Negative feedback is stabilizing. It self-corrects. The classic example is a thermostat: when the room gets too hot, the heat shuts off. In biology, negative feedback governs everything from hormone release to blood sugar regulation to, as we will see shortly, the regulation of our emotions—when they are working properly. In all these cases, the system uses feedback to return to equilibrium. When the heat rises to a set point, or when glucose climbs too high, the response tapers off.

Positive feedback, by contrast, is destabilizing. It pushes a system further and further in the direction it's already going. In rare cases, this is useful—as in childbirth, where uterine contractions trigger the release of oxytocin, which causes more contractions, speeding labor along. But left unchecked, positive feedback leads to what Wiener called "catastrophic" runaway effects—spirals that the system can't stop on its own.

One of Wiener's favorite examples came from winter driving. Picture a car on an icy road. The driver taps the accelerator—just slightly—but instead of inching forward, the tires begin to spin. The car lurches, loses traction, starts to skid. A tiny input (the tap on the gas) is amplified by the system: the loss of friction increases the car's motion, which further reduces control, which further increases the skid. Meanwhile, the usual source of stabilizing feedback—the brakes—is useless. There's nothing to push the system back toward equilibrium. The result is a runaway loop: each attempt to correct only worsens the instability.

In one of the most radical sections of *Cybernetics*, Wiener argued that many so-called functional mental disorders—those not linked to lesions or other physical injuries—were better understood as failures of internal feedback. He described how panic attacks, compulsions, or "malignant worry" could begin with a trivial concern but build into something overwhelming—a self-reinforcing mental loop "totally destructive to the ordinary mental life."

Sadly, Wiener knew the devastating effects of this process firsthand.

He suffered from what would now probably be diagnosed as bipolar disorder. He was often overwhelmed by mood swings and paralyzing despair. According to his daughter Barbara Wiener Raisbeck, during his worst episodes—or "tailspins," as she called them—he would stand in the front hall of their home "shouting and crying," while she tried to pull him back "onto solid ground before he went over the cliff." He regularly threatened to commit suicide. "He would be tearing his hair. Then he would pack his suitcase and say he was going to a hotel and had packed a gun and was going to shoot himself because he was 'no good to anybody.'"

Eventually, she learned that what helped him the most was reminding him that he'd survived such episodes before. "I think he wanted to be told," she said, that "he was not going to just keep on spiraling until he hit the ground."

•••

All throughout this book, I've described feedback effects as anomalies—a kind of structural flaw that shows up now and again in anxiety, or depression, or jealousy, or choking under pressure. But the truth is even more unsettling. Our entire emotional system runs on feedback. When the brain detects a problem—a threat, a violation, a loss—it sends up an emotional signal, which pushes us to act. In a well-functioning system, that signal is self-limiting. Fear heightens vigilance; once the threat passes, the signal shuts off. Sadness slows us down and focuses our attention inward; when we've adapted to the loss, the mood lifts. These are classic negative feedback loops. They might not be pleasant to experience, but they return us to some kind of emotional equilibrium.

But because the feedback system that governs emotions has to be extremely sensitive to new information to work properly, and because the line between negative and positive feedback is a razor's edge, the system is prone, almost by design, to malfunction. Once the balance tips from negative to positive, amplification begins and then we are susceptible to the runaway effects Wiener described.

Why does this happen? Sometimes it's mismatch: our brains evolved for sudden, physical threats but now respond to slow-burning psychological ones. Sometimes it's conditioning: trauma or chronic stress wires the system to stay on high alert, even when the danger is gone. And sometimes the spiral begins not with the emotion itself, but with how we interpret—or misinterpret—it. The result is that a tailspin will inevitably occur right at the moment when the system most needs to stabilize. We slam on the brakes, but the car spins out on the icy road. That, to me, is the essence of what makes misery so miserable.

EPILOGUE

Misery Loves Company

I'm happy only because I don't exist.

—Martin Crimp, *Picture a Day Like This*

Danny

It's a strange thing to have a falling-out with someone you admire. Stranger still when that person is Daniel Kahneman—Nobel laureate, fellow (and far better-known) founder of behavioral economics, and for a time, my friend and intellectual ally. We never yelled at each other or exchanged harsh words. But we did diverge.

It started with an intellectual dispute about a phenomenon that he dubbed "duration neglect." When we judge the quality of extended experiences—vacations, relationships, even colonoscopies in one famous study—we base our overall judgments on two things: the most extreme part of the experience, and its end. According to this "peak-end rule," we ignore pretty much everything else, including, critically, the duration of the experience—how long it lasts. I disagreed with his argument and didn't buy any of the evidence he adduced to support it, and I coauthored an academic article in which I enumerated my misgivings and presented experimental results that provided an alternative, much less interesting, account of his empirical evidence.

To say that Danny was upset by our critique would be an understatement.

He called me repeatedly at home, alternating between begging and ordering me to withdraw the paper before it got published. When my wife was the one to answer the phone (this was in the days before cell phones), she would screw up her face and hand me the receiver with two fingers as if handing off a toxic specimen. The low point of the dispute was when he accused me of having an oedipal complex—a desire to bring down the father (himself in the metaphor). I couldn't entirely reject the charge. I sometimes wish I could look up to figures of authority and prestige. But I have a tendency to kick up and kiss down, the reverse of the classic pattern.

The peak of the extended miserable episode with Danny, which was also its end, was when we agreed to write a joint commentary hashing out our differences and points of agreement. Years later, I was invited to a party celebrating him. I called Danny and asked him if he really wanted me to come, given our disagreements. "Of course," he said. He told me that he felt our differences had been resolved by the joint commentary. What was left unsaid was that we had a tremendous amount of personal contact prior to the dispute and virtually none after it.

I think most people in the field were ignorant of this falling-out until 2008, when it became abundantly clear to everyone in the room. The setting was a conference at the National Bureau of Economic Research (NBER) in Boston. I had been invited to respond to a paper Kahneman had coauthored on National Time Accounting—a system for tracking happiness and quality of life based on how people spend their time and how they feel while doing it. The paper opened with a well-known quote from Robert F. Kennedy, lamenting how economic statistics fail to measure what really matters in life:

> The gross national product does not allow for the health of our children, the quality of their education or the joy of their play. It does not include the beauty of our poetry or the strength of our marriages, the intelligence of our public debate or the integrity of our public officials. It measures neither our wit nor our courage, neither our wisdom nor our learning, neither our compassion nor our devotion to our country. It measures everything, in short, except that which makes life worthwhile.

If GDP misses what matters, they reasoned, why not build a complementary account—one that captures how people actually feel as they move through their days? Not to replace traditional metrics, but to rebalance them. To give policymakers a way to see not just how people are doing economically, but how they're faring emotionally.

This wasn't just academic for Danny. He first started seriously thinking about questions related to happiness and quality of life several years earlier—when we were still friends, so I observed it firsthand. At the time, his mother, who lived far away from him in France, was declining mentally. He agonized about whether and how often to visit her. She had anterograde amnesia, so she would forget his visits almost as soon as they ended. If she wouldn't remember, what would be the point? Then he realized: she would enjoy being with him *in the moment*. Her happiness would be real, even if short-lived. I believe that this was the origin of his view—that he held for many decades and wrote countless papers espousing—that the accrual of such fleeting experiences over a lifetime (what he called "experienced utility") was the truest measure of a person's well-being.

He had a point. But the trouble with using our moment-to-moment happiness to judge whether a person is living a good or bad life is that such feelings are, as I discussed in Chapter 7, highly subject to the forces of adaptation. People adjust to their circumstances, whether they live in extreme deprivation or great luxury. Adam Smith observed this two and a half centuries ago: "In ease of body and peace of mind, all the different ranks of life are nearly upon a level, and the beggar, who suns himself by the side of the highway, possesses that security which kings are fighting for." If measured happiness levels differ only slightly between the privileged and the deprived, it becomes tempting to conclude—wrongly—that deprivation doesn't matter much. In the wrong hands, this way of thinking could serve as a moral alibi for grotesque inequality.

Over time, Danny recognized the limits of his view. He realized that people care about more than just their happiness levels—they care about what they've accomplished, how they're progressing toward their goals, and whether their lives make sense to them. So he adjusted his approach.

"We should give up on the idea of increasing happiness," he said in an interview. "Instead, we should try to reduce suffering." The study I was responding to in Boston—the National Time Accounting project—reflected that new turn in Danny's thinking. It used a new measure, the U-index, to capture the share of the day people spent in negative states like stress, sadness, or frustration. Essentially, it was a misery meter. The hope was to equip policymakers with better data—data that might help them design programs to reduce psychic pain. Danny and I had been arguing about these questions for more than a decade. My own perspective may have had nothing to do with his change of heart, but I still felt, in a smug sort of way, that he'd come around to join me on Team Misery.

Still, I had reservations—and I said so in my talk. To me, the framework didn't account for why we *willingly* suffer in pursuit of things that score high on the U-index: why we raise children, care for dying parents, climb mountains, or endure humiliations in pursuit of greater goals. One example I offered was my father, who spent part of World War II in a French prisoner of war camp, hungry enough to dig up worms for food and chew on shoe leather. It was, by any measure, a miserable time. But he once told me that being in the camp was the peak experience of his life, the crucible out of which he made meaning for the rest of his days. (The Yale psychologist Paul Bloom, incidentally, has a masterful book, *The Sweet Spot*, about the link between suffering and meaning, where he shows why people so often seek out painful or arduous challenges despite the misery involved—or, as in my father's case, find value in enduring unchosen horrors.)

The model couldn't capture any of that. It seemed to confuse bad feelings with bad lives.

When I shared this critique in Boston, Danny was seated three people down from me, on the left. As I spoke, he began to shake his head. Slowly at first, then more vigorously. He scowled. He grimaced. He could not contain his displeasure.

I paused.

"Danny," I said, "if you keep shaking your head and scowling, it makes it impossible for me to present."

"Am I doing that?" he asked, sounding genuinely surprised. "I'll stop."

He did—for about three seconds. Then he started again. So I did the only thing I could think to do: I raised my hand and held it in front of the left side of my face. I delivered the rest of my talk that way, my hand suspended in the air, blocking my view of Kahneman's animated reactions, as nervous laughter filled the room.

To his credit, Danny let me have my say—and published my response immediately following his paper in the final volume. But that afternoon at NBER felt like the final act in a long-running disagreement between us. Also seated at the table was one of Danny's coauthors, the economist Alan Krueger, whose story you might remember from the introduction. As we sat around debating how best to measure suffering, it's poignant to think about how blind we were to *his* misery—which, a few years later, would lead Alan to take his own life.

Matthew

I've met many depressive characters in my life, but one of the most reliably miserable people I've ever known is my friend and collaborator Matthew Rabin. I've stopped asking him how he's doing, since I know the answer is either some variation of "not good" or, more frequently, simply dead silence. John Stuart Mill famously said it's better to be "a human dissatisfied than a pig satisfied," but Matthew begs to differ. He would gladly be a pig, if only it could offer him some relief from the profound depression he regularly sinks into.

What *does* help him cope, I think—even if he wouldn't admit it—is that he isn't ashamed of his feelings. He often shares his misery with others, along with many other interesting thoughts. The two of us have actually studied how people share information, and in the course of that research, Matthew made what I later realized was a quietly profound observation.

He noted how much of what we say to others is information they already know: *Isn't the moon beautiful? Wasn't that a sad movie?*

There's a sizable psychological literature documenting the emotional benefits of exactly this kind of sharing—not because the content is new, but because the experience is mutual. If comparing notes in this way feels good when the emotional stakes are low, the rewards are even greater when we discover that someone else knows what it's like to be racked by self-doubt, or tortured by regret, or consumed by guilt. Why does having these bad things in common feel so good—or, at the very least, so cathartic?

Think of any bad experience. Say you're hungry, take a chance on a new restaurant, and get served a plate of disgusting food. If you're alone, it's miserable. If you're with someone, it becomes something you both endured—a small trauma to laugh about later, or even at the time. I'm often struck, when I go to a party with a good friend, by how much of the social awkwardness and tedium is redeemed by the anticipation, and then the pleasurable reality, of the "post-mortem"—the ritual debrief that recycles an otherwise negative experience into fodder for a funny conversation.

Of course we all know—intellectually—that we're not alone in our misery, that most people at one time or another suffer from depression, jealousy, self-doubt, and the many other afflictions catalogued in this book. But when we hear or read someone else's account of misery, and recognize ourselves in it, the effect is different from mere knowledge. Earlier in the book, I talk about empathy gaps—and how, because of them, it's basically impossible to connect to a feeling that you're not currently experiencing. But when we read or hear about someone else's experience and recognize ourselves in it, we briefly enter the same emotional state. That spark of recognition makes us feel less alone in our misery, and very often, less miserable.

And yet, while we recognize the value of this kind of recognition, we rarely offer it to others. When it comes to the stuff that actually tortures us, that keeps us up at night, that makes us feel small, pathetic, and quietly repellent, we stay silent. Nobody says, "Isn't it terrible how deflated you feel when someone else's child is better at something than yours?" Or: "Isn't it strange how waving at someone who looked right past you can ruin your entire afternoon?"

These private agonies are considered too petty, too self-incriminating—and so we bury them. And because everyone else buries them, too, we don't hear about them, and we begin to believe that no one else has them. Which is, empirically, false.

In a study I conducted with Erin Carbone, Cass Sunstein, and Linda Dezső, we asked participants to report on a range of health- and non-health-related conditions and behaviors—things like incontinence, sexual performance issues, binge-eating, and searching for information about ex-partners on the internet—that, we had determined through pretests, were likely to evoke shame. They reported whether they themselves had the conditions or engaged in the behavior, and then estimated what fraction of respondents to the survey would report the same. What we found was striking: the more ashamed someone felt about a particular experience, the less likely they were to think it was shared with others—and the less likely they were to talk about it. In other words, the more intensely someone suffered, the more convinced they became that they were suffering alone—which only made them more likely to remain silent. We titled our paper "Spirals of Shame."

Daniel, and Me

You may remember the friendship paradox—the statistical quirk that says your friends, on average, are likely to have more friends than you do. I have a rather vivid example of this phenomenon in my friend Daniel, one of the best loved and most socially connected people I know. If you asked me to name the single most popular person in my life, it would be him without hesitation. Daniel took the Misery Survey and told me afterward that he suffered from two afflictions in particular—one of which shocked me: loneliness. This showed me, once again, that feeling lonely has very little to do with being alone.

What struck me even more than Daniel's answer was his reaction to the survey itself. He said it made him feel *good*. Not because he had unburdened himself of some deep sorrow, but because, as he put it, "There were so many I don't have."

One of the unexpected gifts of compiling (and, I hope, reading) this compendium of sorrows is realizing that you don't suffer from all of them. At least not yet. And that, too, is a reason to share our miseries. If we don't feel seen, as discussed above, then we might at least feel spared. That's how I've often felt while reading the responses to the Misery Survey—a kind of mute gratitude: there but for the grace of God (or chance, or dumb luck) go I.

The truth is, we don't all suffer equally, or in the same ways. Misery is personal—painfully so. But the predisposition to it, the patterns of thought and feeling that give rise to it, are widely shared. Most of us fall for the same illusions: that others are doing better than they probably are; that our unhappiness reflects some private failing; and that happiness is a standard we are supposed to meet. At the heart of so many of our miseries is not the fact that we feel bad, but the belief that we should feel otherwise. I've tried to point out the mistake, though I don't pretend it can be fixed. The confusion is part of the wiring. The best we can do is notice it—and remind ourselves, with whatever dark humor we can muster, that we're not the only ones.

Acknowledgments

Completing this book finally gives me the long-overdue opportunity to acknowledge the many people who helped to make it a reality. Jules Lobel and Scott Morgenstern read the whole manuscript and, individually and together (on jogs), talked with me extensively about it. Their combined comments on an early draft improved the book in fundamental ways.

Sincerest appreciation to each and every friend who provided comments on the book and who, in a few cases, provided their own stories about misery: Chiara Aina, Jennifer Blumental-Barby, Ohad Dan, Simon Dedeo, Ava DeMarco, Linda Hassani, Kasia Jasko, Cait Lamberton, Graham Loomes, Andrea Mannberg, Desa Markovic, Sarah Maza, Daniel Mosse, Aidan Pillard, Danica Prelec, Drazen Prelec, Daniel Read, Rocky Schoen, Nicole Steiner, Joachim Vosgerau, Piotr Winkielman, and Homa Zarghamee.

And, special thanks to Matthew Horwitz, to whom the book is dedicated. Mary Shelley wrote in *Frankenstein* that "the companions of our childhood always possess a certain power over our minds which hardly any later friend can obtain." It is a truth that Matthew has confirmed over our sixty-year friendship.

Thank you also to my graduate students, past and present. Working with you, learning from you, and learning about you has been a huge part of the fun of being an academic over the years. You have collectively and individually influenced this book in untold ways. In the chapter on intrusive thoughts, I mentioned my trepidation in the lead-up to a seventieth birthday celebration in summer 2025, when many cherished students joined me in Bellingham, Washington. Though, as I describe in the book, the lead-up had elements of misery, the event itself was one of the most meaningful experiences of my life.

Thanks also to my many research collaborators over the years. If you don't see our joint research discussed in these pages, please stay tuned for the next book!

I'd also like to express my gratitude to my colleagues in the Department of Social and Decision Sciences at Carnegie Mellon University. When I arrive at work each morning, I feel surrounded by a cocoon of intelligence, creativity, and most importantly, goodwill. Wanting to go to work, and being happy when one gets there, has to be one of the best possible gifts one can have in life.

A special thanks to the more than five hundred individuals who completed the Misery Survey. Reading through your responses filled me with a mixture of emotions: gratitude for your willingness to contribute out of the goodness of your heart; admiration for your readiness to open your lives up to me; awe of your insight and eloquence in telling your personal stories. And then there is sympathy. Some of the miseries you have endured are almost unbearably painful to read and that can only be a pale reflection of what it is to suffer them firsthand. Many of these heartrending stories are interlaced in the pages of the book. If you come across your own, I hope it will give you some positive feeling to know that other people will gain from learning about your experiences. If your words didn't make it into the book verbatim, you can be sure that they influenced my thinking and writing. Those of you who permitted me to thank you by name are listed below.*

* **Respondents to the Misery Survey who wished to be publicly recognized:** Tracy Campbell Accardi, Joan Adams, Charles Allen, Gus Andrade, Jake Arpaia, Brian K. Bailey, Sachin Batra, Allan Baumgartner, Cory Bevilacqua, Judith Block, Rob Bogan, Kerry Bowser, John E. Brennan, Lovisa LjungQvist Brinson, Derek Brothers, Arun Buck, Shannon Bumgarner, Mary Pat Campbell, Maura Capps, Andrea Cavalier, Aman Chogle, Susan Claus, Wendy Cohen, Hannah Collier, Jim Cooper, Meredith Crenshaw, Sharon Curcio, Santwana Dasgupta, Aldair De La Rosa, Frank DiCesare, Ben Donnelly, Timothy Durning, Keith Eich, Eric Ewanco, Chris Forland, Charles Frank, Tyreese M. Gayem, Rob Gerritsen, Christine Gervais, Jennifer Getsinger, Anne Goldhammer, Peter Granato, Elijah Gurevich, Isabella Guyott, Val Haskin, Steven Angel Heraz, Hiroshi Higuchi, Emily Horstman, Peter Hunhoff, Jeff Jacobs, Paul Jeffrey, Kyle Jennison, Andrew Jimenez, Anna Johnson, Ken Johnson, Felix Kehr, Patrick Kelly, Chelly Klann, Randall Klarin, Erica Klein,

Speaking of the survey, sincere thanks to Erin Carbone, my amazing colleague, frequent collaborator, and dear friend, who set up the survey for me. Thanks to Christina Sotirescu for organizing the responses to make it easier for me to go through them. And thanks to Emily Cocea, who took my course on public policy as an undergraduate, and as an influencer, taught me almost everything I know about social media. When I wanted to expand the population of young people in the survey, I knew exactly who to ask for help. After making the request to Emily, the number of responses mushroomed.

Hollis Heimbouch, my editor at HarperCollins, saw the merits of a proposal that could easily have been dismissed: Who, several friends asked, would want to read a book about misery? A huge part of my decision to publish with HarperCollins rested on the rapport I felt when we first talked, a judgment that was vindicated in subsequent interactions. Thank you especially, Hollis, for not putting any pressure on me to turn the project into a self-help book, or to end chapters or the book as a whole on an optimistic high note.

Thanks also to my agents for the project, Peter and Amy Bernstein, for negotiating the contract for the book.

Tom Klopack, Ernestine Kuhr, Mary Kunzmann, Beth Laffey, Fred Langan, Mary LaPlante, Steven Lapp, Brandy Larson, Rob Laymon, Johanna Ledesma, Edward Levine, Alanna Libbrecht, Zara Lindquist, Steve Lucente, Amanda Marano, Laura Martinez, Owen Feryl Masters, Chad O. McMahill, Elizabeth McNutt, Dixie Meeks, Alexander Meseguer, David Mills, Claire Mitchell, Thomas Moore, Peggy Morrissette, Susannah Mowris, Lorraine Murray, Colton Nelson, William Newton, Linda Nielsen, Maggie O'Toole, Gregory Patterson, Nathanael Pena, Luke Peterson, Jim Pinsky, Ann Plicque, Vicki Porter, Bryan Price, Carson Price, Kathleen Rai, Neeharika Rao, Trinidad Regaspi, Lisa Reinhart, Jamie Richards, Lenore Riegel, Jim Roberts, Kate Roberts, Josh Rodriguez, Fernando Rossi, Steve Rubinstein, John Russell, Joe Sabo, Jesper Sahlin, Olga Salodini, Stuart Schupack, Kim Sikes, Edwin Soledad, Vikki Stefans, Cristen Stephansky, Mark Steppel, Eric Strauss, Henry Strobel, Meghan Sweeney, Mark Tabish, Lisa Thimas, Aiden Tkac, Cindy Tonkin, Elisabetta Torossi, Jim Tragakis, Ryan Tupper, Joseph Tyler, Sheila Tyler, Nora Vencill, Gerry Wasserman, Trey Webb, Lily Whitford-Philippou, Jeremiah Will, Bella Williams, Tara Williams, Timothy Williams, Katie Wilson, Sawyer Wilson, and Dennis Woo.

I've deliberately delayed thanking the individual who provided by far the greatest input on the book: Stephen Heyman. Steve didn't ghostwrite the book, but calling him an "editor" doesn't do justice to his contributions. Steve and I started working together on the book in June 2023, and we quickly found our stride. I would write a first draft of each chapter, then he would transform it from stilted academic-speak into what I hope you will agree is elegant prose.

I'll end with a few words of thanks for my family.

First, my mother, Sophie, who died four years ago. So much in life comes back to our mothers. She had a difficult childhood, which shaped her life in ways good and less good. My sisters, Andrea and Dania, both read drafts of the book, and I am grateful for their suggestions and support. I'd also like to acknowledge Caroline, my wonderful nearest-in-age cousin. Caroline's father, Walter, was Sophie's brother and shared her difficult childhood. During World War II, Sophie and Walter were cruelly separated, a trauma that rippled through the family for generations. Andrea, Dania, and I often lament that some of Sophie's outsized character rubbed off on us, again for better and for worse. But, if any of my observations about misery are insightful, I have my mother to thank. A psychologist / social worker, she posed psychological riddles to me almost as soon as I could talk. She was happy that I became an academic and always wanted me to author a book (as she herself did). When, as an adult, I would visit her at her house in a suburb of Boston, I would know that at some point during the visit she would drop *the book question*. I'm not one for the afterlife but—who knows?—perhaps she's out there somewhere pondering the psychological riddle of why my first book appeared only after she died.

Second, my children and grandchildren: my daughter, Rosa; my son, Max; my daughter-in-law, Susanna; and their two little darlings, Zoey and Georgia. They provide the love, the unexpected, the fun, the chaos, and the profound human connection that make life worthwhile.

Third, my wife, Donna. She read the book cover to cover and provided some of the most helpful—and blunt—comments. As she has through all of my downs and ups during our forty-five years together, Donna provided the warmth and encouragement that made this project possible. In the book I talk about envy, and about how we aren't always as joyful about our friends' accomplishments as we think we should be. There is incredible value, therefore, in having someone who you know will take complete pleasure in your accomplishments—such as writing a book!

Finally, a word about Donna's father, Henry Harsch, one of the sweetest, most supportive individuals on earth, who was always there for his children, not to mention anyone he crossed paths with. At some point I mentioned to him an article I wrote about mountaineering, and a quote from the climber David Roberts: "Nobody on his death bed ever said, 'I wish I had spent more time at the office.'" I said it to him late in his life, meaning to make him feel good about the things he had prioritized in his life. I was surprised when he responded: "I have one great regret in life: that I didn't write a book." Henry, this is for you, too.

About the Misery Survey

Readers can take the Misery Survey themselves—and sign up to contribute to future research—by visiting oppositeofhappiness.com.

The Misery Survey was an open-ended, qualitative study of the experiences people find most psychologically painful. More than five hundred participants, recruited through academic and public channels in late 2024 and early 2025, were invited to describe in their own words a time when they felt truly miserable. The survey was designed to encourage introspection and narrative detail. Respondents wrote freely about feelings such as shame, rejection, anger, regret, loneliness, and anxiety, often blending personal stories with more general reflections on different kinds of suffering.

The survey was unpaid and anonymous, partly relying on volunteers who had previously expressed interest in participating in my research. Each participant was randomly assigned one of the twelve negative emotions examined in Part 2 of the book, and then asked whether they suffered from that kind of misery in particular. If they said no, another emotion was presented, again at random, until they either found one that resonated or exhausted the list (which almost never happened). Those who identified with an emotion were asked to tell a story about it, rate how bad it was on a zero-to-ten scale, and share any insights they had. Basic demographic information was also collected.

Respondents ranged in age from 18 to 88, with a roughly even split between younger (18–44) and older (45–88) respondents. About 58 percent identified as male (323), 42 percent as female (238), and a small number identified as nonbinary or preferred not to say. Most were married or in domestic partnerships, though a sizable minority were single or divorced.

Notes

INTRODUCTION

xvi **women unburden themselves to others:** Erin Carbone, George Loewenstein, Irene Scopelliti, and Joachim Vosgerau, "He Said, She Said: Gender Differences in the Disclosure of Positive and Negative Information," *Journal of Experimental Social Psychology* 110 (2024): 104525, https://doi.org/10.1016/j.jesp.2023.104525.

xvii **ranks second only to public speaking:** Steven Soifer and Richard Ziprin, "Paruresis or Shy Bladder Syndrome: The Little Known Social Phobia," *The Behavior Therapist* 23, no. 10 (2000): 217–218.

xvii ***No one must ever know*:** Adam Green, "How Derren Brown Remade Mind Reading for Skeptics," *New Yorker*, September 30, 2019, https://www.newyorker.com/magazine/2019/10/07/how-derren-brown-remade-mind-reading-for-skeptics.

xviii **"are mere trinkets of frivolous utility":** Adam Smith, *The Theory of Moral Sentiments* (London and Edinburgh, 1759; reprint, Prometheus Books, 2000), 260–261.

xix **"It is this deception which rouses":** Smith, *The Theory of Moral Sentiments*, 264.

CHAPTER 1 Because Misery Is the Price of Survival

3 **"Life for the emotional is":** Alain de Botton, *On Love* (Grove Press, 1993), 151.

5 **costs of pregnancy and child-rearing:** David M. Buss, "Sex Differences in Human Mate Preferences: Evolutionary Hypotheses Tested in 37 Cultures," *Behavioral and Brain Sciences* 12, no. 1 (1989): 1–49, https://doi.org/10.1017/S0140525X00023992.

6 **a deeper, more intricate system:** Joseph E. LeDoux, *The Emotional Brain* (Simon & Schuster, 1996).

6 **flip familiar decision-making patterns:** Jennifer S. Lerner, Deborah A. Small, and George Loewenstein, "Heart Strings and Purse Strings: Carryover Effects of Emotions on Economic Decisions," *Psychological Science* 15 (2004): 337–341.

7 **"superordinate programs":** Leda Cosmides and John Tooby, "Evolutionary Psychology and the Emotions," in *Handbook of Emotions*, 2nd ed., eds. Michael Lewis and Jeannette M. Haviland-Jones (Guilford Press, 2000), 91–115, https://cognitionandculture.net/wp-content/uploads/10.1.1.140.7434.pdf.

8 **"Natural selection does not give a fig":** Randolph M. Nesse, *Good Reasons for Bad Feelings: Insights from the Frontier of Evolutionary Psychiatry* (Penguin Press, 2019), 49.

8 **a way to read people's minds:** Tom M. Mitchell et al., "Predicting Human Brain Activity Associated with the Meanings of Nouns," *Science* 320, no. 5880 (May 30, 2008): 1191–1195, https://doi.org/10.1126/science.1152876.

10 **patterns in their brain activity:** Karim S. Kassam, Amanda R. Markey, Vladimir L. Cherkassky, George Loewenstein, and Marcel Adam Just, "Identifying Emotions on the Basis of Neural Activation," *PLOS ONE* 8, no. 6 (June 19, 2013): e66032, https://doi.org/10.1371/journal.pone.0066032.

11 **Research on autobiographical memory:** Katie Hoemann, Yeasle Lee, Peter Kuppens, Maria Gendron, and Ryan L. Boyd, "Emotional Granularity Is Associated with Daily Experiential Diversity," *Affective Science* 4, no. 2 (2023): 291–306.

11 **But the asymmetry is striking:** Michel Cabanac, "Sensory Pleasure," *The Quarterly Review of Biology* 54, no. 1 (1979): 1–29.

12 **more than a third of a second:** Felicia Pratto and Oliver P. John, "Automatic Vigilance: The Attention-Grabbing Power of Negative Social Information," *Journal of Personality and Social Psychology* 61, no. 3 (1991): 380.

12 **drop a cockroach into a vat:** Paul Rozin and Edward B. Royzman, "Negativity Bias, Negativity Dominance, and Contagion," *Personality and Social Psychology Review* 5, no. 4 (2001): 296–320, https://doi.org/10.1207/S15327957PSPR0504_2.

13 **"negativity bias":** Roy F. Baumeister, Ellen Bratslavsky, Catrin Finkenauer, and Kathleen D. Vohs, "Bad Is Stronger Than Good," *Review of General Psychology* 5, no. 4 (2001): 323–370, https://doi.org/10.1037/1089-2680.5.4.323.

13 **"a more pungent sensation":** Smith, *The Theory of Moral Sentiments*, 176–177.

13 **"What are positive feelings?":** Charles Carver and Michael F. Scheier, "Origins and Functions of Positive and Negative Affect: A Control-Process View," *Psychological Review* 97, no. 1 (1990): 19–35.

13 **"psychology's knowledge base":** Barbara L. Fredrickson, "What Good Are Positive Emotions?," *Review of General Psychology* 2, no. 3 (1998): 300–319, https://doi.org/10.1037/1089–2680.2.3.300.

14 **to make sense of them:** Bernard Weiner, "An Attributional Theory of Achievement Motivation and Emotion," *Psychological Review* 92, no. 4 (1985): 548.

14 **"What is commonly called happiness":** Arthur Schopenhauer, *The World as Will*

and Idea, vol. 1 of 3, translated by R. B. Haldane and J. Kemp (Project Gutenberg, 2011), 410, PDF file, accessed at https://www.gutenberg.org/files/38427/38427-pdf.

14 **"We're not normal animals":** Robert M. Sapolsky, *Why Zebras Don't Get Ulcers: Stress and Health*, lecture recorded September 22, 2016, at the Krannert Center for the Performing Arts, University of Illinois, https://www.youtube.com/watch?v=D9H9qTdserM.

CHAPTER 2 Because We Can't Bridge the Empathy Gap

17 **"We feel in one world":** Marcel Proust, *In Search of Lost Time: The Guermantes Way*, trans. C. K. Scott Moncrieff and revised by D. J. Enright (Vintage, 1996), 49.

18 **"I could do nothing":** Mike Stroud, *Shadows on the Wasteland: Crossing Antarctica with Ranulph Fiennes* (Jonathan Cape, 1993), 109.

18 **"It is clear that Gibson's audience":** David B. Morris, *The Culture of Pain* (University of California Press, 1991), 13.

19 **"We conceive in a much more lively":** Smith, *The Theory of Moral Sentiments*, 37.

19 **"When we condole with our friends":** Smith, *The Theory of Moral Sentiments*, 65–66.

19 **"creative writers are valuable allies":** Sigmund Freud, "Delusion and Dream in Jensen's *Gradiva*," in *Writings on Art and Literature* (Stanford University Press, 1997), 4.

20 **"The awful, terrible act of his dying":** Leo Tolstoy, *The Death of Ivan Ilyich and Other Stories*, trans. Constance Garnett (New American Library, 1960), 131–132.

20 **"It *islands* you":** Christian Wiman, *My Bright Abyss: Meditation of a Modern Believer* (Farrar, Straus and Giroux, 2013), excerpt read by Wiman in interview with Terry Gross, *Fresh Air*, NPR, July 15, 2024, https://www.npr.org/transcripts/1218953700.

20 **The term that I came up with:** George Loewenstein, Drazen Prelec, and Catherine Shatto, "Hot/Cold Intrapersonal Empathy Gaps and the Under-Prediction of Curiosity," unpublished manuscript, Carnegie Mellon University, 1998, https://www.andrew.cmu.edu/user/gl20/GeorgeLoewenstein/Papers_files/pdf/Hot:ColdIntraEmpathyGap.pdf.

21 **"The *memory deficit*":** Stroud, *Shadows on the Wasteland*, 178.

22 **I once presented eighty male undergraduates:** George Loewenstein, Daniel Nagin, and Raymond Paternoster, "The Effect of Sexual Arousal on Expectations of Sexual Forcefulness," *Journal of Research in Crime & Delinquency* 34, no. 2 (1997): 209–228.

23 **MacKinnon, the feminist legal theorist:** "*New Yorker* Articles on Analyst Harmed Their Relationship, His Ex-Lover Tells Jury," *New York Times*, May 25, 1993, https://www.nytimes.com/1993/05/25/us/new-yorker-articles-on-analyst-harmed-their-relationship-his-ex-lover-tells-jury.html.

24 **the "morning after syndrome":** Loran F. Nordgren, Joop van der Pligt, and Frenk

van Harreveld, "Evaluating Eve: Visceral States Influence the Evaluation of Impulsive Behavior," *Journal of Personality and Social Psychology* 93, no. 1 (July 2007): 75–84, https://doi.org/10.1037/0022-3514.93.1.75.

25 **in the aftermath of the 9/11 attacks:** More recently, as I edit the final version of this book, the Trump administration has, for the first time in US history, voted against the UN General Assembly's periodic resolution condemning torture. Argentina and Israel were the only other countries to do so; 169 countries voted in favor. https://www.justsecurity.org/126649/does-united-states-oppose-torture/#:~:text=Listen%20to%20Article,169%20countries%20voted%20in%20favor.

25 **"The living organism cannot entirely withstand":** "Communist Interrogation and Indoctrination of 'Enemies of the State'": *Archives of Neurology and Psychiatry* 76 (August 1956): 115–174.

26 **Rumsfeld scoffed at objections:** Scott Shane, interview by Terry Gross, *Fresh Air*, NPR, June 6, 2007, https://www.freshair.com/segments/scott-shane-us-interrogation-techniques.

26 **gaps affect perceptions of torture:** Loran F. Nordgren, Mary-Hunter Morris McDonnell, and George Loewenstein, "What Constitutes Torture? Psychological Impediments to an Objective Evaluation of Enhanced Interrogation Tactics," *Psychological Science* 22, no. 5 (May 2011): 689–694, https://doi.org/10.1177/0956797611405679.

27 **committed war crimes:** Evan Wallach, "Drop by Drop: Forgetting the History of Water Torture in U.S. Courts," *Columbia Journal of Transnational Law* 45, no. 3 (2007): 468–472.

28 **"it's absolutely torture":** Erich "Mancow" Muller, "Mancow Waterboard (Live On-Air 2009)," YouTube video, May 22, 2009, https://www.youtube.com/watch?v=qUkj9pjx3H0.

28 **"If waterboarding isn't torture":** Christopher Hitchens, "Believe Me, It's Torture," *Vanity Fair*, August 2008, https://www.vanityfair.com/news/2008/08/hitchens200808.

28 **victims of Stalin's terror:** Irina Scherbakova, personal communication.

28 **"disabling effects of guilt":** Albert D. Biderman, "Communist Techniques of Coercive Interrogation," Air Force Personnel and Training Research Center Development Report No. TN-56-132 (Lackland Air Force Base, TX: US Air Force, December 1956).

29 **"Our very survival as a species":** Francine Prose, "Boarding a Plane, Staying the Course," *New York Times*, September 23, 2001, https://www.nytimes.com/2001/09/23/travel/boarding-a-plane-staying-the-course.html.

30 **"at Auschwitz 40 years later":** Diego Gambetta, "Primo Levi's Plunge: A Case Against Suicide," *New York Times*, August 7, 1999, https://www.nytimes.com/1999/08/07/arts/primo-levis-plunge-a-case-against-suicide.html.

30 **"I know that this phase":** Ian Thomson, *Primo Levi: A Life* (Vintage, 2003), 526.

31 **"will to live is highly unstable":** Harvey Max Chochinov, Douglas Tataryn, Jennifer J. Clinch, and Deborah Dudgeon, "Will to Live in the Terminally Ill," *The Lancet* 354,

no. 9181 (1999): 816–819. The researchers also found that as patients' death drew nearer, psychological variables were replaced by physical variables (e.g., shortness of breath) as predictors of will to live.

31 **think about their lives differently:** Alisha C. Holland and Elizabeth A. Kensinger, "Emotion and Autobiographical Memory," *Physics of Life Reviews* 7, no. 1 (2010): 88–131.

31 **prone to impulsive behavior:** J. John Mann et al., "Toward a Clinical Model of Suicidal Behavior in Psychiatric Patients," *American Journal of Psychiatry* 156, no. 2 (February 1999): 181–189, https://doi.org/10.1176/ajp.156.2.181.

31 **"regret their decision in midair":** Tad Friend, "Jumpers," *New Yorker*, October 13, 2003, https://www.newyorker.com/magazine/2003/10/13/jumpers.

32 **94 percent were either still alive:** Richard H. Seiden, "Where Are They Now? A Follow-Up Study of Suicide Attempters from the Golden Gate Bridge," *Suicide and Life-Threatening Behavior* 8, no. 4 (Winter 1978): 203–216.

32 **"It is always thus, impelled":** Marcel Proust, *Within a Budding Grove*, trans. C. K. Scott Moncrieff (Project Gutenberg Australia, originally posted March 2003), https://gutenberg.net.au/ebooks03/0300401h.html.

CHAPTER 3 Because Our Self-Worth Is Shaped by Others

33 **"Nature, when she formed man":** Smith, *The Theory of Moral Sentiments*, 170.

34 **"I have observed in myself":** Thomas C. Schelling, "The Mind as a Consuming Organ," in *Decision Making: Descriptive, Normative, and Prescriptive Interactions*, eds. David E. Bell, Amos Tversky, and Howard Raiffa (Cambridge University Press, 1988), 349.

35 **"forever requiring the helium":** Alain de Botton, *Status Anxiety* (Pantheon Books, 2004), 14.

35 **"relational value" to other people:** Mark R. Leary, "Sociometer Theory and the Pursuit of Relational Value: Getting to the Root of Self-Esteem," *European Review of Social Psychology* 16 (2005): 75–111, https://doi.org/10.1080/10463280540000007.

36 **"the sociometer":** Charles Horton Cooley, a sociologist, articulated a closely related idea more than a century earlier in his account of the "looking-glass self." In *Human Nature and the Social Order* (1902), Cooley argued that what we would now call self-esteem emerges from a three-step social process: imagining how we appear to others, imagining their judgments of us, and experiencing corresponding feelings such as pride or shame.

37 **to avoid the emotional risk:** Roland Bénabou, Ania Jaroszewicz, and George Loewenstein, "It Hurts to Ask," *European Economic Review* 171 (2025): article 104911, https://doi.org/10.1016/j.euroecorev.2024.104911.

39 **interviewing incarcerated violent criminals:** Leonard Berkowitz, "Is Criminal Violence Normative Behavior? Hostile and Instrumental Aggression in Violent Incidents," *Journal of Criminal Justice* 6, no. 2 (1978).

40 **"that miserable sinking feeling":** Roy F. Baumeister, *Evil: Inside Human Violence and Cruelty* (Henry Holt, 2015), 178. See also Botond Kőszegi, George Loewenstein, and Takeshi Murooka, "Fragile Self-Esteem," *The Review of Economic Studies* 89, no. 4 (2022): 2026–2060, https://doi.org/10.1093/restud/rdab060.

40 **In a 1989 study:** Michael H. Kernis, Barbara D. Grannemann, and Lee C. Barclay, "Stability and Level of Self-Esteem as Predictors of Anger Arousal and Hostility," *Journal of Personality and Social Psychology* 56, no. 6 (June 1989): 1013–1023.

40 **the phenomenon of precarious masculinity:** Joseph A. Vandello, Jennifer K. Bosson, Dov Cohen, Rochelle M. Burnaford, and Jonathan R. Weaver, "Precarious Manhood," *Journal of Personality and Social Psychology* 95, no. 6 (2008): 1325.

41 **choose to hit a punching bag:** Jennifer K. Bosson and Joseph A. Vandello, "Precarious Manhood and Its Links to Action and Aggression," *Current Directions in Psychological Science* 20, no. 2 (2011): 82–86.

41 **"attention? sympathy? respect? dominance?":** Robert A. Caro, *The Path to Power: The Years of Lyndon Johnson* (Alfred A. Knopf, 1982), 112, 363.

41 **"a mass of insecurities":** Ron Chernow, *Alexander Hamilton* (Penguin Press, 2004), 145.

41 **"mixture of ego and insecurity":** Walter Isaacson, *Kissinger: A Biography* (Simon & Schuster, 1992), 13.

42 **This reflexive tendency to compare:** Leon Festinger, "A Theory of Social Comparison Processes," *Human Relations* 7, no. 2 (May 1954): 117–140.

43 **sparking a research project:** Jae Jeon Chang and George Loewenstein, "(Mis)perceptions Within Hierarchical Relationships," working paper, Carnegie Mellon University, 2025.

44 **those comparisons are usually unfavorable:** Scott L. Feld, "Why Your Friends Have More Friends Than You Do," *American Journal of Sociology* 96, no. 6 (May 1991): 1464–1477.

45 **may lead to eating disorders:** Rubinia Celeste Bonfanti et al., "The Association Between Social Comparison in Social Media, Body Image Concerns, and Eating Disorder Symptoms: A Systematic Review and Meta-Analysis," *Body Image* 52 (March 2025): 101841, https://doi.org/10.1016/j.bodyim.2024.101841.

45 **"Facebook fostering unfavorable social comparisons":** Luca Braghieri, Ro'ee Levy, and Alexey Makarin, "Social Media and Mental Health," *American Economic Review* 112, no. 11 (2022): 3660–3693.

CHAPTER 4 Because We Have Feelings About Feelings

48 **"For a moment he felt good":** Douglas Adams, *So Long, and Thanks for All the Fish*, quoted in Natasha H. Bailen, Haijing Wu, and Renee J. Thompson, "Meta-Emotions in Daily Life: Associations With Emotional Awareness and Depression," *Emotion* 19, no. 5 (2019): 776–787, https://doi.org/10.1037/emo0000488.

50 **"second-order desires":** Harry G. Frankfurt, "Freedom of the Will and the Concept of a Person," *Journal of Philosophy* 68, no. 1 (January 14, 1971): 5–20, quoted in Daniel Immerwahr, "What If the Attention Crisis Is All a Distraction?," *The New Yorker*, January 20, 2025, https://www.newyorker.com/magazine/2025/01/27/the-sirens-call-chris-hayes-book-review.

51 **"his face on a stamp":** Colm Tóibín, "My God the Suburbs," *London Review of Books* 31, no. 21 (November 5, 2009): 17–19, https://www.lrb.co.uk/the-paper/v31/n21/colm-toibin/my-god-the-suburbs.

51 **"If I followed my instincts":** Blake Bailey, *Cheever: A Life* (Alfred A. Knopf, 2009), 77.

52 **wished they took *more* risks:** Linda Thunström, Andrea Mannberg, Ben Gilbert, and George F. Loewenstein, "(Dis)satisfaction with Risk Preferences," SSRN working paper, September 20, 2024, https://doi.org/10.2139/ssrn.4939893.

53 **the "bodily appetites":** Smith, *The Theory of Moral Sentiments*, 34.

54 ***tyranny of the shoulds*:** Karen Horney, *Neurosis and Human Growth: The Struggle Toward Self-Realization* (W. W. Norton, 1950), 81–82.

55 **"We remind ourselves repeatedly":** Joan Didion, *The Year of Magical Thinking* (Vintage International, 2007), 191–192.

55 **greater resilience and emotional intelligence:** John M. Gottman, Lynn F. Katz, and Carole Hooven, *Meta-Emotion: How Families Communicate Emotionally* (Lawrence Erlbaum Associates, 1997).

55 **"depression about depression":** John D. Teasdale, "Psychological Treatments for Depression: How Do They Work?," *Behaviour Research and Therapy* 23, no. 2 (1985): 157–165, https://doi.org/10.1016/0005-7967(85)90024-5.

55 **a recent experience-sampling study:** Bailen et al., "Meta-Emotions in Daily Life."

56 **a sample of over three hundred medical students:** Horst Mitmansgruber, Thomas N. Beck, Stefan Höfer, and Gerhard Schüssler, "When You Don't Like What You Feel: Experiential Avoidance, Mindfulness and Meta-Emotion in Emotion Regulation," *Personality and Individual Differences* 46, no. 4 (2009): 448–453, https://doi.org/10.1016/j.paid.2008.11.013.

CHAPTER 5 Because We Crack Under Pressure

57 **"While gambling at checkers":** Walter Isaacson, *Benjamin Franklin: An American Life* (Simon & Schuster, 2003), 49–50.

59 **"What Cro-Magnon man needed":** Joan Acocella, "The Fear: How to Beat Stage Fright," *New Yorker*, May 7, 2012, https://www.newyorker.com/magazine/2012/05/14/the-fear.

60 **levels of arousal affected learning:** Robert M. Yerkes and John D. Dodson, "The Relation of Strength of Stimulus to Rapidity of Habit-Formation," *Journal of Comparative Neurology and Psychology* 18, no. 5 (1908): 459–482.

62 **"He could work":** Leo Tolstoy, *Anna Karenina*, trans. Louise and Aylmer Maude (Carefully Crafted Classics, Kindle ed.), 755.

62 **"I wasn't nervous":** Bob Harig, "Masters Meltdown Seared into Golf History," *ESPN*, April 12, 2009, https://www.espn.com/golf/columns/story?columnist=harig_bob&id=4031953.

63 **"carry a gun with me":** Paul Kimmage, "And That Was It Right There: The Masters Was Done on That Hole," *Irish Independent*, April 9, 2017, https://www.independent.ie/sport/golf/paul-kimmage-and-that-was-it-right-there-the-masters-was-done-on-that-hole/35607182.html.

63 **golf to study why people choke:** Richard S. W. Masters, "Knowledge, Knerves and Know-How: The Role of Explicit Versus Implicit Knowledge in the Breakdown of a Complex Motor Skill Under Pressure," *British Journal of Psychology* 83, no. 3 (1992): 343–358.

65 **experiment in a rural Indian village:** Dan Ariely, Uri Gneezy, George Loewenstein, and Nina Mazar, "Large Stakes and Big Mistakes," *The Review of Economic Studies* 76, no. 2 (2009): 451–469.

66 **study of NBA free-throw performance:** Zheng Cao, Joseph Price, and Daniel F. Stone, "Performance Under Pressure in the NBA," *Journal of Sports Economics* 12, no. 3 (2011): 231–252, https://doi.org/10.1177/1527002511404785.

67 **operating while listening to music:** Michael El Boghdady and Beatrice Marianne Ewalds-Kvist, "The Influence of Music on the Surgical Task Performance: A Systematic Review," *International Journal of Surgery* 73 (2020): 101–112, https://doi.org/10.1016/j.ijsu.2019.11.012.

67 **baseball players performed significantly better:** Brooke Castaneda and Rob Gray, "Effects of Focus of Attention on Baseball Batting Performance in Players of Differing Skill Levels," *Journal of Sport & Exercise Psychology* 29 (2007): 60–77.

67 **"The best swing thought":** Holly Brubach, "Doc Rotella's Cure for the Thinking Athlete," *New York Times Magazine*, November 2, 1997, 46–49.

68 **took nearly 60 percent longer:** Kenneth O. McGraw and John P. McCullers,

"Evidence of a Detrimental Effect of Extrinsic Incentives on Breaking a Mental Set," *Journal of Experimental Social Psychology* 15, no. 3 (1979): 285–294.

68 **"home disadvantage":** Ken Harb-Wu and Alex Krumer, "Choking Under Pressure in Front of a Supportive Audience: Evidence from Professional Biathlon," *Journal of Economic Behavior & Organization* 166 (2019): 246–262, https://doi.org/10.1016/j.jebo.2019.09.001.

68 **solved substantially fewer anagrams:** Ariely et al., "Large Stakes and Big Mistakes."

69 **had used beta-blockers to manage:** Acocella, "The Fear."

69 **Barry Manilow T-shirts:** Thomas Gilovich, Victoria Husted Medvec, and Kenneth Savitsky, "The Spotlight Effect in Social Judgment: An Egocentric Bias in Estimates of the Salience of One's Own Actions and Appearance," *Journal of Personality and Social Psychology* 78, no. 2 (2000): 211–222.

69 **chance to do something embarrassing:** Leaf Van Boven, George Loewenstein, Edward Welch, and David Dunning, "The Illusion of Courage in Self-Predictions: Mispredicting One's Own Behavior in Embarrassing Situations," *Journal of Behavioral Decision Making* 25, no. 1 (2012): 1–12, https://doi.org/10.1002/bdm.706.

CHAPTER 6 Because Our Thoughts Have a Mind of Their Own

72 **"The devil! . . . what beastly incidents":** Eugene O'Neill, *The Plays of Eugene O'Neill: Volume 3* (Modern Library, 1982), 25.

73 **"Now and then his thoughts":** Marcel Proust, *Swann's Way*, trans. C. K. Scott Moncrieff and Terence Kilmartin (Random House, 1981), 300.

73 **unable to think of anything else:** Daniel M. Wegner, *White Bears and Other Unwanted Thoughts: Suppression, Obsession, and the Psychology of Mental Control* (Viking, 1989).

73 **clusters that we forage over:** Thomas T. Hills, Michael N. Jones, and Peter M. Todd, "Optimal Foraging in Semantic Memory," *Psychological Review* 119, no. 3 (2012): 431–440.

74 **the brain's *default network*:** Robert P. Spunt, Meghan L. Meyer, and Matthew D. Lieberman, "The Default Mode of Human Brain Function Primes the Intentional Stance," *Journal of Cognitive Neuroscience* 27, no. 6 (2015): 1116.

74 **involuntary memory in post-traumatic stress disorder:** Craig Steel and Emily Homes, "The Role of Involuntary Memories in Posttraumatic Disorder and Psychosis," in *Involuntary Memory*, ed. J. Mace (John Wiley & Sons, 2007).

77 **"after nothingness":** Natasha Dow Schüll, *Addiction by Design: Machine Gambling in Las Vegas* (Princeton University Press, 2012), 12–13.

78 **neurobiology behind this phenomenon:** Greg Murray, "Why Do We Wake Around 3am and Dwell on Our Fears and Shortcomings?," *The Conversation*, October 6, 2021, https://theconversation.com/why-do-we-wake-around-3am-and-dwell-on-our-fears-and-shortcomings-169635.

80 **"the falsity of its antecedent":** Neal J. Roese, "Counterfactual Thinking," *Psychological Bulletin* 121, no. 1 (1997): 133–148.

81 **spontaneously generate counterfactual thoughts:** Roese and James M. Olson, "Counterfactual Thinking: A Critical Overview," in *What Might Have Been: The Social Psychology of Counterfactual Thinking* (Lawrence Erlbaum Associates, 1994).

CHAPTER 7 Because Pain Is Stickier Than Pleasure

82 **"There is neither happiness":** Alexandre Dumas, *The Count of Monte Cristo* (Modern Library, 2005), 1461.

86 **the "squishing problem":** Max Bennett, *A Brief History of Intelligence: Evolution, AI, and the Five Breakthroughs That Made Our Brains* (Mariner Books, 2023), 35.

86 **"Some people faint and grow sick":** Smith, *The Theory of Moral Sentiments*, 37.

88 **a review of hedonic adaptation:** Shane Frederick and George Loewenstein, "Hedonic Adaptation," in *Well-Being: The Foundations of Hedonic Psychology*, eds. Daniel Kahneman, Ed Diener, and Norbert Schwarz (Russell Sage Foundation, 1999), 302–329.

89 **She documented her experiences:** Stephanie Byram, Jennifer Matesa, and Charlee Brodsky, *Knowing Stephanie* (Carnegie Mellon University Press, 2003).

90 **spawned decades of follow-up research:** Philip Brickman, Dan Coates, and Ronnie Janoff-Bulman, "Lottery Winners and Accident Victims: Is Happiness Relative?," *Journal of Personality and Social Psychology* 36, no. 8 (1978): 917–927.

90 **the psychology of mountaineering:** George Loewenstein, "Because It Is There: The Challenge of Mountaineering . . . for Utility Theory," *Kyklos* 52, no. 3 (1999): 315–344.

90 **"After Chimney Rock":** Peter Potterfield, *In the Zone: Epic Survival Stories from the Mountaineering World* (The Mountaineers, 1996), 233.

91 **they surveyed assistant professors:** Daniel T. Gilbert, Elizabeth C. Pinel, Timothy D. Wilson, Stephen J. Blumberg, and Thalia P. Wheatley, "Immune Neglect: A Source of Durability Bias in Affective Forecasting," *Journal of Personality and Social Psychology* 75, no. 3 (1998): 617–638.

91 **paraplegia, below-the-knee amputation, colostomies:** George Loewenstein and Peter A. Ubel, "Hedonic Adaptation and the Role of Decision and Experience Utility in Public Policy," *Journal of Public Economics* 92, no. 8–9 (2008): 1795–1810; Heather P. Lacey, Angela Fagerlin, George Loewenstein, Dylan M. Smith, Jason Riis, and Peter A.

Ubel, "Are They Really That Happy? Exploring Scale Recalibration in Estimates of Well-Being," *Health Psychology* 27, no. 6 (2008): 669.

92 **"to live on a hedonic treadmill":** Philip Brickman and Donald T. Campbell, "Hedonic Relativism and Planning the Good Society," in *Adaptation-Level Theory*, ed. M. H. Appley (Academic Press, 1971), 287.

92 **"In spite of the complete fulfillment":** Tolstoy, *Anna Karenina*, 739.

93 **"I've been a real estate developer":** Tom Wolfe, *A Man in Full* (The Dial Press, 2001), 721.

94 **more than twenty-four thousand Germans:** Richard E. Lucas, Andrew E. Clark, Yannis Georgellis, and Ed Diener, "Reexamining Adaptation and the Set Point Model of Happiness: Reactions to Changes in Marital Status," *Journal of Personality and Social Psychology* 84, no. 3 (2003): 527–539.

94 **(like persistent unemployment):** Richard E. Lucas, Andrew E. Clark, Yannis Georgellis, and Ed Diener, "Unemployment Alters the Set Point for Life Satisfaction," *Psychological Science* 15, no. 1 (2004): 8–13, https://doi.org/10.1111/j.0963-7214.2004.01501002.x.

95 **"If a nematode is exposed":** Bennett, *A Brief History of Intelligence*, 73.

96 **Without sustained emotion, action withers:** Daniel Schwartz and George Loewenstein, "The Chill of the Moment: Emotions and Proenvironmental Behavior," *Journal of Public Policy & Marketing* 36, no. 2 (2017): 255–268.

96 **"The first body":** Jon Krakauer, *Into Thin Air: A Personal Account of the Mount Everest Disaster* (Anchor Books, 1998), 139.

96 **famous obedience experiments:** Stanley Milgram, *Obedience to Authority: An Experimental View* (Harper & Row, 1969).

96 **"the most difficult thing":** Chris Hedges, "Croatian's Confession Describes Torture and Killing on Vast Scale," *New York Times*, September 5, 1997, https://www.nytimes.com/1997/09/05/world/croatian-s-confession-describes-torture-and-killing-on-vast-scale.html.

97 **study of Nazi doctors:** Robert Jay Lifton, *The Nazi Doctors: Medical Killing and the Psychology of Genocide* (Basic Books, 1986).

97 **"This very adaptability":** René Dubos, *Man Adapting* (Yale University Press, 1965), 278.

CHAPTER 8 Because Hope Refuses to Die

98 **"Any parent who has had to confront":** Dominique Browning, "Reefer Madness," *New York Times Book Review*, August 30, 2009, https://www.nytimes.com/2009/08/30/books/review/Browning-t.html.

100 **higher survival rates:** David B. Feldman and Benjamin W. Corn, "Hope and Cancer," *Current Opinion in Psychology* 49 (2023): 101506.

100 **"Only hope remained there inside":** Hesiod, *Theogony and Works and Days*, trans. M. L. West (Oxford University Press, 1988), 40.

100 **"Zeus did not wish man":** Friedrich Nietzsche, *Human, All-Too-Human: A Book for Free Spirits*, trans. Helen Zimmern (Russell & Russell, 1964), 82.

102 **"The irony is deep":** Nesse, *Good Reasons for Bad Feelings*, 107.

102 **"He made it sound as if":** Ari Shapiro, "What It's Like to Be Held Hostage by Somali Pirates for 2 1/2 Years," *NPR*, July 24, 2018, https://www.npr.org/2018/07/24/631941716/what-its-like-to-be-held-hostage-by-somali-pirates-for-2-1-2-years.

103 **82 percent of physicians:** Lisa I. Iezzoni et al., "Physicians' Perceptions of People with Disability and Their Health Care," *Health Affairs* 40, no. 2 (2021): 297–306, https://doi.org/10.1377/hlthaff.2020.01452.

104 **end-stage renal disease:** Jason Riis, George Loewenstein, Jonathan Baron, Christopher Jepson, Angela Fagerlin, and Peter A. Ubel, "Ignorance of Hedonic Adaptation to Hemodialysis: A Study Using Ecological Momentary Assessment," *Journal of Experimental Psychology: General* 134, no. 1 (2005): 3–9, https://www.cmu.edu/dietrich/sds/docs/loewenstein/IgnoranceHedonicAdapt.pdf.

104 **Peter and his team recruited 107 patients:** Dylan M. Smith, George Loewenstein, Aleksandra Jankovich, and Peter A. Ubel, "Happily Hopeless: Adaptation to a Permanent, but Not to a Temporary, Disability," *Health Psychology* 28, no. 6 (2009): 787–791, https://doi.org/10.1037/a0016624.

107 **"The medicines of the physician":** Smith, *The Theory of Moral Sentiments*, 213.

CHAPTER 9 Impatience

111 **"She was waiting for something":** Gustave Flaubert, *Madame Bovary*, trans. Geoffrey Wall (Penguin Classics, 2007, Kindle ed.).

113 **"Friday limped on":** Lena Andersson, *Willful Disregard: A Novel About Love* (Pan Macmillan, 2016), 86.

113 **"What she must definitely not":** Andersson, *Willful Disregard*, 87.

114 **to get their shock *sooner*:** John Oliver Cook and Lehman W. Barnes, "Choice of Delay of Inevitable Shock," *Journal of Abnormal and Social Psychology* 68, no. 6 (1964): 669–672, https://doi.org/10.1037/h0047127.

115 **"suffering twice":** Elizabeth Strout, *My Name Is Lucy Barton* (Random House, 2016), 76.

116 **when we experience dread:** Gregory S. Berns, Jonathan Chappelow, Milos Cekic,

Caroline F. Zink, Giuseppe Pagnoni, and Megan E. Martin-Skurski, "Neurobiological Substrates of Dread," *Science* 312, no. 5774 (2006): 754–758; Carey K. Morewedge, Daniel T. Gilbert, and Timothy D. Wilson, "The Least Likely of Times: How Remembering the Past Biases Forecasts of the Future," *Psychological Science* 16, no. 8 (2005): 626–630.

116 **Japanese practice of executing:** Daisuke Sato, "Focus: Japan Criticized as Treating Death Row Inmates Inhumanely," *Kyodo News*, September 16, 2024, https://english.kyodonews.net/articles/-/49931.

116 **"cruel, inhuman and degrading":** "Death Row Prisoners in Japan Sue over Same-Day Notice of Executions," Death Penalty Information Center, November 5, 2021, https://deathpenaltyinfo.org/news/death-row-prisoners-in-japan-sue-over-same-day-notice-of-executions.

117 **"Christopher Robin said":** A. A. Milne, *The House at Pooh Corner* (E. P. Dutton, 1928; Kindle ed., 2011).

119 **"pleasure like a future pain":** Annie Ernaux, *Simple Passion*, trans. Tanya Leslie (Seven Stories Press, 2011), 33.

122 **"Waiting is a form of imprisonment":** Lance Morrow, "Waiting as a Way of Life," *TIME*, July 23, 1984.

122 **tends to produce negative evaluations:** Chezy Ofir and Itamar Simonson, "In Search of Negative Customer Feedback: The Effect of Expecting to Evaluate on Satisfaction Evaluations," *Journal of Marketing Research* 38, no. 2 (2001): 170–182.

122 ***slips* . . . and *skips*:** Richard C. Larson, "Perspectives on Queues: Social Justice and the Psychology of Queueing," *Operations Research* 35, no. 6 (1987): 895–905.

123 **first documented in the 1930s:** Clark L. Hull, "The Goal-Gradient Hypothesis and Maze Learning," *Psychological Review* 39, no. 1 (1932): 25–43.

124 **a surprising number of prison escapes:** Richard F. Culp and Elizabeth Bracco, "Examining Prison Escapes and the Routine Activities Theory," *Corrections Compendium* 30, no. 3 (2005): 1–5. Also highlighting the importance of expectations for prison escapes, a common finding in the literature is that escapes are more likely following events adverse to the convict's situation—e.g., unfavorable parole decisions. See, for example, Bryce Elling Peterson, Adam Fera, and Jeff Mellow, "Escapes from Correctional Custody: A New Examination of an Old Phenomenon," *The Prison Journal* 96, no. 4 (2016): 511–533.

124 **to satisfy rising expectations:** James C. Davies, "Toward a Theory of Revolution," *American Sociological Review* 27, no. 1 (1962): 5–19.

125 **"The most perilous moment":** Alexis de Tocqueville, *Alexis de Tocqueville on Democracy, Revolution, and Society*, eds. John Stone and Stephen Mennell (University of Chicago Press, 1980), 230.

125 **"sacrifice a real tranquility":** Smith, *The Theory of Moral Sentiments*, 192–193.

CHAPTER 10 Boredom

126 **"In between the periods of sexual excitement":** Graham Greene, *A Sort of Life* (Pocket Books, 1973), 105.

127 **to shift our attention:** George Loewenstein and Zachary Wojtowicz, "The Economics of Attention," *Journal of Economic Literature* 63, no. 3 (2025): 1038–1089.

127 **"My boredom might be described":** Alberto Moravia, *Boredom*, trans. Angus Davidson (New York Review Books, 2011), 5.

129 **largest studies of boredom:** Alycia Chin, Amanda Markey, Saurabh Bhargava, Karim S. Kassam, and George Loewenstein, "Bored in the USA: Experience Sampling and Boredom in Everyday Life," *Emotion* 17, no. 2 (2017): 359–368, https://doi.org/10.1037/emo0000232.

132 **borrowed a term from economics:** Zachary Wojtowicz, Nick Chater, and George F. Loewenstein, "Boredom and Flow: An Opportunity Cost Theory of Motivational Attention," *SSRN* (March 13, 2019), https://doi.org/10.2139/ssrn.3339123.

133 **boredom steadily rose:** Megan E. Weybright, John E. Schulenberg, and Linda L. Caldwell, "More Bored Today than Yesterday? National Trends in Adolescent Boredom from 2008–2017," *Journal of Adolescent Health* 66, no. 3 (2020): 360–365.

133 **report feeling bored more often:** Zibei Gu, Chen Yang, Qian Su, and Yuan Liang, "The Boredom Proneness Levels of Chinese College Students Increased over Time: A Meta-Analysis of Birth Cohort Differences from 2009 to 2020," *Personality and Individual Differences* 215 (December 2023): 112370, https://doi.org/10.1016/j.paid.2023.112370.

134 **who has studied dream reports:** Simon DeDeo, "Possibility Architectures: Exploring Human Communication with Generative AI," presentation, Santa Fe Institute, March 10, 2023, https://www.youtube.com/live/B8y_t0jjnL8?si=R5Ozoy94BmlsKMDd.

135 **it was *something to do*:** Timothy D. Wilson et al., "Just Think: The Challenges of the Disengaged Mind," *Science* 345, no. 6192 (2014): 75–77, https://doi.org/10.1126/science.1250830.

135 **substance abuse:** Nicole LePera, "Relationships Between Boredom Proneness, Mindfulness, Anxiety, Depression, and Substance Use," *The New School Psychology Bulletin* 8, no. 2 (2011): 15–25.

135 **compulsive gambling:** Alex Blaszczynski, Neil McConaghy, and Anna Frankova, "Boredom Proneness in Pathological Gambling," *Psychological Reports* 67, no. 1 (1990): 35–42, https://doi.org/10.2466/pr0.1990.67.1.35.

135 **reckless driving:** Eric R. Dahlen, Ryan C. Martin, Katie Ragan, and Myndi M. Kuhlman, "Driving Anger, Sensation Seeking, Impulsiveness, and Boredom Proneness in the Prediction of Unsafe Driving," *Accident Analysis & Prevention* 37, no. 2 (2005): 341–348, https://doi.org/10.1016/j.aap.2004.10.006.

135 **experimental findings:** Erin C. Westgate and Timothy D. Wilson, "Boring Thoughts and Bored Minds: The MAC Model of Boredom and Cognitive Engagement," *Psychological Review* 125, no. 5 (2018): 689–713, https://doi.org/10.1037/rev0000097.

135 ***"Wars, pogroms, and persecutions"*****:** Bertrand Russell, *The Conquest of Happiness* (George Allen & Unwin, 1930), 61.

CHAPTER 11 Anger

137 **"Alice could feel *rage* rising":** John Steinbeck, *The Wayward Bus*, in *John Steinbeck: Travels with Charley and Later Novels, 1947–1962*, ed. Robert DeMott (Library of America, 2007), 25.

137 **"I started writing this a million":** 2025 email from a colleague to the author; name withheld to protect her privacy.

139 **someone else's wrongful action:** James R. Averill, *Anger and Aggression: An Essay on Emotion* (Springer-Verlag, 1982). Averill conducted a series of survey-based studies asking participants to report on their own experiences of anger—what triggered it, how they responded, and what followed. His goal was to examine how anger connects to aggression as well as the typical targets, triggers, and consequences of anger. Averill found that the majority (59 percent) of the angering incidents reported by the community residents and university students in his investigation followed "a voluntary and unjustified act."

139 **"One does not become angry":** Anthony Trollope, *He Knew He Was Right* (Oxford University Press, 1998), 919.

139 **the machines fell on them:** Michael Q. Cosio, "Soda Pop Vending Machine Injuries," *Journal of the American Medical Association* 260, no. 18 (1988): 2697–2699, https://doi.org/10.1001/jama.1988.03410180105039.

140 **participants who hit a punching bag:** Brad J. Bushman, "Does Venting Anger Feed or Extinguish the Flame? Catharsis, Rumination, Distraction, Anger, and Aggressive Responding," *Personality and Social Psychology Bulletin* 28, no. 6 (2002): 724–731, https://doi.org/10.1177/0146167202289002.

142 **"Someone who becomes enraged":** Robert H. Frank, *Passions Within Reason: The Strategic Role of the Emotions* (W. W. Norton, 1988), 53.

143 **"careless or even self-destructive attitude":** Thomas C. Schelling, *The Strategy of Conflict* (Harvard University Press, 1980), 17.

143 **two decades of left-right brain research:** Iain McGilchrist, *The Master and His Emissary: The Divided Brain and the Making of the Western World* (Yale University Press, 2019).

144 **from a specific kind of harm:** Richard S. Lazarus, "Progress on a Cognitive-Motivational-Relational Theory of Emotion," *American Psychologist* 46, no. 8 (1991): 819–834.

144 **"the basic motive to preserve":** Richard S. Lazarus, *Emotion and Adaptation* (Oxford University Press, 1991), 222.

144 **"Anger is not always":** Maria Popova, "Philosopher Martha Nussbaum on Anger, Forgiveness, the Emotional Machinery of Trust, and the Only Fruitful Response to Betrayal in Intimate Relationships," *The Marginalian*, May 9, 2016, https://www.themarginalian.org/2016/05/03/martha-nussbaum-anger-and-forgiveness/.

146 **"Anger, if not restrained":** Seneca the Younger, "On Anger," in *Anger, Mercy, Revenge*, trans. Robert A. Kaster and Martha C. Nussbaum (University of Chicago Press, 2010).

CHAPTER 12 Envy

151 **"A common soldier bears no":** David Hume, *A Treatise of Human Nature* (1739), ed. L. A. Selby-Bigge (Clarendon Press, 1896; digital edition, ETH Zurich, 2007), 198, https://www.files.ethz.ch/isn/125487/5010_Hume_Treatise_Human_Nature.pdf.

151 **"We do not envy a good fortune":** Russell, *The Conquest of Happiness*, 91.

152 **economists at the University of California, Berkeley:** David Card, Alexandre Mas, Enrico Moretti, and Emmanuel Saez, "Inequality at Work: The Effect of Peer Salaries on Job Satisfaction," *American Economic Review* 102, no. 6 (2012): 2981–3003, https://doi.org/10.1257/aer.102.6.2981.

154 **this is a *focusing illusion*:** Ed O'Brien, Alexander C. Kristal, Phoebe C. Ellsworth, and Norbert Schwarz, "(Mis)Imagining the Good Life and the Bad Life: Envy and Pity as a Function of the Focusing Illusion," *Journal of Experimental Social Psychology* 75 (March 2018): 41–53, https://doi.org/10.1016/j.jesp.2017.10.002.https://doi.org/10.1016/j.jesp.2017.10.002.

156 **documenting the asymmetry:** Irene Scopelliti, George Loewenstein, and Joachim Vosgerau, "You Call It 'Self-Exuberance'; I Call It 'Bragging': Miscalibrated Predictions of Emotional Responses to Self-Promotion," *Psychological Science* 26, no. 6 (2015): 1–12, https://doi.org/10.1177/0956797615573516.

156 **less likely to perspective-take:** Leaf Van Boven, George Loewenstein, David Dunning, and Loran F. Nordgren, "Changing Places: A Dual Judgment Model of Empathy Gaps in Emotional Perspective Taking," in *Advances in Experimental Social Psychology*, vol. 48, eds. J. M. Olson and M. P. Zanna (Elsevier), 117–171.

157 **"evidence of the inner drama":** de Botton, *Status Anxiety*, viii.

CHAPTER 13 Jealousy

161 **51 percent of divorced men:** Martin Daly, Margo Wilson, and Suzanne Weghorst, "Male Sexual Jealousy," *Ethology and Sociobiology* 3, no. 1 (1982): 11–27, citing Alfred C. Kinsey et al., *Sexual Behavior in the Human Female* (Saunders, 1953).

161 **men reacted more strongly:** David M. Buss, Randy J. Larsen, Drew Westen, and Jennifer Semmelroth, "Sex Differences in Jealousy: Evolution, Physiology, and Psychology," *Psychological Science* 3, no. 4 (1992): 251–255, https://doi.org/10.1111/j.1467-9280.1992.tb00038.x.

161 **measured physiological responses:** Robert H. Pietrzak, James D. Laird, David A. Stevens, and Nicholas S. Thompson, "Sex Differences in Human Jealousy: A Coordinated Study of Forced-Choice, Continuous Rating-Scale, and Physiological Responses on the Same Subjects," *Evolution and Human Behavior* 23, no. 2 (2002): 83–94.

162 **youth or physical attractiveness:** Buss et al., "Sex Differences in Jealousy."

162 **large study of Finnish twins:** Tom R. Kupfer, Morgan J. Sidari, Brendan P. Zietsch, Patrick Jern, Joshua M. Tybur, and Laura W. Wesseldijk, "Why Are Some People More Jealous than Others? Genetic and Environmental Factors," *Evolution and Human Behavior* 43, no. 1 (2022): 26–33, https://doi.org/10.1016/j.evolhumbehav.2021.08.002.

164 **over two hundred college students:** Steven Arnocky, Kayla Kubinec, Megan MacKinnon, and Dwight Mazmanian, "An Experimental Test of Jealousy's Evolved Function: Imagined Partner Infidelity Induces Jealousy, Which Predicts Positive Attitude Towards Mate Retention," *Evolutionary Psychology* 22, no. 3 (2024): 1–12, https://doi.org/10.1177/14747049241267226.

165 **"There is no doubt that":** Alain de Botton, *How Proust Can Change Your Life* (Pantheon, 1998), 165.

165 **may actually be a good thing:** Jeremy Dugosh, "On Predicting Relationship Satisfaction: What Role Does Jealousy Play?," *Current Research in Social Psychology* 5 (2000): 252–263.

165 **a "subordinate passion":** David Hume, *Four Dissertations* (A. Millar, 1757), "Of the Passions," sec. 2.27, https://davidhume.org/texts/empl1/tr#27.

CHAPTER 14 Rejection

168 **"Methinks I have a plan":** Plato, *Symposium*, trans. Benjamin Jowett, sec. 191a, *The Internet Classics Archive*, MIT, http://classics.mit.edu/Plato/symposium.html.

168 **"nearest to the physical":** Diana Athill, *Instead of a Letter: A Memoir* (Doubleday, 1962), 108.

168 **memory for physical pain:** Stephen Morley, "Vivid Memory for 'Everyday' Pains," *Pain* 55, no. 1 (1993): 55–62.

169 **two basic components:** Ronald Melzack and Kenneth L. Casey, "Sensory, Motivational, and Central Control Determinants of Pain: A New Conceptual Model," *The Skin Senses* 1 (1968): 423–443.

169 ***focus* on the pain:** Howard Leventhal, Donald Brown, Saya Shacham, and Gretchen

Engquist, "Effects of Preparatory Information About Sensations, Threat of Pain, and Attention on Cold Pressor Distress," *Journal of Personality and Social Psychology* 37, no. 5 (1979): 688

169 **among the "worst events":** Scott M. Monroe, Paul Rohde, John R. Seeley, and Peter M. Lewinsohn, "Life Events and Depression in Adolescence: Relationship Loss as a Prospective Risk Factor for First Onset of Major Depressive Disorder," *Journal of Abnormal Psychology* 108, no. 4 (1999): 606–614, https://doi.org/10.1037/0021-843X.108.4.606.

169 **Over 40 percent of people struggle:** Jack Mearns, "Coping with a Breakup: Negative Mood Regulation Expectancies and Depression Following the End of a Romantic Relationship," *Journal of Personality and Social Psychology* 60, no. 2 (1991): 327–334, https://doi.org/10.1037/0022-3514.60.2.327.

170 **Heart attacks and strokes:** In the context of divorce, see Janice Kiecolt-Glaser et al., "Marital Quality, Marital Disruption, and Immune Function," *Psychosomatic Medicine* 49, no. 1 (1987): 13–34, https://doi.org/10.1097/00006842-198701000-00002.

170 **Discussing not a romantic breakup:** Andrew Solomon, *The Noonday Demon: An Atlas of Depression* (Scribner, 2011), 45.

172 **"They just stopped throwing it":** Kipling D. Williams, "Social Rejection, Ostracism," YouTube video, 3:32, from the documentary *REJECT*, posted by @REJECTfilm, June 29, 2011, https://www.youtube.com/watch?v=A3UTXsJzAj4.

172 **hurt, confusion, lowered self-esteem:** Kipling D. Williams, "Ostracism," *Annual Review of Psychology* 58 (2007): 425–452, https://doi.org/10.1146/annurev.psych.58.110405.085641.

173 **In one study . . . when rejection-sensitive:** Geraldine Downey and Scott Feldman, "Implications of Rejection Sensitivity for Intimate Relationships," *Journal of Personality and Social Psychology* 70, no. 6 (1996): 1327.

174 **rated their partner more negatively:** Sandra L. Murray, John G. Holmes, Geoff MacDonald, and Phoebe C. Ellsworth, "Through the Looking Glass Darkly? When Self-Doubts Turn into Relationship Insecurities," *Journal of Personality and Social Psychology* 75, no. 6 (1998): 1459–1480, https://doi.org/10.1037/0022-3514.75.6.1459.

174 **the contents of their dorm room:** Sandra L. Murray, Paul Rose, Gina M. Bellavia, John G. Holmes, and Anna Garrett Kusche, "When Rejection Stings: How Self-Esteem Constrains Relationship-Enhancement Processes," *Journal of Personality and Social Psychology* 83, no. 3 (2002): 556–573, https://doi.org/10.1037/0022-3514.83.3.556.

177 **"If I had known him":** Athill, *Instead of a Letter*, 110.

CHAPTER 15 Guilt

184 **Even when explicitly instructed:** Colin Camerer, George Loewenstein, and Martin Weber, "The Curse of Knowledge in Economic Settings: An Experimental Analysis," *Journal of Political Economy* 97, no. 5 (1989): 1232–1254, https://doi.org/10.1086/261651.

184 **As Edgar Allan Poe's:** Edgar Allan Poe, "The Tell-Tale Heart," *The Pioneer: A Literary and Critical Magazine*, January 1843. Cass Sunstein, Russell Golman, and I coined the term the *telltale heart effect* in our paper reviewing the impact of mandatory information disclosure policies, to refer to situations in which firms faced with the prospect of information disclosure about their products improve their products or product offerings out of exaggerated fear about how consumers will react to the disclosed information. George Loewenstein, Daylian M. Cain, and Sunita Sah, "Disclosure: Psychology Changes Everything," *Annual Review of Economics* 6, no. 1 (2014): 391–419.

184 **research I did with Shereen Chaudhry:** Shereen J. Chaudhry and George Loewenstein, "Thanking, Apologizing, Bragging, and Blaming: Responsibility Exchange Theory and the Currency of Communication," *Psychological Review* 126, no. 3 (2019): 313–344, https://doi.org/10.1037/rev0000139.

184 **an *outside observer*:** Chaudhry and Loewenstein, "Thanking, Apologizing, Bragging, and Blaming."

CHAPTER 16 Shame

187 **"Being forgiven creates a peculiar shame":** Alice Munro, *Lives of Girls and Women* (Vintage, 2001), 65.

188 **"Compared with the contempt of mankind":** Smith, *The Theory of Moral Sentiments*, 83.

188 **"Ignominy is universally acknowledged":** Jon Ronson, *So You've Been Publicly Shamed* (Riverhead Books, 2015), 54.

189 **"Honours like these produce":** Maria Popova, "John Quincy Adams on Impostor Syndrome and the True Measure of Success," *The Marginalian*, June 3, 2024, https://www.themarginalian.org/2024/06/03/john-quincy-adams-impostor-syndrome-success. I have known various people who received the MacArthur "genius award" when they were young, and hadn't really yet "proven themselves"—i.e., largely on the basis of promise. My observation is that this has not necessarily been a good thing for them.

189 **"After a lull of almost 180 years":** Ronson, *So You've Been Publicly Shamed*, 9.

191 **"The train station at Cambridge":** 2025 email from a friend to the author; name withheld for privacy.

191 **"guilt cultures" and "shame cultures":** Ruth Benedict, *The Chrysanthemum and the Sword: Patterns of Japanese Culture* (Houghton Mifflin, 1946).

CHAPTER 17 Anxiety

195 **the book on anxiety:** David H. Barlow, *Anxiety and Its Disorders: The Nature and Treatment of Anxiety and Panic* (2nd ed., Guilford Press, 2002).

195 **one early case from 1787:** Simon Wessely, "Mass Hysteria: Two Syndromes?," *Psychological Medicine* 17, no. 1 (1987): 109–120. See also Robert E. Bartholomew and Simon Wessely, "Protean Nature of Mass Sociogenic Illness: From Possessed Nuns to Chemical and Biological Terrorism Fears," *The British Journal of Psychiatry* 180, no. 4 (2002): 300–306.

197 **Stranger anxiety:** Ross G. Menzies and J. Christopher Clarke, "The Etiology of Phobias: A Nonassociative Account," *Clinical Psychology Review* 15, no. 1 (1995): 23–48, https://doi.org/10.1016/0272-7358(94)00039-5.

198 **phenomenon of *spontaneous recovery*:** Mark E. Bouton, "Conditioning, Remembering, and Forgetting," *Journal of Experimental Psychology: Animal Behavior Processes* 20, no. 3 (1994): 219–231, https://doi.org/10.1037/0097-7403.20.3.219; Mark E. Bouton and Dale Swartzentruber, "Sources of Relapse After Extinction in Pavlovian and Instrumental Learning," *Clinical Psychology Review* 11, no. 2 (1991): 123–140, https://doi.org/10.1016/0272-7358(91)90091-8.

199 **It had been overwritten:** Maria A. Morgan and Joseph E. LeDoux, "Differential Contribution of Dorsal and Ventral Medial Prefrontal Cortex to the Acquisition and Extinction of Conditioned Fear in Rats," *Behavioral Neuroscience* 109, no. 4 (1995): 681–688.

199 **"I would die during the night":** Email to the author; name withheld for privacy.

203 **"Now every kind of fear grows worse":** Russell, *The Conquest of Happiness*, 78.

CHAPTER 18 Regret

209 **"adversarial collaboration":** Thomas Gilovich, Victoria H. Medvec, and Daniel Kahneman, "Varieties of Regret: A Debate and Partial Resolution," *Psychological Review* 105, no. 3 (1998): 602–605.

209 **"in full 1960s lingerie":** Email to the author; name withheld for privacy.

210 **"I wish I'd had the courage":** Bronnie Ware, *The Top Five Regrets of the Dying: A Life Transformed by the Dearly Departing* (Hay House, 2011).

211 **they took *too few* risks:** Thunström et al., "(Dis)satisfaction with Risk Preferences."

212 **rafting on the Green River in Utah:** Melanie Thernstrom, "A Father's Wrenching Memoir of Death, Guilt and Reckoning," *New York Times*, February 3, 2017, https://www.nytimes.com/2017/02/03/books/review/disaster-falls-stephane-gerson.html.

212 **Mr. Adams was involved in an accident:** Daniel Kahneman and Amos Tversky, "The Psychology of Preferences," *Scientific American* 246, no. 1 (1982): 160–173.

213 ***hindsight bias*:** Baruch Fischhoff, "Hindsight ≠ Foresight: The Effect of Outcome Knowledge on Judgment Under Uncertainty," *Journal of Experimental Psychology: Human Perception and Performance* 1, no. 3 (1975): 288–299, https://doi.org/10.1037/0096-1523.1.3.288.

215 **"takeover aversion":** Erik Hoelzl and George Loewenstein, "Wearing Out Your Shoes to Prevent Someone Else from Stepping into Them: Anticipated Regret and Social Takeover in Sequential Decisions," *Organizational Behavior and Human Decision Processes* 98, no. 1 (2005): 15–27.

216 **"If the summer jackpot":** Marcel Zeelenberg, "The Science of Regret," *TEDx-CollegeofEuropeNatolin*, YouTube video, 16:24, posted September 27, 2016, https://www.youtube.com/watch?v=ZPCV3Oe1fYw.

216 **complete health risk assessments (HRAs):** Emily Haisley, Kevin G. Volpp, Thomas Pellathy, and George Loewenstein, "The Impact of Alternative Incentive Schemes on Completion of Health Risk Assessments," *American Journal of Health Promotion* 26, no. 3 (2012): 184–188.

216 **they gained back the weight:** Kevin G. Volpp, Leslie K. John, Andrea B. Troxel, Laurie Norton, Jennifer Fassbender, and George Loewenstein, "Financial Incentive–Based Approaches for Weight Loss: A Randomized Trial," *Journal of the American Medical Association* 300, no. 22 (2008): 2631–2637; Leslie K. John, George Loewenstein, Andrea B. Troxel, Laurie Norton, Jennifer E. Fassbender, and Kevin G. Volpp, "Financial Incentives for Extended Weight Loss: A Randomized, Controlled Trial," *Journal of General Internal Medicine* 26, no. 6 (2011): 621–626.

218 **"Being with you":** Geoff Dyer, *Out of Sheer Rage: Wrestling with D. H. Lawrence* (Farrar, Straus and Giroux, 2014), 152–168.

CHAPTER 19 Loneliness

219 **"Lizzie felt herself alone":** Anthony Trollope, *The Eustace Diamonds* (Floating Press, 1872/2010), 539.

219 **"In different ways, people tell":** Vivek H. Murthy, *My Parting Prescription for America*, U.S. Department of Health and Human Services (Washington, DC, January 7, 2025), 11.

220 **"We can start by reaching out":** Murthy, *My Parting Prescription for America*, 15.

220 **"connection rituals":** Vivek H. Murthy, *Our Epidemic of Loneliness and Isolation: The U.S. Surgeon General's Advisory on the Healing Effects of Social Connection and Community* (Washington, DC: U.S. Dept. of Health and Human Services, 2023), https://www.hhs.gov/sites/default/files/surgeon-general-social-connection-advisory.pdf.

220 **the figure rises to 43 percent:** Katherine V. Bruss et al., "Loneliness, Lack of Social and Emotional Support, and Mental Health Issues—United States, 2022," *Morbidity and Mortality Weekly Report* 73, no. 24: 539–545, https://www.cdc.gov/mmwr/volumes/73/wr/mm7324a1.htm.

221 **fifth leading cause of death:** Maria Carmenza Mejia, Charles H. Hennekens, Robert S. Levine, and Panagiota Kitsantas, "Deaths of Despair: A Major and Increasing

Contributor to United States Deaths," *Advances in Preventive Medicine and Health Care* 7 (2024): 1062, https://doi.org/10.29011/2688-996X.001062. See also, https://www.fau.edu/newsdesk/articles/deaths-of-despair-study.php.

221 **CDC notes that lonely adults:** Bruss et al., "Loneliness, Lack of Social and Emotional Support."

222 **meta-analysis of loneliness-reduction programs:** Christopher M. Masi, Hsi-Yuan Chen, Louise C. Hawkley, and John T. Cacioppo, "A Meta-Analysis of Interventions to Reduce Loneliness," *Personality and Social Psychology Review* 15, no. 3 (2011): 219–266.

222 **the late John T. Cacioppo:** "Addressing Negative Thoughts Most Effective in Fighting Loneliness," press release, *UChicago News*, September 10, 2010, https://news.uchicago.edu/story/addressing-negative-thoughts-most-effective-fighting-loneliness.

223 **"without redeeming features":** Robert S. Weiss, *Loneliness: The Experience of Emotional and Social Isolation* (MIT Press, 1973), 15.

224 **elevated rates of mortality:** R. Sai Prathap Yadav, Faizah Ansari, Neha Bera, Clement Kent, and Pavan Agrawal, "Lessons from Lonely Flies: Molecular and Neuronal Mechanisms Underlying Social Isolation," *Neuroscience & Biobehavioral Reviews* 156 (2024): 105504.

224 **smoking fifteen cigarettes a day:** Julianne Holt-Lunstad, Timothy B. Smith, and J. Bradley Layton, "Social Relationships and Mortality Risk: A Meta-Analytic Review," *PLOS Medicine* 7, no. 7 (2010): e1000316; John T. Cacioppo, Louise C. Hawkley, Greg J. Norman, and Gary G. Berntson, "Social Isolation," *Annals of the New York Academy of Sciences* 1231, no. 1 (2011): 17–22; and Nicole K. Valtorta, Mona Kanaan, Simon Gilbody, and Barbara Hanratty, "Loneliness, Social Isolation and Risk of Cardiovascular Disease in the English Longitudinal Study of Ageing," *European Journal of Preventive Cardiology* 25, no. 13 (2018): 1387–1396.

224 **"Loneliness kills":** Liz Mineo, "Good Genes Are Nice, but Joy Is Better," *Harvard Gazette*, April 11, 2017, https://news.harvard.edu/gazette/story/2017/04/over-nearly-80-years-harvard-study-has-been-showing-how-to-live-a-healthy-and-happy-life/.

224 **"Being a stay-at-home mom":** Barbara Kingsolver, *Flight Behavior* (Harper, 2012), 81.

227 **In one study, lonely students:** Craig A. Anderson, Leonard M. Horowitz, and Rita deSales French, "Attributional Style of Lonely and Depressed People," *Journal of Personality and Social Psychology* 45, no. 1 (1983): 127–136.

228 **"Real relief from loneliness":** John T. Cacioppo and William Patrick, *Loneliness: Human Nature and the Need for Social Connection* (W. W. Norton, 2008), 37.

228 **Lonely individuals tend to form:** Steve Duck, Kris Pond, and Geoff Leatham, "Loneliness and the Evaluation of Relational Events," *Journal of Social and Personal Relationships* 11, no. 2 (1994): 253–276, https://doi.org/10.1177/0265407594112004.

228 **Lonely people may push away:** Louise Hawkley, Kristopher J. Preacher, and

John T. Cacioppo, "Multilevel Modeling of Social Interactions and Mood in Lonely and Socially Connected Individuals: The MacArthur Social Neuroscience Studies," in *Oxford Handbook of Methods in Positive Psychology*, eds. Anthony D. Ong and Manfred H. M. van Dulmen (Oxford University Press, 2007), 559–575, https://doi.org/10.1093/oso/9780195172188.003.0039. See also, John T. Cacioppo, James H. Fowler, and Nicholas A. Christakis, "Alone in the Crowd: The Structure and Spread of Loneliness in a Large Social Network," *Journal of Personality and Social Psychology* 97, no. 6 (2009): 977–991.

229 **facial muscle activity was measured:** Andrew J. Arnold and Piotr Winkielman, "Smile (but Only Deliberately) Though Your Heart Is Aching: Loneliness Is Associated with Impaired Spontaneous Smile Mimicry," *Social Neuroscience* 16, no. 1 (2021): 26–38.

CHAPTER 20 Depression

232 ***lachesism . . . Altschmerz*:** John Koenig, *The Dictionary of Obscure Sorrows* (Simon & Schuster, 2021), 45, 228.

233 **"laid low by the disease":** William Styron, *Darkness Visible: A Memoir of Madness* (Vintage, 1992), 36–37.

233 **evolutionary accounts:** Randolph M. Nesse, "Is Depression an Adaptation?," *Archives of General Psychiatry* 57, no. 1 (2000): 14–20.

234 **"Modern populations are increasingly overfed":** Brandon H. Hidaka, "Depression as a Disease of Modernity: Explanations for Increasing Prevalence," *Journal of Affective Disorders* 140, no. 3 (2012): 205–214, https://doi.org/10.1016/j.jad.2011.12.036.

234 **"People died of feelings all the time":** Edward St. Aubyn, *The Patrick Melrose Novels: Never Mind, Bad News, Some Hope and Mother's Milk* (Picador, 2012), 633.

235 **"the wish for a more visible illness":** Andrew Solomon, *The Noonday Demon: An Atlas of Depression* (Scribner, 2001), 71.

236 **"indescribably different from, actual pain":** Styron, *Darkness Visible*, 16.

237 **"When a person is depressed":** Carol Ezzell, "Why? The Neuroscience of Suicide—Brain Chemistry Might Explain Why Some People Impulsively Choose to End Their Lives," *Scientific American*, February 2003, 28, 44–51.

237 **discontinue medications like lithium:** Jan P. Scott and Marie Pope, "Nonadherence with Mood Stabilizers: Prevalence and Predictors," *Journal of Clinical Psychiatry* 63 (2002): 384–390.

239 **"I knew my life to be a shambles":** Solomon, *The Noonday Demon*, 265.

240 **94 percent were still alive:** Seiden, "Where Are They Now?"

241 **about one in ten:** Ronald C. Kessler, Patricia Berglund, Guilherme Borges, Matthew Nock, and Philip S. Wang, "Trends in Suicide Ideation, Plans, Gestures, and Attempts in

the United States, 1990–1992 to 2001–2003," *JAMA* 293, no. 20 (May 25, 2005): 2487–2495, https://doi.org/10.1001/jama.293.20.2487.

241 **"The more episodes you have":** Solomon, *The Noonday Demon*, 265.

243 **Depressed individuals tend to evoke discomfort:** Nesse, *Good Reasons for Bad Feelings*, 186–187; James C. Coyne, "Depression and the Response of Others," *Journal of Abnormal Psychology* 85, no. 2 (1976): 186–193.

243 **"When one suffers a misfortune":** Javier Marías, *The Infatuations* (Vintage International, 2012), 64.

247 **"totally destructive to the ordinary mental life":** Flo Conway and Jim Siegelman, *Dark Hero of the Information Age: In Search of Norbert Wiener, the Father of Cybernetics* (Basic Books, 2005, Kindle ed.), 94–96, 179–180.

EPILOGUE Misery Loves Company

249 **"I'm happy only because":** Martin Crimp, *Picture a Day Like This*, libretto for the opera by George Benjamin, premiered July 5, 2023, Aix-en-Provence Festival.

250 **"The gross national product does not":** Alan B. Krueger, Daniel Kahneman, David Schkade, Norbert Schwarz, and Arthur A. Stone, "National Time Accounting: The Currency of Life," in *Measuring the Subjective Well-Being of Nations: National Accounts of Time Use and Well-Being*, ed. Alan B. Krueger (University of Chicago Press, 2009), 9–86, http://www.nber.org/chapters/c5053.

251 **"In ease of body and peace of mind":** Smith, *The Theory of Moral Sentiments*, 264–265.

251 **"We should give up":** Amir Mandel, "Why Nobel Prize Winner Daniel Kahneman Gave Up on Happiness," *Haaretz*, October 7, 2018, https://www.haaretz.com/israel-news/2018-10-07/ty-article-magazine/.premium/why-nobel-prize-winner-daniel-kahneman-gave-up-on-happiness/0000017f-e650-df5f-a17f-ffde36ed0000.

252 **link between suffering and meaning:** See Paul Bloom, *The Sweet Spot: The Pleasures of Suffering and the Search for Meaning* (Harper, 2021).

254 **incontinence, sexual performance issues:** Erin Carbone, George Loewenstein, Cass R. Sunstein, and Linda Dezső, "Spirals of Shame: The Bi-directional Relationship Between Shame and Disclosure," Harvard Public Law working paper, forthcoming, February 7, 2025, https://papers.ssrn.com/sol3/papers.cfm?abstract_id=5141799.

Index

Index page references in italics refer to graphics.